*1992 – Strategies
for the Single Market*

1992

STRATEGIES FOR THE
SINGLE MARKET

JAMES W DUDLEY

GUILD PUBLISHING LONDON

This edition published in 1989 by
Guild Publishing
by arrangement with Kogan Page Ltd

Typeset by the Spartan Press Ltd
Printed and bound in Great Britain by
Richard Clay Ltd, Bungay, Suffolk

British Library Cataloguing in Publication Data
Dudley, James W.
  1992 – strategies for the single market.
  1. International marketing. Effects of economic
  integration of European Community countries.
  I. Title.
  658.8′48
  ISBN 1 85091 240 8

This book is dedicated to
my daughters
Sarah and Susannah

Acknowledgements

In writing this book I have to thank the following people and organisations for their enthusiasm, help and material. Without their support the book would have been considerably more difficult.

Tracy Newbold helped me put the text together; Lynda Muldoon typed and corrected much of the manuscript. Professor Martin Christopher from Cranfield School of Management and Professor Bernard Taylor from Henley The Management College for their help and counsel. Companies and organisations that provided information and support were *The Economist*; the *Financial Times*; The Institute of Marketing; Peter Sheperdson, Pilkington Glass PLC; The Boots Company PLC; Glaxo Holding PLC; *Sunday Times*; Colin Milbourne, Wilkinson Sword Ltd; The Institute of Directors; *Marketing Week*; Frank Harrision, Saatchi and Saatchi World Advertising PLC; Ann Brunton, Wellbeck PR; Euromonitor; The DTI (in particular Tim Abrahams of the Internal European Policy division); BOTB and the various departments within the European Commission.

Note

This book contains a number of references to companies and people. In the context they exemplify approaches and views and should in no way be construed as a judgement of good or bad business practice. The author has taken pains during his research to ensure that the facts in these cases are correct, or were correct at the time of research, or refer to facts published by others.

Contents

List of Figures

List of Tables

Foreword

So much has already been written and said about 1992 that the reader might be forgiven some hesitation in picking up this book. The fact is, however, that the Single Market in Europe has a symbolic and a practical importance that has major implications, both within and outwith the 12 member countries. The unique commitment that now exists to remove the remaining barriers to trade and commerce and to seek to standardise fiscal and regulatory practices, represents a great step forward in the history of European integration.

Nevertheless, there still remain substantial issues to be resolved and, indeed, a number of national differences which will endure. Certainly some would claim that a truly integrated market is not possible whilst language and cultural difficulties exist – removing the formal barriers to trade will not be sufficient to overcome the barriers of taste, preference and habit.

It was Peter Drucker who once wrote 'there are no problems, only opportunities', and in a sense, this could be the motto of the astute executive when viewing the prospect of 1992. To the ignorant and unconcerned a unified European market might indeed be a threat – if 1992 provides a single point of entry for a British Company, remember it also provides a single point of entry for an overseas competitor.

Perhaps the biggest opportunities for business lie in the ability to exploit the marketing and logistics economies that are available in a vastly expanded 'home' market. Already companies are making plans for European production facilities with flexible manufacturing capabilities to produce the 'standard' products in a diversity of forms, eg packages, formulations, sizes and so on. Companies adopting a European strategy will, in effect, be capable of achieving both a volume-based cost advantage over their more local competitors and, at the same time, be capable of achieving differentiation by catering for local requirements through flexible manufacturing.

To prepare the executive for the challenge of 1992, James Dudley has written this highly practical guide for action. It is more than just another review of the '300 Directives'. Rather it focuses our attention upon how strategy should be formulated with the world's biggest-spending market place in mind. 1992 is just around the corner: this book will help us in our anticipation of the view that might await us round that corner.

Martin Christopher
Professor of Marketing & Logistics
Cranfield School of Management

Introduction

'Within Europe the preparation for 1992 will hot up, with companies seeking dominant market share, buying up brand names and pursuing economies of scale'

Financial Times 21.5.1988

The Single European Act (SEA) heralds a new era of opportunity. An environment will be created which fosters wealth and job creation across the whole of the European Community. Yet above all it will create a fiercely competitive business environment driving down prices, pushing up demand and reducing inflation. The effects will ripple across the entire globe.

1992 is not an option. It is a challenge. For many companies the challenge may well be a struggle for survival. The massive benefits pointed out by Paolo Cecchini's study will only occur after a major period of industry restructuring. For many companies this will mean not only new competitors but changes in their customer profiles and suppliers.

The Single European Act is designed to break the log jam of legislation which has piled up for nearly a decade through the internecine rivalry of quarrelsome and competing governments. This legislation (plus much more that is being added) is designed to break down barriers which have hitherto prevented the European Community from becoming potentially the largest single market in the free world.

The act is a catalogue of activities needed to open markets, free the movement of goods, capital and people. It is a pot-pourri of economic, business, environmental and social legislation. Its aim is to unify the Community: making it a true economic union through providing a body of law; strengthening the powers of the European Commission, the Council and European Parliament. It does not only facilitate internal trade but also harmonises many of the aspects of national norms and legal issues whose inconsistencies have stood in the way of making the European Community a market for free and fair trade between member states.

The changes which will come about in the Single Market make it imperative for firms to find strategies, compete within it, exploit opportunities and influence the political and legal processes the Single European Act has initiated. The Single Internal Market is being brought about through legal and political activity in which firms are openly invited to participate.

Whilst this book focuses on the European Community's business environment, it also extends to global issues and opportunities. It does so for two reasons:

- The Single Market environment will touch every business in terms of legal issues, threats and opportunities.

- The European Community, whilst offering potentially the largest domestic market in the free world, is part of the global market place in which many firms operate. Thus synergies and advantages created by the Single Market for individual firms make the global market more attainable.

The text, therefore, asks managers to examine their firms' competitive positions and offers a number of strategic and operational options. Appreciating that each company will have different sets of problems and priorities, the book offers no prescriptive formula other than to emphasise the need to find criteria against which to achieve competitiveness.

In writing the book, it was necessary to look at both the US market (a model referred to by the Cecchini study group) and the business strategies adopted by the 'blue chip' Japanese companies. Whilst neither are true analogues of a future European market nor models for business theory, they both provide a scenario against which market competition and business strategies can be viewed. Peter Drucker's and Philip Kotler's examples, conclusions and views of the Japanese dynamo and its impact on the North American market are thus referred to as instances of highly organised foreign competition impacting on an intensely competitive marketing environment.

The book also mentions a number of examples from the pharmaceutical industry. This is not only because of the author's intimate knowledge of the industry but because it is one of the truly international industries requiring a global market upon which to fund its research and development (R & D). Furthermore, it is a demand-based highly competitive industry in which competition is truly global. It is also an industry in which European companies excel competitively in a wider world.

There are also a considerable number of examples drawn from the fast-moving consumer goods (fmcg). These too not only reflect the author's apprenticeship in marketing but more importantly, exemplify excellence in promotional marketing. They provide a comparison against which to evaluate alternative international and nationally responsive marketing communications.

Lastly, the industrial or business-to-business market provides examples of the way structure, innovation and service can be brought to bear on their markets. No book embracing international business would be complete without looking at the ways in which companies like IBM continue to hold their position against national or international competition. ·

I

The Trauma of the Single Market

On 1st July 1987 the Single European Act came into force. In so doing it unleashed an avalanche of change designed to sweep before it all nationalistic self-interest which has hitherto prevented the European Community from becoming a Single Internal Market. By the end of 1992 companies within the Community will be able to share a single home market potentially larger than any in the free world.

Most commentators, politicians and economists predict that the European Community business environment will offer greater opportunities for firms, yet will be very competitive and turbulent after 1992. The hysterical lather they have worked up to urge businesses to become more competitive and internationally orientated serves little purpose in the cool reality of making business decisions. The problem for most business people is not inactivity but separating the reality of the Single Market from the proliferation of myths and conflicting political innuendoes in circulation.

It is the aim of this book to help managers gain some understanding of what the Single European Act means to them in terms of changes it will bring to their business environment. Its purpose is to assist them to tackle the complexities of threats and opportunities to their domestic, European and global markets.

It will provide some of the tools necessary to help them decide whether to use the Single Market to grow and dominate in the Community and into the global arena beyond, or to retain a protected niche in a region or market segment. It will provide some insights into the operational aspects of diversifying into the Community's markets and then into wider international markets. It will also bring to managers' attention the less obvious opportunities the Single Market affords them in their domestic and other existing markets.

It points to the effects created externally by the Single European Act on such global issues as competition, product standards and norms and pricing, amongst many.

There is an urgency for companies to start doing something about the Single Market. Yet there is little purpose in rushing into hasty decisions at the expense of doing something which has been clearly thought through. Making wholesale changes to a company's business strategies and working practices are pointless unless they are aimed at achieving specific goals in response to identifiable changes in the business environment.

Unfortunately, the time for pondering and deliberation is fast running out. Despite the fact that in reality the creation of the Single Market provides companies with a gradually expanding opportunity in the Community market, the excitement of the 1992 prospect has begun to force the pace. A zest for mergers and takeovers has already been sparked off (see Figure 1.1).

Companies both from within the Community and from outside, particularly the US, Switzerland, Austria, Sweden and Japan, are rushing for acquisitions to give them the bases from which to spread across the Community. The effect will not only contribute to the intensification of competition but, as we will see in Chapter 2, it will change both customers and suppliers for many companies.

There is a need, therefore, for companies to look much more closely at developing a strategy for the Single Market. For even if only half the benefits so publicly acclaimed by the European Commission actually accrue, the factors of change will bring with them both new threats and opportunities.

Companies will need, therefore, to reassess their capabilities within their existing markets as well as their abilities to contest the wider domestic market of the European Community. The opportunities and threats, as we will see, are not just those associated with new opportunities and direct competition from Europe. They are to do with changes in the composition of customers, suppliers and competition. They are to do with changing product standards and norms. Changes in the financial environment, transport and frontier controls. They are also concerned with the shifts in political power from governments to Brussels, as well as the growing influence of the European Court of Justice in forcing governments and institutions to conform to laws long forgotten.

So how should companies begin to form some strategy for the Single Market?

Figure 1.2 shows in outline the approach needed to assess the impact of the Single Market and to formulate strategies to deal with changes to

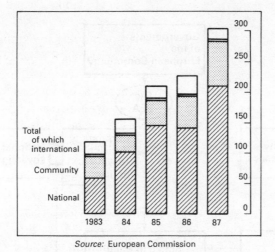

Source: European Commission

By kind permission of *The Economist* (Survey Europe's Single Market) July 9 1988

Figure 1.1 The acceleration of mergers and acquisitions involving EC-based companies

the business environment. What the figure brings out which may be new to many companies is the need to develop a political strategy. Without access to the Community's legal decision-makers now plotting the future of the legal and political framework, companies will have to accept *carte blanche* rules and regulations handed down to them. In many cases these will have been influenced by companies astute enough to realise the competitive advantages.

Yet the Single European Act is about providing a market place for companies. The machinery exists for them to bring issues to a forum and contribute to such areas as product standards, health and safety regulations, protection of sensitive industries and considerable social legislation concerning trade unions and personnel policies. There are a legion of political, social and environmental issues which will impact on companies operating in the Community. It is important, therefore, to take the lead from Wisse Dekker of Philips, and others whose endeavours have had such an influence on persuading community governments for the need for an open internal market.

Will the European Community be a single internal market unfettered by hidden barriers to trade? Can the costly bureaucracy and internecine quarrels between member states be eliminated by the end of 1992?

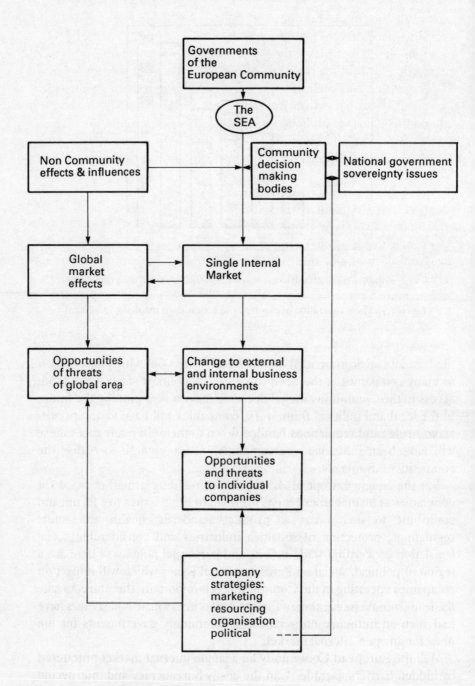

Figure 1.2 Scheme for a strategic response to the creation of the Single Internal Market

Certainly the Single European Act puts into a legal framework all the activities necessary to create a single internal market within the European Community. It provides a time-scale for 300 pieces of legislation to be enacted. The deadline is 31 December 1992.

There is at last a realisation by Community member governments that imminent decay hangs over Europe. The knowledge that within a decade the common market could be enslaved as the 'screwdriver' economy of its North American and Far Eastern competitors has forced a crisis which has enabled the processes for the formation of the Single Internal Market to begin.

The aims and objects of the Single European Act are to provide an economic environment in which its industries can become more competitive on the world stage. It provides a legal framework which will enable 60 per cent of the decisions required for its fulfilment to be made by qualified majority decisions of the European Council of Ministers. It does not create a European federation, a Community currency or provide the architecture for a protective customs cordon around the Community.

Yet, more and more, both economists and politicians are becoming aware that the faster the Community moves towards the creation of the Single Market the more traumatic will be its impact on business life. The Battle of the Somme will be re-enacted for a whole generation of companies. Through the forces of competition they are driven towards opportunities across a battlefield from which some of the mines and much of the barbed wire has been removed.

Despite the vast amount of information, views and comment surrounding the Single Market concept, it is difficult for many people to understand what it all really means and how it will affect their business.

This chapter, then, deals with the European Community, the Single European Act and forming a political strategy.

The European Community – a coalition of self-interest

The EC first came into being through the Treaty of Rome in January 1958, the six founding members being Belgium, France, Germany, Italy, Luxembourg and the Netherlands. In 1973, three more countries – Great Britain, Ireland and Denmark – joined. Greece joined in January 1981 and Spain and Portugal in 1986.

Half the world's trade is conducted in the European Community. The combined gross domestic product (GDP) of all its members make it the second largest economic block in the world, behind North America. The EC has an approximate population of 323 million people, making it the second largest populated market in the free world behind India.

It has 228 of the top 1000 companies in the world – behind Japan with 310 and the US with 345. Europe has 115 companies with profits exceeding $200 million compared with Japan with 58 and the US with 205. Even so the EC has a technology deficit of $10.6bn with its competitors mainly Japan and North America. It is this deficit which has had a major influence on governments to agree to the formation of the Single Market.

The Community is made up of 12 separate states ranging in size from 366,000 in Luxembourg to more than 60 million in Western Germany. Amongst its member states are the richest and some of the poorest in Europe.

Despite its size the Community has continued to lose ground against its principal competitors, the USA and Japan. The reason is largely associated with the Community's fragmented nature. It does not provide a unified and homogenous home market in which companies of member states can grow to become competitive in innovation cost and price in the way of Japanese or US companies.

The Community spends at least as much in R & D as Japan, yet the dispersion of effort and the sums spent on trying to match and adapt products to meet the myriad differences in product standards dissipate energies. Member country companies are therefore less competitive than their global competitors in terms of technological and production development.

The obstacles to the free movement of goods through the hidden barriers to trade (namely: varying national specifications, health and safety standards, environmental controls, quality controls and differences in VAT) have discouraged many companies from making a complete commitment to developing a pan-Community business. Many multinational companies have plumbed for the more open and lucrative North American market rather than attempt to invest in the Community.

In the past, many attempts to create a unified Europe have run into considerable problems. They have run into conflict with individual national governments on sensitive issues of national sovereignty such as taxation, financial and foreign policy. For example, the Fouchet plan of 1961 – which provided a vision of a joint European foreign policy – failed because it conflicted with the sovereignty aspirations of individual member states. The Werner plan in the early 1970s attempted to achieve an economic and monetary union by 1980. Its aims and objects cut straight into those very sensitive nationalistic issues which were so dear to the independence of individual member governments. Even so, from the ashes of its demise the European Monetary System (EMS) was kindled in 1979.

The Tindemans concept of a European Union was yet another initiative for unification which died on the vine.

The preoccupation with nationalism and protectionism by governments and lobbyists from major industries against both internal and external competition has created massive resistance to unification. This was particularly so during the economic recession of the 1970s. In the meantime Japanese and North American companies have stolen a competitive march on EC industry.

The structure of European industry reflects the fragmented nature of the market and national attitudes. Whilst many Community companies sell their products within the EC the need to adapt and modify products to meet individual market restrictions makes it difficult for them to rationalise production and compete on cost. The perpetuation of the manufacture of separate products for each individual market has hitherto discouraged many companies from committing resources to the Community market. Hence for many there is no trained management base to take on the market. Nor have companies been able to scale up to take advantage of the collective scientific, technical and industrial capacity within the Community market.

The Single European Act

The heads of state agreed in 1985 to a programme comprising 300 separate pieces of legislation which would lead to a unified single market by 1992. The timetable of activity was based on a period between 1985 and 1992. Legislation was to be front-loaded to allow time for individual states to enact their own legislation in order to bring each into conformity with EC law by 1992.

Whereas in the past, progress of legislation has moved at the speed of the slowest dissenting nation member, the Single European Act overcomes this problem. The Act replaces the unanimity provided within the original treaties. It permits decisions to be made by a qualified majority*

*Qualified majority means that 54 out of a total of 76 votes are required. Abstention does not count towards making a qualified majority. It does not, however, prevent unanimity where that is required.

of ministers in regard to measures which have the establishing and functioning of the internal market as their principal objectives.

The Act covers a broad spectrum of Community law. It sets out to amend a number of the original treaties. It covers such diverse areas as:

- economic and social cohesion;
- environment;
- co-operation between institutions; and
- political co-operation.

The most important feature of the Act in achieving the internal market is the fact that, ratified by all member states, it provides the legal framework and facilitates the political impetus to create a unified market by 1992. The adoption of the Act demonstrates, at least superficially, that there is some universal political will within the Community to dispense with the inefficiencies of fragmentation and to provide a unified market in which companies and people can share in the collective, scientific, technical and industrial capacity of the EC.

Sharing the wealth

The Commission is concerned with ensuring that the whole Community shares the benefits of the Single Internal Market. It recognises that certain regions have greater economic advantages than others. The south-east of Britain, northern France, the Ruhr and Benelux are amongst the areas with excellent infrastructures and existing industrial strengths to benefit from the internal market. Yet the Act attempts to ensure that other areas on the periphery of the Community are also gainers. Large amounts of aid will be made available to those areas which are seen as disadvantaged. This measure will provide considerable opportunities for the development of the less prosperous areas as well as creating further competitive pressures on countries and companies within the Community.

Community law and member countries

For the Single European Act to be totally effective the legal framework has to be conceived and enacted correctly. Member states must be committed and involved at all stages of development. Although 300 pieces of legislation were agreed, nearly 10 per cent have been dropped or replaced and each will have to be translated into the laws of each member state.

It would, however, be erroneous to assume that unity within the Community can be achieved through the enactment of legislation alone. For there is even now a considerable amount of Community common law, the enforcement of which will be just as important.

Deregulation through regulation

The original White Paper emphasised the need to deregulate areas which restrict the free movement of products, people, services and financial services in order to open the market. Furthermore the need to harmonise indirect taxation and customs procedures is seen as a prerequisite to reducing the restrictions and incumbencies which contribute to the delays in shipping goods across Europe.

The need for companies and their legal councillors to be cognisant of their rights under Community law is also an area focused upon in the White Paper. The Commission is aware that many companies have become resigned to accepting the restrictive barriers to trade within certain EC countries. It understands the frustration and the fact that a number of businesses have actually given up on some markets, unaware that many of the restrictive practices are illegal under Community law. Few companies want to take on governments; even fewer are aware of the existence of the means to begin proceeding.

Cassis de Dijon ruling

In 1979 the European Court ruled that the restrictions on the import of a product – Cassis de Dijon – into the Federal Republic of Germany were contrary to the definition of freedom of trade between member states. The West Germans had indeed banned the import of Cassis de Dijon because it did not meet German criteria as liquor and was in competition with a German product of similar description. The court ruled that Cassis de Dijon could not be restricted on the basis that it did not meet a German criterion. Thus arose the concept that what was legally sold in one member state was legally fit for sale in another.

The ramifications of this ruling were to expose the myriad petty restrictions which prevented or discouraged the freedom of movement of products between member states. The ruling was to permit movement of previously affected products and, more importantly, it was to focus attention on the problem of product regulations covering standards and descriptions across member states.

The complexity of product-standards regulations stems from the primary concern of governments to protect consumers and the environment from harm. Yet the temptation to add economic criteria to such regulations has escaped few governments. The Community has wrestled with the problem for decades. It has reached the ludicrous point where harmonisation of standards has reached the statutes long after the subject technology has become obsolete.

Under the new proposals the abolition of differential standards is a target. The areas under focus are:

- individual product regulations and standards;

- safety standards;

- health and environmental standards; and

- consumer protection.

The combination of interpretation and sheer abuse of standards regulations by governments presently means that such items as televisions and cars have to be modified a hundred times over to meet individual state rules. British chocolate cannot be marketed in a number of EC countries. Beers brewed outside Germany cannot be imported into Germany because they are full of additives deemed to contravene the German purity for beer which go back to the sixteenth century. (Despite the fact that German brewers add the same additives to their export products.)

The Commission is painfully aware that all these regulations add extra costs to production and distort production patterns. They discourage business co-operation and reduce individual company and hence Community competitiveness. They inhibit and penalise attempts for companies to operate on a European scale.

Under the future legislation the Commission exploits the concept that that which is legally sold in one member state should in principle be legally sold in another. A ban can only be applied if it is proved that a product fails to satisfy a narrow range of public interest criteria such as environmental or consumer protection.

In principle, it will soon no longer be possible for countries to prevent the import of products which compete with their national industries just because they are deemed to be slightly different from theirs.

Above all the consumer is to be given the right of choice. This is a fundamental right and a stimulus for competition. However, the consumer also has the right to safety and environmental protection. There is no principle, however, which suggests or should be interpreted as suggesting that the consumer should be protected from other member states' products because of possible injury to the competitive position of the national industry concerned.

The Commission therefore is adopting the axiomatic solution of harmonising health and safety regulations across the Community. This leaves individual manufacturers the freedom of design and manufacturing skills to offer a wide range of consumer choice within the parameters of a universally acceptable range of standards – the concept of *mutual recognition*.

There is also an emphasis on avoiding the idiotic concept of 'Euro products', ie a narrow standard criteria which forces suppliers to provide identical products with identical components across the Community. Such a policy is now seen as contrary to the concept of consumer choice without which a healthy competitive environment for business cannot exist.

Competition

It has been a basic aim of the Community to prevent market distortion. Considerable amounts of statute work have gone into preventing collusion between companies to distort prices and share trade within the Community. Yet governments have overtly and covertly taken measures which have favoured particular firms and industries. Such activities .have ranged from public procurement policy to special tax advantages to outright aid.

The view adopted by the Commission is that any activity which is deemed anti-competitive is not legal. The Commission's belief is that a strong competitive policy is not only politic but is vital to the successful creation of an internal market.

The overriding objective of the Commission is to hammer home regulations combating anti-competitiveness and bring offending companies and governments to heel where necessary. The correct and equitable application of Community law is crucial if the universal commitment to be a unified market and all its stages of development are to be tested.

Movement of goods

Frontier controls are both frustrating and costly to all shippers. Delays, bureaucracy and the weight of documentation have in the past added considerable costs to the movement of goods within the Community. A figure of nearly $9bn per year has been put on the combined costs for the internal movement of goods.

Whilst recognising the need for vehicles to be stopped and checked to prevent smuggling and comply with agricultural health and hygiene requirements as well as counter-terrorism measures there is a general recognition that the paperwork should be reduced.

In 1988 the Single Administrative Document (SAD) was introduced, thereby making redundant some 70 administrative forms within the Community. Complications, however, still exist. Two problem areas are: monetary compensation amounts (MCA's) and value added tax (VAT).

Monetary compensation amounts are in effect compensation paid to food and agricultural producers. Their aim is to reduce the relative effects of currency exchange where distortions would otherwise be influential on the movement of agricultural products.

VAT is more difficult. The rate of VAT is different on different products in each country. It is one of the most contentious issues in the 1992 proposals. The question of approximating the rates of VAT within the EC is one of the features of the unification process which cuts into nationalistic interests. Yet it is a crucial viewpoint if the internal frontiers are to be removed. The fiscal proposals cover two areas: changes in the administration and enforcement of VAT and excise duties once the frontier posts have been abolished; and the rate of VAT and excise duties that member states can levy.

Much of the energy and time of customs authorities in member states is concerned with collecting VAT on goods shipped between countries. Because VAT is raised on the end-user and exports are thus zero-rated. Customs authorities have to guard against the possibility that goods are moved around the market and back to their country of origin without any VAT being charged. Thus a truck carrying goods from France to Italy and then illegally returning unloaded might escape VAT if the probability of detection were not a restraint. Permitting VAT to be charged on the supplier and cleared within the Community so that tax revenue flows back to the individual states is the one suggestion most favoured by the Commission. At the time of writing, however, this proposal was still not accepted by governments across the Community.

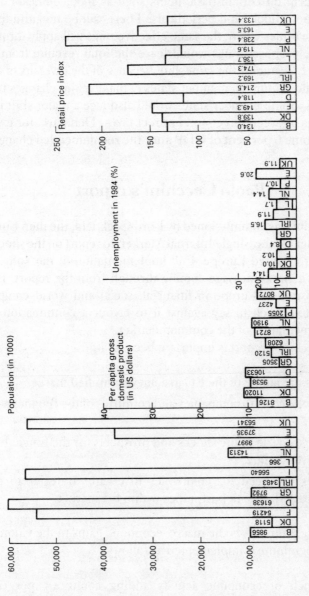

Reprinted from *Europe Without Frontiers* – completing the Internal Market Periodical 4/1987. Office for Official Publications of the European Communities 1987

B. Belgium; DK. Denmark; F. France; D. W Germany; IRL. Ireland; L. Luxembourg; NL. The Netherlands; P. Portugal; E. Spain; UK. United Kingdom

Figure 1:3 European Community member states: basic statistics

It is proposed that member states will have two VAT rates, a standard rate in the band 14 per cent–20 per cent and a lower rate in the band 4 per cent–9 per cent on certain basic items such as food, domestic energy, public transport, books and periodicals. There will be no latitude in the case of excise duties where the same effective rates will apply throughout the EC. The proposed rates would leave the total revenue from excise duties in the EC roughly the same, but, because of the diversity of rates at present, would require all member states to make major changes to some of their rates. Some member states would also face a major shift in their tax burden as between direct and indirect taxes. Denmark, for example, would lose some 6 per cent of GDP after the recommended changes.

Paolo Cecchini's report

Paolo Cecchini was commissioned by Lord Cockfield, the then European Commissioner for the Single Internal Market, to report on the shocks and prospects for a united Europe. Full implementation of the 1985 White Paper is the general message coming through from the report. For the costs of a disunited Europe in financial, social and world-competitive terms have too much to say against it to favour a continuation of the present fragmentation of the common market.

Paolo Cecchini's report is important because it:

- Highlights the failing of the EC to achieve a unified market;
- points out the costs to companies and countries of the fragmentation of the EC;
- provides a scenario of the shocks and prospects for the Single Internal Market beyond 1992;
- emphasises the need for companies to create strategies to remain competitive and seize opportunities within the market.

The report summarises the macro-economic gains to the Community if the full programme is implemented as follows:

- the relaunch of economic activity adding about 4.5 per cent to Community GDP;
- reduction of inflation – average consumer prices will fall by 6.1 per cent;

- improvement in the balance of public finances by about 2.2 per cent of GDP and thus the increase in the Community's external position by 1 per cent of GDP;
- reduction of unemployment by creating upwards of 1.8 million new jobs.

It is through these savings and their psychological effect on industry managers that will, according to Cecchini, initiate a massive supply-side shock upon which the gains will have been based.

In assessing the probable gains for the European Community from the formation of the Single Market, taking Paolo Cecchini's calculations is insufficient. For these are based on complete implementation of the White Paper. The 1992 report itself emphasises that 'Implementation of half the actions proposed [in the White Paper] will deliver much less than half the total benefits'. It acknowledges the psychological importance of convincing managers that the whole programme has to be implemented.

If we take four aspects of the 1992 effect in which Cecchini describes the catalysts for the economic explosion and examine these in the light of the practicalities of implementing them, we can see the extent to which the plausibility of the arguments for the full benefits of the Single Market is compromised.

The four main catalysts for creating the supply-side shock emanating from the Act are, according to Paolo Cecchini's conclusions:

- removal of border controls;
- opening of public procurement markets;
- liberalisation of financial services; and
- supply-side effects of business strategies reacting to a new competitive environment.

Removal of border controls

The effects on the macro-economy will be more to do with the psychological effect that the open market will have than the actual reduction in costs hitherto incurred in border delays and documentation.

Cost savings in moving goods around the Community can be passed on in terms of price reductions, helping goods produced in one country to be competitively priced with those produced in the importing country. This will lead to goods produced within the EC becoming substitutes for nationally produced products. At the same time competitive pricing will enable goods to compete with those produced outside the Community – thus having a beneficial effect on the Community's trade balance.

The removal of border controls is to be the symbol of unification. It is to be the psychological trigger for commercial activity. Yet it is the biggest gamble the Commission is taking, for it opens an arena where the compromises national governments will have to make are outweighed on three fronts.

- There will be resistance by national governments to harmonising or relaxing their individual anti-smuggling, gun laws, anti-terrorist, immigration laws, and the movement of livestock and agricultural products.

- The harmonisation of indirect taxation (VAT and duty) will have to be put into effect before frontier controls can be abolished. This in itself is a highly contentious issue as far as individual governments are concerned and unlikely to be resolved in a time-frame short enough.

- Article 115, which allows governments to shield themselves from 'economic difficulties' provides a whole basketful of opportunities for individual governments not only to block direct imports from non-member countries, but also to prevent intra-community trade in such imports once they have been legally imported elsewhere in the Community.

It is the removal of border controls in the 1992 timetable which is most likely to upset the schedule for the true unification of the Community. So much weight is placed on its importance as both the symbol of 1992 and the psychological trigger for the macro-economic benefits, that its outcome must be considerably more assured than it is at the time of writing.

Even so, relaxation of transport regulations should at least reduce the artificial frontiers created for the transport industry, bringing down costs for shippers.

Transport in the community will face a major shake-up as the 1992 deadline approaches. The fact that in 1985 the European Court found that the Community's transport requirement was illegal points to the iniquities and inefficiencies under which the present system operates.

Road transport carries the highest share of intra-Community trade by value. About half of all cross-border road movements are covered by bilateral arrangements negotiated between member states. They are rationed on a trip-by-trip basis measured in tonne-kilometres.

Only about 16 per cent of truck trips are permitted under community-wide permits. Under present regulations, the West Germans seem to benefit the most and have proffered considerable resistance to change. However, with the 1985 European Court ruling as support, the Commission aims to increase the number of Community permits by some 40 per cent per year until 1990.

The effects will be threefold.

- Cost should come down considerably. The same sort of inter-state deregulation of transport in the US in 1980, for example, reduced costs by about 10 per cent.
- The growth in transport services will lead inextricably to more mergers and takeovers within the transport industry.
- The transport infrastructure will become more congested than it is even today which could exacerbate delays through customs procedures.

If the latter could be removed by 1992 transport costs will come down dramatically. For not only will the basic costs per metre-tonne be reduced, the reduced time factor caused by removing frontier delays will again add to higher efficiency savings, which under competitive conditions will be passed on. Much depends, therefore, on the abolition of frontier controls if the cost savings created by competitive forces are not to be squandered on delays caused by an overcrowded infrastructure being exacerbated by frontier hold-ups.

Air transport regulations are another issue altogether. The Community-wide resistance to opening air transport to competitive forces is reinforced by long-standing binational treaties created in the 1946 Bermuda agreement. It is unlikely, therefore, that even the Commission will be able to coax member governments to give up a system which, although illegal, is financially in their interests to preserve. Whilst there is likely to be some future relaxation on air transport costs, they will still continue to run substantially higher than those of the USA. At present US costs are a third lower than comparable EC costs.

Rail costs and services will alter substantially. The opening of the Channel tunnel between continental Europe and Britain will provide a viable alternative to truck transport. This will add to the competitive forces in the transport industry, particularly between Britain and the continent.

Opening of public procurement markets

Cecchini points to this as having a major economic impact. Public procurement affects some 15 per cent of Community GDP. The advantages of opening procurement markets will create benefits to the Community's economy for three reasons:

- it will reduce costs to major public utilities, transport and telecommunications through the opening of Community-wide competitive bidding;

- public administration will save costs which can either be passed on through tax reductions or through infra-structure investment; and

- companies supplying public markets will need to become more competitive once their cosy relationship with sponsoring procurers is eliminated. Those who can reduce costs and compete will have the competitive propensity to expand their markets beyond their traditional customers. Thus they will increase the competitive intensity in private sector markets as well as offering competitive products and prices to customers outside the Community.

The impact of opening procurement is expected to increase GDP by 0.5 per cent and create 400,000 new jobs, the report says. The downward pressure on prices by public bodies is expected to have a negative inflationary impact of as much as 1.4 per cent over time.

The Community's public sector has been under legal obligation to open procurement since 1971 for large construction contracts (exceeding 1M ECUs) and for large purchasing tenders (exceeding 200,000 ECUs) since 1977. Yet in ten years barely a fraction of such regulated contracts has gone to contractors from outside the purchaser's borders. With the exception of mainframe computer suppliers, few sectors have enjoyed the open procurement policy of the Community. Telephone suppliers are an example. Restrictions and standards regulations have hindered the ability of companies to supply handsets to different national governments. For exchange suppliers there are seven different digital switching systems, five of which are backed by large national companies under the sponsorship of their governments. A study by the commission showed that consumers pay between $225 and $500 for a telephone installation across the Community.

The procurement policy kicks open a hornets' nest of nationalistic interests. This is inevitable when you consider its aims of broadening the scope of legislation and closing the loopholes which have appeared; providing powers for the commission to police its regulations; improving redress of tenderers who believe they have been illegally discriminated against; and extending policy to new areas previously exempt, namely, energy, transport, water and telecommunications.

The regulations not only attack the anti-competitive and discriminatory activities of public procurement authorities, they also bring some large private companies into the net, and herein lies the problem. It means that affected companies will need to be seen to be offering their procurement to competitive tender. It ignores the many non-financial business decisions which go into procurement that relationships built up over time endow, such as reliability, inter-personal understandings, proximity to production sites and so forth.

The 'remedies' directive, so far in draft, changes the procedure for complaints to be lodged. Present policy demands that the aggrieved party complains to the European Commission which first investigates then complains to the central government in question. Final redress is taken to the European Court. The proposal is to demand that individual countries set up some form of court to handle complaints.

The question then is: will the proposals on public procurement be compromised? Their intrusion into the private sector will in effect give the Commission a say in the running of enterprises without accountability in terms of costs and profitability.

Liberalisation of financial services

The Commission's aim is to open up the financial services market on three fronts, namely:

- freedom of capital movement;
- the right to sell financial services across the Community; and
- the right for financial organisations to set up in other Community countries.

The Cecchini report outlines the principal benefits to the macro economy from the liberalisation of financial services.

By releasing competitive forces in such sectors as banking, insurance and security services the Community can expect an increase of 1.5 per cent to GDP, a deflationary effect of 1.4 per cent and an improvement in public finances equivalent to 1 per cent of GDP.

The effects of liberalising financial services will occur through:

- reduction in prices charged to customers by financial institutions;

- lower interest charges leading to greater productive investment and greater household consumption; and

- wider availability of credit enabling companies and private individuals to avail themselves of credit offered competitively within the Community.

This will stimulate domestic demand by increasing purchasing power. In turn, it should help firms become more competitive in meeting external demand.

The dangers of overheating of domestic economies and the effects that consumer credit will have in sucking in imports and affecting external trade balances are dealt with summarily in the report. In short, the gains in European competitivity will hold in balance both downsides!

Critical to the success of the free movement of capital and financial services is the relaxation of exchange controls. Presently Italy, France, Greece, Spain, Portugal and Ireland have strict controls on the movement of foreign exchange by their nationals. By 1990 Italy and France will have lifted their restrictions. Yet the four remaining countries are unlikely to fall in line until 1992.

Even so, there has been little movement towards the harmonisation of withholding taxes which are raised on interest payments. Obviously if these are not harmonised across the community, the savings will flow to areas where taxes are lowest, affecting especially both Denmark and France.

The importance of the EMS will be even more greatly emphasised. The need for the fixed currency provisions will need to be applied to the major economies in the community to control the flow of money between West Germany, France and Italy. It will be crucial for Britain to join if the EMS is to act as moderating agency in the flow of the relative rates of exchange. Furthermore, governments will have to co-operate in settling interest rates if the EMS is to withstand the impact of free movement of

European prices for financial services

Per cent above or below the average of the lowest four national prices found.

Table 1.1 The relative cost of financial services in the EC

Standard Service	Belgium	W Germany	Spain	France	Italy	Luxem-bourg	The Netherlands	UK
Banking services								
Consumer credit — Annual cost of consumer loan of 500 ECU. Excess interest rate over money market rates	-41	136	39	na	121	-26	31	121
Mortgages — Annual cost of home loan of 25,000 ECU. Excess interest rate over money market rates	31	57	118	78	-4	na	-6	-20
Foreign-exchange drafts — Cost to a large commercial client of purchasing a commercial draft for 30,000 ECU	6	31	196	56	23	33	-46	16
Commercial loans — Annual cost (including commissions and charges) to a medium sized firm of a commercial loan of 250,000 ECU	-5	6	19	-7	9	6	43	46
Insurance services								
Life insurance — Average annual cost of term (life) insurance	78	5	37	33	83	66	-9	-30
Home insurance — Annual cost of fire and theft cover for house valued at 70,000 ECU with 28,000 ECU contents	-16	3	-4	39	81	57	17	90
Commercial fire and theft — Annual cover for premises valued at 390,000 ECU and stock at 230,000 ECU	-9	43	24	153	245	-15	-1	27
Brokerage services								
Private-equity transactions — Commission costs of cash bargain of 1,440 ECU	36	7	65	-13	-3	7	114	123
Institutional-equity transactions — Commission costs of cash bargain of 288,000 ECU	26	69	153	-5	47	68	26	-47

Source: EC Commission
By kind permission of The Economist

funds within the Community, for it will have to take on many of the roles of a common currency by proxy!

Effects of business strategies

Supply-side effects of business strategies reacting to a new environment will have a major impact on the European economy according to Cecchini – 'all the macro-economic consequences of the supply-side shock' derive from companies competing in cost and price, leading to better dispositions and management of resources. This will have the effect of increasing domestic demand and boosting external demand through resultant industry competitiveness. This has to be balanced by the short-term impact of job losses during the restructuring which will occur before the competitive position settles down. Yet for many companies, product standards and norms are still bedevilled with inconsistencies between community markets.

The problems of finding common product standards which will enable products to be sold freely across the Community are far from being solved. For despite the case law from the Cassis de Dijon ruling and the acceptance that what is legally fit for sale in one member state is fit for sale in another, a number of practical problems persist.

Three factors come into play:

- national regulations;
- national standards; and
- certification

Before the Cassis de Dijon ruling, it could take many years before a common standard could be agreed unanimously by all the governments in the Community. Each product standard had to be agreed in great detail and each aspect voted on under the rules of unanimity. A European regulation very often took so long to evolve that it was out of date by the time everyone had agreed to it.

The concept of mutual recognition enables regulations to focus on the aspects of safety needed to permit products to be offered for sale in any of the Community's member states. The Community's standard-making institutions, CEN and CENELEC, would then bring together the various national standards bodies for example, DIN (West Germany), BSI (UK) and AFNOR (France).

The problems still affecting the harmonisation of standards are decribed below.

- The difficulty of persuading government standard-fixing authorities to regulate in terms of aims rather than specific description (eg a machine should have a general safety factor under full capacity, not a quantified percentage of insulation here or be made of fireproof material there).

- The absence of an adequate Community-wide certificating system to provide incontestable evidence of meeting safety regulations.

- European safety regulations do not in practice ensure that a product can be sold openly across the internal market. Whereas a product may well be considered safe under European guidelines, it may still find that it will not be accepted by another Community country because it does not conform to usage regulations or it affects local insurance regulations.

- There is considerable concern amongst the smaller countries that they will be compromised by the voting for regulations by the larger, more dominant German, French and British – whose output of new standards accounts for a little under 90 per cent in any year.

The facts as they emerge therefore indicate that despite the Commission's aims for common safety regulations, there is little that can be done to forcibly remove product norms as a means of protection. In addition it will need the enthusiasm of industry to force the pace for harmonising standards and product norms. This is already beginning in food additives, computers, high definition televisions and mobile telephones. The initiatives in many other industries are also leading to pre-commercial agreements of standards and norms. This will obviously save considerable time and effort where standards and norms are agreed at the outset rather than going through the process of harmonisation after commercialisation in individual markets.

Will the Single Market deliver for business?

The principal factors undermining the 1992 report scenario which may moderate the success of the Single Market and even lead to catastrophic economic consequences are:

- the lack of common policy for external trade;
- the period of adjustment;
- the inward looking approach to creating a competitive environment; and
- the lack of a common currency.

The lack of a common policy for external trade

Article 115 of the Treaty of Rome provides the 'bolt-hole' in which member states can shelter if they don't like the consequences of the Single Market. It enables each state to initiate measures to protect themselves from 'economic difficulties'. Yet the very existence of Article 115 means that a whole volume of considerations has been largely ignored. These considerations involve the inconsistencies in formulating a policy for foreign competition.

Whilst in generalities the 1985 White Paper stated that Community firms should be the principal beneficiaries, no common policy on foreign competition exists. This will act against the success of the Single Market in two ways. Firstly, there is no negotiating basis for the EC to represent itself as one of the three largest economic units in the world. With a disparate foreign trade policy, there is no unity to combine with the USA and Japan. Secondly, intra-trade between products and services legally created in one country from foreign origins cannot take place. Italy and France restrict the number of Japanese car imports. The multi-fibre arrangement is conducted on a country-by-country basis. Britain has special trading relationships with its former colonies bringing meat from New Zealand, bananas from the Caribbean and so forth. Yet under Article 115, which allows countries to make unilateral decisions on external trade, trade in these items between the importing country and the rest of the Community cannot take place.

The effects of Article 115 are not only to exacerbate the difficulties of abolishing frontier controls as already pointed out, they mitigate against the negotiation of bilateral arrangements between the Community and other trading blocks.

Without liberal trade between the EC and the rest of the world, the diversion of trade would be catastrophic to the principal aim of the Act – to regenerate industry on a global competitive basis. Yet without having negotiated Community-wide bilateral arrangements with external countries ahead of the internal market, particularly for sensitive trade sectors, the Community opens itself for these to be swamped by foreign companies prepared to find ways of overcoming the country-by-country barriers piecemeal. This they will achieve through building dominant positions in markets where they have relatively free access and expanding outwards through legitimately recognised incorporated companies in the Community.

The period of adjustment

All the scenarios so far produced indicate that a period of adjustment will occur between the triggering of activity and the benefits which will accrue.

It involves convincing people, trade unions, firms and political parties that the superordinate gains involve sacrifice. It involves convincing early losers (people losing jobs, firms losing markets, countries seeing others doing better) that their losses are for the good of the Community as a whole. Yet for the vast majority of enfranchised people in the Community, 1992 has very little direct relevance in daily life. There are political parties openly averse to Community unity within the EC and thus any political exploitation of the period of adjustment could lead to new faces at the conference table – hostile to its short-term effects.

The temptation of governments to override EC policy and attempt to manage the period of adjustment with the instruments of political and economic management they still retain will be great. The fact that the period of adjustment will affect different countries in different ways for longer or shorter periods of time will magnify the propensity for individual countries to unilaterally effect short-term economic measures – thus compromising the economic outcome.

Many member states will enter 1992 with adverse balances of payments, budget deficits, inflation and high unemployment figures. Whilst the Single Market should in the longer term remedy these ills the period of adjustment will exacerbate them. Early increases in unemployment, rising imports (both intra-Community and from external countries) foreign exchange fluctuation and stock market instability will create a period of turbulence and uncertainty. The psychological factor (upon which recovery is based) could well turn inward through politicians losing their nerve, trade union pressure and pressures from money and stock markets. The propensity for the population to sack their governments should the trauma of change impact on their daily lives would spell ruin for the Single Market's principal aim – economic recovery.

The temptation to rush into a 1992 deadline is already being tempered by governments and within the European Parliament. A more cautious and less traumatic move towards creating the Single Market is therefore likely. Such an approach will give more lasting benefits.

The inward-looking approach to internal competition

The European Commission's attitude to competition is wholly inward in approach. It supposes that by creating internal competition companies will become leaner and fitter to contest external competition. Yet it ignores the fact that many global Japanese and North American organisations are already so strongly competitive that they may become the major beneficiaries in the Single Market. Thus too great an invasion by foreign predators may undermine both the political credibility of the Single Market and influence governments to take unilateral action against it. Such action may lead to disunity within the Community.

Comparison between EC and Japanese industrial strategies

In comparing the Single Market to Japanese industrial strategy it can be seen that the aims of the Single Market differ widely from the more focused industrial strategy of the Japanese. It is useful to compare Japanese strategy to the aims of the SEA. The Japanese have after all been the most successful of all post-war economies. Japan's meteoric growth makes it a net creditor nation controlling more than 20 per cent of world trade.

Both Japan's and the European Community's industrial strategies are based on increasing industrial activity. They differ in a number of critical areas. The most important of these is that Japan has been able to focus a unified management policy of exploiting the most favourable global opportunities open to it by concentrating on its limited competitive advantages in a limited number of key industries.

Through infrastructure and government encouragement of certain industries it has focused its international success through a narrow range of industrial activities – barely employing 20 per cent of Japan's entire work-force. Japan took an early lead through setting up a single ministry (Ministry of Internal Trade and Industry – MITI) to mastermind Japanese recovery.

MITI built up a relationship with Japanese companies through:

- initiating takeovers and mergers of particular companies in key industries in Japan to provide strength and resources to tackle international markets – it encouraged the development of dominant companies;

- providing subsidies and incentives for strategic businesses to expand internationally;

- creating barriers to foreign competition and controlling foreign investment to protect key companies in the Japanese domestic market thus enabling them to earn high profits at home to finance exports;

- setting up an international research base effectively underwriting all the export marketing intelligence costs of Japanese companies;

- encouraging banks to support companies on a long-term market-building basis thus providing a high availability of capital at low cost; and

- an orientation towards high-technology industries ensuring that priorities and funds are channelled into those companies with an R & D commitment – 1.6 per cent of all industrial R & D comes from the Japanese government.

The European Community and its individual member states on the other hand have acted quite differently.

- Companies are discouraged from occupying dominant positions by attempts to control mergers.

- The Community discourages subsidies and incentives to its companies as these are believed to distort internal trade. Even so Community companies have to compete in the wider world against heavily subsidised competitors.

- Far from creating effective barriers to foreign firms the Commission in effect encourages them – despite its activities to prevent dumping and the creation of 'screwdriver' factories. This has the effect of weakening the potential for Community companies in sensitive sectors to develop to a competitive level before opening the market to competition.

- The Community has no global network for intelligence gathering on anything like the scale of MITI. It is left to the resources of individual governments to promote and subsidise market research in export markets.

- The Community has no real policy for bringing banking sector and industry together on the Japanese scale. The increased level of banking competition through the Single Market may well discourage banks from taking on major investment risks by encouraging them to compete for soft credit opportunities.

- The Community shares the aim to invest in high-technology areas of industry. Through its various machineries it encourages and subsidises co-operative R & D in automotive, computer, information technology, and aerospace industries among several major R & D initiatives – but even so it does so on a broad scale with only marginally greater investment in total terms than Japan.

The principal difference between Japanese and Community industrial strategies are that Japan is focused, outward-looking and protective of Japanese companies while the European Commission's strategy is wide-ranging, inward looking and non-protective of EC industry. Japan concentrates on creating and reinforcing competitive advantages for its industries. The European Community seeks to force its industries to adopt a cost-orientated approach regardless of those they may have in R & D and organisational ability. It would therefore appear that in many respects Community industry policy is the obverse of Japanese strategy. Yet the Japanese have proved theirs with success whilst the Community has yet to enact its policy.

The lack of common currency

The lack of common currency and the machinery to manage it through a Community central bank are major weaknesses of the Single Market. For, despite the EMS, variations in foreign exchange have the propensity to:

- distort trade in terms of production and markets despite relative efficiencies of competing industries;

- increase foreign exchange risks for firms operating across the Community;

- stimulate competition between countries to protect their trade balances (thus continuing to promote mercantilism within the Community); and

- exacerbate money market turbulence particularly during the period of adjustment.

The lack of a common currency, then, undermines the Single Market. Such a market creates shocks which, without a single currency, individual member states and companies operating in the market have no collective machinery to absorb. It penalises competitive industries through their location.

Decision-making in the Community

An important factor is the greater powers of influence which the SEA affords the European Parliament. The European Parliament will have more teeth. It will be able to influence the voting of the Council of Ministers.

There are four main groups which influence community decision-making.

The Commission

This is the executive of the community. It is headed by 17 commissioners (two each from France, Italy, Spain, the United Kingdom and West Germany and one each from the remaining seven states). Each commissioner has a cabinet of advisors.

The Council of Ministers

In effect the combined group of foreign secretaries from each member state who are responsible for all the major decisions affecting the Community. Detailed decision-making involves the relevant ministers for the subjects under discussion – for example, industry, transport, finance and agriculture and fishery.

The European Parliament

Made up of elected members from all over the Community. The Parliament has the powers to either approve the Council's position on a proposal or to take no position at all. It has no power of veto. Through parliamentary procedures Parliament can seek amendments or reject proposals. Where this occurs the Council of Ministers can only override the Parliament by unanimous decision.

The Economic and Social Committee

The fourth and important element in Community decision-making. This acts in an advisory capacity to the Council of Ministers. It is made up of employers, trade unions and independent representatives of the 12 states. It is here that proposals by the Commission are discussed so that the ramifications of proposals can be put to ministers.

Table 1.2   Composition of the Economic and Social Committee

Member State	No of seats
Luxembourg	6
Denmark	9
Ireland	9
Belgium	12
Greece	12
The Netherlands	12
Portugal	12
W Germany	24
France	24
UK	24
Italy	24
Spain	24

Under Article 195 countries have to nominate twice as many candidates as there are seats on the Committee.

The decision-making process within the Community thus emanates with a proposal from the European Commission. This involves consultation with the Council of Ministers. The proposal then goes to the Economic and Social Committee for its opinions before the Council of Ministers can begin its deliberations. If the Council adopts a common position on the proposal the European Parliament will have taken a position on the proposal within about three months. Where the Parliament agrees to the proposal by an absolute majority the proposal is adopted into legislation by the Council of Ministers.

Where a proposal is rejected or amended the proposal is returned to the Commission which will review it in the light of Parliament's views. The proposal is then passed once more to the Council of Ministers which may adopt the Commission's Proposal by qualified majority or seek to impose the amendments made by the European Parliament if these have not been proposed by the Commission. For the latter, unanimity is required within the Council.

THE DECISION-MAKING PROCESS IN THE EUROPEAN COMMUNITY

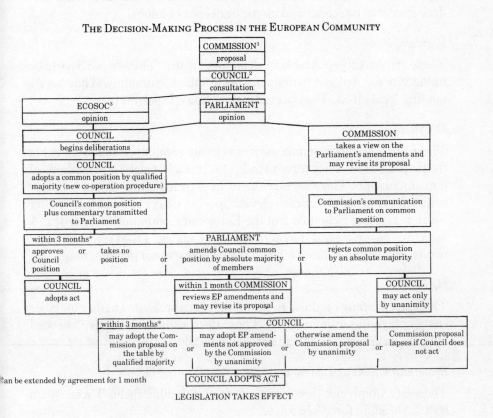

Figure 1.4 The decision-making process in the EC

Footnotes

1. The Commission is the executive arm of the Community, headed by 17 Commissioners appointed by the member states (two each from the UK, France, Spain, Italy and West Germany, one each from the other seven states). There are 22 Directorates-General.
2. The Council of Ministers for major decisions is the Foreign Secretary of each member state. For detailed decision-making it comprises the relevant Ministers for the issue under discussion, such as agriculture, industry, transport, finance.
3. The Economic and Social Committee is a body of employers, trade unions and independent representatives from each of the 12 member states.

Reproduced with permission of the Institute of Directors

Types of Community Legislation

Article 189 of the EC Treaty (Article 161 of the Euratom Treaty), stipulates that the Council and Commission may make directives; take decisions; make recommendations; or deliver opinions.

Regulations

These are directly applicable in all member states. They do not have to be ratified by the national parliaments within the Community. They have a binding legal effect. They prevail over national legislation.

Directives

These are binding on member states as to the result to be achieved within the period stated. They leave to individual member states the methods of implementation. This may take the form of primary legislation, statutory instruments made under the relevant specific powers or an Order under Section 2(2) and Schedule 2 of the European Communities Act 1972. A directive has no legal force in member states. However, particular provisions may take direct effect if the directive is not implemented.

Decisions

These are binding on those to whom they are directed, whether member states companies or individuals. Those decisions which impose financial obligations are enforceable in national courts.

Recommendations and opinions

These are simply the views of the institution issuing them. These issues have no binding force whatsoever.

The legislative power in the Community is provided by the Council. Some legislation may, however, be issued by the Commission; this, however, is confined to the implementation of earlier Council regulations and is usually of a technical or routine nature.

The European Court of Justice

The role of the European Court is very much in evidence through the growing amount of case law it is contributing. The Cassis de Dijon ruling in itself has had a major influence on ending trade barriers. Its judgements on financial services and transport have brought inconsistencies to light. Case law is an important part of the Community's development in terms of a legal system.

Developing a political strategy

With such an amount of change being brought about by the SEA a new feature of company strategy development will be the need to become adept at the political level. The European Community recognises the need for companies to become involved in the development of a number of legal areas. It encourages their participation in the processes of eliminating discriminatory anti-competitive activity. It provides forums for the views of industry to be heard. It provides the machinery for firms to involve themselves with product standards and so on.

The Small and Medium Enterprise (SME) Task Force was set up by the Commission in 1986. This, amongst its other duties of providing assistance to SMEs, monitors the EC's Fiche de 'Impact' System under which all Commission proposals must be accompanied by an assessment of their likely impact on Community businesses.

There are a number of other issues, including protection of sensitive and vulnerable industries from non-Community competition, takeovers and merger policies, taxation and foreign relations.

Companies need, therefore, to put a political strategy somewhere towards the top of their agenda. They will need to understand the political motivations of the different member states within the Community and the workings of the Community's executive and legislative. Competition is no longer a mere market phenomenon, it is exercised at the political level. Companies, therefore, not having their views and interests represented will have to accept what is handed out to them whether or not it is in their interests.

Companies will need to assess what interests they need to preserve and seek a route to political access. This is not as difficult as it may seem. On-line data is available through agencies such as Spearhead to provide information on the progress of legislation. This will enable managers to watch for developments. Trade associations mindful of their members' interests are also researching members' attitudes and providing a system for alerting members to developments. The ways of gaining political access to decision-making are also less formidable than might be perceived. The following list gives some of the routes open to companies.

- Sponsoring executives to sit on the various Commission's committees.
- Participating in trade association lobbies and national standards authorities initiatives.
- Contacts through national members of parliament.
- Contacts through members of the European Parliament.
- Contacting the SME Task Force.*
- Accessing the European Social and Economic Committee.
- Employing political consultants.

The importance of a political strategy cannot be over-emphasised. Even where trade associations are becoming involved it is imperative that companies clearly make their own interests known and pursue them either individually or collectively. It is vital too that companies ensure that their rights of free and fair competition are upheld. It will, therefore, be incumbent on companies and their legal advisors to keep abreast of legal developments in the community and to file protests and complaints where abuse is detected.

*The SME Task Force: Commission of the European Communities, 80 Rue d'Arlon, Brussels 1040, Belgium.

2

Competitive Challenges of the Single Market

The most obvious outcome of the Single Market is the change it will bring about in competition, suppliers and customers. In this chapter we will look at the underlying features of competition in the European Community and its impact on changing both industry structures and customers. We will then deal with the question of how companies can assess the competitive position in relation to these changes.

Competitive intensity is likely to increase in most industrial sectors. Cecchini points to a major shake-up in food, automotive, telecommunications and financial services. The Henley Forecasting Centre report indicates that high-technology areas will be vulnerable once the barriers are down. Add too, the impact on the Single Market price-levelling on the pharmaceutical industry and the internal and external competition within the textile industries, and straight away it shows that few industries will remain untouched by change.

The changes in public sector procurement policy will have a quite determinable impact for it accounts for some 15 per cent of the Community's GDP. By creating competition between suppliers it will mean that many companies will lose their large public sector markets.

The consequences will mean that not only will companies who have lost government contracts assert a greater intensification of competition on the private sector but, no less importantly, those companies which have been traditional suppliers to government contractors may suddenly find that their customer profiles have changed. The disappearance of four or five of Europe's major telecommunication exchange suppliers (which is not an outcome easily dismissed), will have massive effect on the structure of an industry worth more than $7bn in the EC.

Companies which have yet to determine the impact of a barrier-free

European Community need look at the effects which a change in customers and competition is likely to bring. Not only will some industries be affected by increased competitor-rivalry, the emergence of new market entrants is inevitable. This intensity will change both customer buying habits and, where industry restructuring occurs, it will also change the profiles of the customer base for many component and service industries.

In order for companies to determine the impact of competition on their business they must focus first of all on their customers rather than on competition. It is of paramount importance to forecast the likely changes in industry structure and the effects these are likely to have on buying behaviour and customer composition.

The main areas to examine therefore are:

• the direct opportunities for competition to exploit product and service weakness perceived by a firm's loyal customers;

• the propensity for existing and loyal customers to shop around the market; and

• the probability that competitive pressures will force an amount of industry restructuring, thus changing the customer profiles for their suppliers.

An understanding of customer behaviour is a fundamental rule of business. Identifying those windows of opportunity afforded to competitors by the shortcomings of a company to meet fully its customers' needs will be a critical discipline for companies. This is basic marketing.

Yet the point often missed by managers is that whilst they themselves are at pains to provide for their customers competitively, it is more often than not their intermediate customers who are not supplying consumers with what they want. So, in studying customers, it is important to research their propensity to remain competitive.

Survival for a firm may well depend more on meeting its customers' competitors' needs than doggedly adjusting product specifications to meet the needs of an uncompetitive customer. The automotive industry in the UK was an example. Its near demise crippled many components manufacturers not smart enough to have developed a market with their customer's competitors. Take the Pilkington Glass Group: its polished lens division identified the propensity for the Japanese to overtake the global camera market. By the time that it did Pilkington was supplying nearly all the lenses for Japanese cameras.

Whilst this idea is extremely important for component suppliers and business-to-business marketing organisations, it also has relevance to consumer product producers. Channels of distribution have the ability to change markets. The loss of share by US television-makers in North America is a case in point. Some of the multiples in the USA began to source own label televisions from Japan. The competition between multiples to provide televisions at competing prices had two effects on US manufacturers. Firstly, they lost share of television sales through the multiples to Japanese suppliers. Secondly, their loyal customers lost share to multiples offering own-label sets.

In examining the issues of competition it is necessary to examine its sources and its impact on industry structures. This will provide a reasoned basis for analysing competition which managers can use in the prognosis for their own business. It is important, therefore, to look briefly at the features of principal potential competitors and their characteristics. It will be their impact on the Single Market which will most affect industry structures. We will look, therefore, briefly at:

- the impact of Japanese competiton;
- North American competition;
- competition from the Pacific basin;
- European competition;
- small business competition; and
- the effects of competition on industrial value systems.

The impact of Japanese competition

Japanese competition has been a major catalyst for the Single Market. Its rapid industrial expansion displaced West Germany and the USA as leaders in world trade in ten years between 1975 and 1985. Its emergence as the second largest economic force in the world has forced the creation of the Single Market.

It will be the way in which Japanese companies adapt their strategies to the Single Market which will set the pace of future competitive intensity in many sectors. The Japanese companies have the global scale, the will and the determination to succeed in dominating high-technology industries in Europe.

A study carried out in Britain by the Henley Forecasting Centre indicates that the vast, fragmented barrier-prone industries in the Community, where the gains are greatest, are the fast-growing technological sectors. These are the ones in which the Japanese excel.

It is realistic to believe that the Japanese have both the capability and propensity to establish positions in Europe comparable to those which US companies achieved in the 1950s and 1960s.

- Japanese companies have created total commitment to total quality management (TQM) – this concept permeates to every area of each company. Yet the Japanese have managed to twin this commitment to that of high productivity, ensuring lower production costs are not at the price of quality loss.

- Japanese companies work to lower current rates of return and longer payout periods than their competition. Japanese companies tend to be highly geared (using low-cost bank borrowings), thus reducing shorter-term pressures brought to bear by equity holders.

As a result price/earnings ratios of Japan's largest companies are around 94 per cent against returns in capital of about 8 per cent.

This is further illustrated by the fact that despite the large market

Table 2.1 Top automotive companies

Company	Sales ($m)	Ranking of sales	Profits ($m)	% of Sales	Ranking of profits	Return on equity %	Ranking of return on equity	Country of incorporation
General Motors	101,782	1	171	0.2	8	10.0	8	USA
Ford	71,643	2	4630	6.4	1	26.0	3	USA
Toyota	**53,380**	**3**	**2080**	**3.9**	**2**	**8.6**	**9**	**Japan**
Daimler Benz	39,093	4	1035	2.6	6	31.7	2	W Germany
Nissan	**34,170**	**5**	**163**	**0.5**	**10**	**4.6**	**10**	**Japan**
Fiat	30,200	6	1850	6.1	3	24.7	4	Italy
Chrysler	26,277	7	1290	4.9	4	20.1	6	USA
Honda	**22,930**	**8**	**692**	**3.0**	**7**	**12.6**	**7**	**Japan**
Peugeot	20,300	9	1150	5.6	5	49.7	1	France
Volvo	15,476	10	171	1.1	8	21.2	5	Sweden

The table is based on latest available data (31 May 1988)

Source: *Business Week*, Morgan Stanley Capital International

shares Japanese companies enjoy across the world only 51 have profits of $200 million dollars or more, compared to 58 British and 205 US companies. The Japanese reinvest profits in the R & D, quality and market investment. This is what fuels their expansion.

The automotive industry provides an example of the relative perform-ance of Japanese companies compared with their global rivals as Table 2.1 shows.

The Japanese see the European Community as a single market. Until 1985 the low value of the yen and the excellent exporting infras-tructure provided by Japan's 6,000 or so trading companies (*Sogo Shosha*, 16 of which control 55 per cent of Japanese exports and just over a third of Japan's GNP) gave Japan an edge in exporting to the Community.

Lately, in response to the rising yen and to avoid trade friction, many Japanese companies are locating in Europe. Not only are production units arriving but many, like Mazda, are establishing R & D in Europe.

The impact that Japanese companies will have on the Community markets is mixed. Firstly, dominant companies will have to slug it out with their Japanese rivals in terms of cost, R & D and marketing to remain competitive. Yet at the same time more and more Japanese companies are under pressure to source from outside Japan. Hitachi for example has procurement offices in London, New York, and Hong Kong to identify suppliers. This provides opportunities for components and service suppliers in the Community.

Suppliers to companies under threat to Japanese competition will be forced to meet Japanese quality and service standards if they are to survive. This is simply because their European customers will need to match Japanese standards to compete in terms of quality and price. At the same time many potential Japanese customers will want to source from companies who can meet their quality and service specifications.

The other factor which will impact on Europe as a result of greater Japanese competition is the quality of their marketing. The Japanese spend heavily on advertising, they price aggressively and provide high levels of customer support. Their marketing very often stems from a great depth of market research to find the weakness of their competition in terms of meeting customer needs. A good example of their potential threat is seen in the way Toyota entered the US car market.

Having studied the small car market Toyota found that it could enter the US market by positioning its small car against Volkswagen's Beetle and did so through:

- designing a small car which met US consumers' expectations more closely than Volkswagen (a compact American car);

- ensuring a better service organisation than Volkswagen; and

- providing superior margins to its distributors.

Japanese entry strategies tend to be successful. The list below gives some idea of how and why.

- They establish critical definitions of success, determined by exhaustive research, against which criteria they will permit no shortfall – whether to do with product performance, promotional activities, service levels, price levels etc.

- Though they do not always use established distribution networks, the Japanese always ensure that there is a competitive edge to availability and to customer service.

- Effective Japanese market entry strategies will tend towards outspending competitors and, where possible, orientation towards television advertising with the aim of creating a competitive edge towards competition.

- They are prepared to accept long periods of investment before payout is achieved.

- They bring a unified marketing attack to bear, ensuring that activities are sequenced for maximum impact.

Each market entry strategy is worked out from minute examination of the markets and the role that each element in the strategy will play. Planning tends to be bottom-up. Rather than relying upon tiers of home-based staff functionaries the Japanese are adept at using nationals in their own markets to effect strategies.

Yet not all Japanese activity consists of head-on assaults on rival companies. They also have joint ventures and informal collaboration agreements across nearly every business sector. For example: Toshiba has links with Siemens and GE; Honda with British Leyland; and Nissan with Volkswagen. The reason is described by senior executive vice president Sakae Shimizu of Toshiba: 'As the distance between countries is shortened and technology grows more complex, one company simply cannot cope with all aspects of technology development.'

The potential Japanese threat to Europe's industries will, however, apply to a limited range of industries only. For the strengths of Japanese internationalism are so far found in high-profile industries only.

High-profile Japanese companies in the key industrial sectors such as car making, watches, cameras, electronics and calculators present an impression that all Japanese enterprises are very efficient in terms of cost, quality, output and marketing. Yet according to Kenichi Ohmae less than 15 per cent of the Japanese working population are employed in the high-technological blue chip companies. The general impression that all Japanese companies are so successfully run is incorrect.

Areas such as chemicals, food processing, cement and aluminium are far less competitive than many Western companies. Pharmaceutical companies, though beginning to reshape, are still many and small. Aerospace is still far behind US and European competitors. The Japanese service industries such as retailing, airline, insurance and distribution, have much lower productivity than those found for example in Britain or the USA. The banking sector is expanding very rapidly though, fuelled by Japan's tremendous financial surplus.

In relative sales terms, Mitsubishi chemical, Japan's largest chemical company, is worth about $3bn while companies like ICI and Hoechst have sales in excess of $20bn.

Outside the principal blue chip companies it would be a myth to suggest that Japanese companies are by and large better managed and more productive than those in the West. Yet it would be true to say that the strength of the Japanese economy in export terms is highly dependent on the success of companies employing less than 20 per cent of the total labour force.

North American competition

Nearly 40 per cent of the world's 1,000 largest companies are North American. The US has 345 and Canada 35. Most of them already operate in the EC.

North American companies have co-existed with Community companies for decades. In fact since 1945 they have played no small part in European recovery. Many large US companies such as IBM, Procter and Gamble, Nabisco, Ely Lilley and Caterpillar have provided the training grounds for European management. Management education is largely based on the curricula of US business schools such as Harvard.

The linkages between Europe and North American companies are largely through Multinational Enterprise (MNE) ownership although the USA enjoys a positive trade balance through exports to the community. Even so the European Commission sees North America along with Japan as a major competitor – particularly in terms of technological innovation and global presence.

Table 2.2 The EC's share of global companies – Top 1,000

Country	No of companies	No in oil gas utilities	No with capitalisation greater than $2bn	No with sales greater than $2bn**	No with profits greater than $200m
Belgium	11	1	6	4	4
Denmark	1	–	–	–	–
France	25	2	18	20	16
Italy	17	–	10	5	11
Ireland	–	–	–	–	–
The Netherlands	11*	1	6	5	7
Portugal	–	–	–	–	–
Spain	16	3	9	4	6
W Germany	35	4	22	19	13
UK	112*	6	82	97	58
Japan	310	17	260	172	51
USA	345	45	259	240	205

* including 2 Anglo-Dutch Companies
** Excluding banks

Source: *Business Week*, Morgan Stanley International

The need for American companies to operate globally to compete at home makes the Community very attractive both for investment and to growing exports from the USA. The impact of the Single Market will provide US companies (which have scale advantages) with the opportunity to compete more effectively in the Community than many Community companies. The harmonisation of products and freedom of movement for goods across such a large market provides ample opportunities for firms with large, cost-effective capacity.

North American companies already established in Europe have an intimate knowledge of the market and have adequate dispositions through which to exploit the Single Market. They have tremendous R & D resources and their new hunger and motivation to export will cause more and more US firms to look at Europe, especially as it is one of the few remaining areas in the global market prepared to accept bilateral trade agreements of equal advantage and at the same time be able to pay for their products in hard currency.

With the advent of the Single Market the very size of the European Community will force North American managers to look at Europe as a single entity rather than as a collection of small countries. The mode of entry into the Community by US firms is typically by acquisition. This will undoubtedly alter the ownership patterns within the Community.

The styles of North American companies contrast strongly with Japanese. They are more likely to go for quick returns on investment. Stockholder pressure is much more severe for US companies. Price/ earnings ratios for the largest US companies are about 22 per cent, 6 per cent higher than for principal European companies although their return on equity is on average 4 per cent lower at 15.2 per cent.

There is considerable unease in North America that a 'fortress Europe' will emanate from the Single Market. Many North American companies in anticipation of such a prospect are rapidly acquiring, forming alliances with, or acquiring equity in, Community companies. IBM has had companies throughout the Community for decades but is already emphasising the 'Britishness' or 'Germaness' etc of its products in each market.

The dominance of many large North American companies already established in Europe will mean that competition in their sectors will not be greatly disturbed by the Single Market save where their capacity advantages enable them to exploit scale opportunities afforded by the harmonisation of standards.

However, larger US companies have already deployed production into centres of excellence across the Community to produce products or components in countries or regions where they can be most beneficially made.

One interesting feature of North American investment in Europe will be to create a new sunbelt high-technology area in Spain, Italy, Portugal, and possibly the southern regions of France. By recreating California in Europe it will shift high-value-added and high-technology production and R & D to the warmer areas of Europe.

Competition from the Pacific basin

In their recent book, *The New Competition*, Philip Kotler et al describe the threats not only from Japan but potentially from the Pacific basin.

Korea, Taiwan, Singapore, and Hong Kong are following the Japanese model for expansion. Indonesia, Thailand and Malaysia together with the Philippines are slowly awakening as potential global competitors with cheap labour, technology and the Japanese model for global expansion. Many of these countries already provide low cost Original Equipment Manufacture (OEM) manufacture for US, Japanese and European companies. They are acquiring technology and product expertise.

In Korea for instance, production technology is rapidly advancing beyond 'screwdriver' status and R & D is already taking place in high technology. It has for example the most efficient steelmaking industry in the world feeding its rapidly expanding automotive industry.

The major impact of Pacific basin competition will be to attack vulnerable low-technology European industries and provide a low-cost alternative for OEM production. Surprisingly, these countries have a massive marketing capability created for them by the large international trading companies, many of them based in Hong Kong and Singapore.

European companies that are the targets of threats from this region's exports will need to lobby for protection and improve on cost, product quality and reliability to compete.

Kotler et al also point out the threat from India and China: the two largest national populations on earth. India needs only to shake off political inertia and social and economic mismanagement to join the league table of rapidly expanding countries. It has an educated commercial elite, a cheap source of labour and a technological infrastructure. It only needs a kick start.

And China, 'the sleeping giant' – what will happen when the billion or so Chinese begin to tread the wheel of their industrial dynamo. In 1997 Hong Kong will become a province of China and a gateway to the world for Chinese products.

Australia too has a rapidly growing industrial base. Its larger companies in food, beverage, media and financial services have been very acquisitive in both Europe and the USA. Outside its agricultural and extractive industries Australian majors occupy global positions in broadcasting, food, brewing and household products.

As a principal member of the British Commonwealth, Australia enjoys both national links and a political status in the British economy. The tendency therefore will be for Australian companies to expand into Europe through their bases in Britain.

European competition

To try and estimate the impact that potential European competitors will have on each other's markets ignores the presence of external competition. Yet in terms of estimating changes in the customer base two features of European competition emerge.

- Companies within the Community forming mergers or collaborative arrangements may bring about a change to customer profiles. It is rare indeed that procurement is shared proportionately between the suppliers of two or more companies following a merger or acquisition.
- Companies will make efforts to become more international in marketing terms. As a consequence they will tend to become more international in procurement.

In looking at the nature of European Community competition we can see some distinct differences between those countries with larger companies and those without. Britain has 112 of the world's top companies; Germany 35, France 25, Italy 17, Spain 16 and the Netherlands and Belgium 11 each.

There has been a great emphasis placed on investment in the USA by the larger European companies. This is basically because investment in North America is relatively less encumbered by red tape than Europe and the US market offered considerably more potential than the barrier-strewn Community. Yet in a number of fields, especially the pharmaceutical sector in which Europe still retains a competitive position, entry into the USA remains an important goal in their Single Market strategy. Jean-François Dehecq, chairman of Samoti SA, interviewed by *Business Week* said: 'We absolutely must be in the US market by 1992 to sell the new drugs our research labs will be producing.'

The combined advantages of a North American and a free European Community market put a number of major European companies on to a competitive global footing with their North American and Japanese competitors. No doubt this will be reinforced by the tremendous financial capacity such a position allows to make further acquisitions within the Community.

The desire for non-Community European companies to enter the Community through acquisition and collaboration is already greatly in evidence particularly by Swiss and Swedish concerns. Companies such as

Swedish Match, Atlas Copco and Nestlé have long operated in the Community through acquired subsidiary companies. The furore over the Swiss company Nestlé's acquisition of Rowntree Mackintosh in the UK was much heralded as a sign that Nestlé was securing a greater base in the Community. Yet for the world's largest food producer, which already has indigenously-incorporated companies throughout the Community, the move was probably more to secure a greater global opportunity than to create additional dispositions in the Community. Yet the non-community European companies do realise they need to take a stake within it.

Small- and medium-sized businesses

The importance of small- and medium-sized businesses is not to be underestimated. The impact of the Single Market has been forecast as the death knell for many. Yet the reverse is likely. Evidence gathered in the US for example shows quite clearly that smaller companies not only survive quite well in North America, they have the propensity to compete with large companies.

The Small and Medium Sized Business Task force is a European Commission organisation aimed at providing support for this sector. Its creation of the Business Co-operation Network has been designed to enable organisations to find contacts for collaboration. This enables small firms to continue to do what they are best at – namely sub-optimising larger firms.

This they achieve through their flexibility and lower costs which enable them to exploit narrow niches in the markets that would be uneconomic for larger-scale firms. Smaller firms too can be far more regionally organised to meet specific and peculiar customer needs much more closely than organisations operating on a pan-European scale.

The effects of the Single Market will be adverse on small companies where these are component or own-label suppliers to large domestic customers who restructure, begin to shop around the Community, or move their production bases. Companies thus affected will need to do some restructuring of their own or develop an exporting capability to follow their customers. The danger is that some small companies may overstretch their capabilities by spreading their operations too thinly across the Community. This will result if, rather than focusing on narrow niches or regions they are best able to exploit, they dilute their activities. Stretched financial resources may be a greater threat to their survival than being overwhelmed by competitors.

The effects of competition on industry structures

The intensification of business activity triggered by the creation of the Single Market will have a number of effects on the shaping of industry structures across the community. The main elements will be:

- the exit of a number of firms due to competitive intensity;
- the relocation of production by companies needing to produce more competitive products in recognised centres of excellence or needing to find lower cost production centres;
- the acquisition by predatory companies of firms located within Community markets to provide or strengthen their marketing and manufacturing dispositions in target markets or to acquire essential technology;
- acquisition of smaller companies which may in themselves be at a competitive disadvantage but are attractive enough for them to successfully offer themselves to larger firms;
- acquisitions by external Community firms as a means of creating an indigenous presence;
- acquisition and mergers for vertical integration reasons to control upstream and downstream elements of their industry's value system; and
- mergers and joint ventures to reinforce the strength and position of companies in the face of the need to scale up activities, collaborate on distribution, meet R & D needs etc.

It is these potential changes to industry structures which will affect the competitive conditions under which both suppliers and customers will have to operate. It is vital, therefore, that managers look more closely at the risks of change and the impact they will bring to their individual firms.

Industry structures in which companies compete are transaction points within an overall industry value system. The relationship between, say, a finished product manufacturer and its channels of distribution are just as much affected by the costs the manufacturer pays for its raw materials as the competition the company faces itself in supplying the distribution channels.

If we consider that an industry is part of an overall value system through which the movement of raw materials pass in various stages of added value until they reach the final customer then we have a model upon which to assess the risks of change to a firm.

Figure 2.1 is a simplified value system which can be used to assess the probabilities of change which will have an effect on suppliers, customers and competition.

Industry value system model

The model shows the components of an industry as a *value system* and the transaction points along it. These transaction points represent the industry structures in which companies compete as sellers and buyers. An industry structure is therefore affected by changes in competitive intensity in two ways. First, the actual intensity within the structure at a given transaction point, and secondly the effects of change at other transaction points.

For example, if the number of finished product manufacturers were to increase without a corresponding increase in the number of component suppliers then the latter's control over prices and services would increase because they would exert supplier power over the manufacturers. If, at the same time, the competitive intensity of the distribution channels were not to increase, the dominance of buyers would be to command buying power over the manufacturers. The effect would be to reduce prices and margins on the one hand and to increase costs on the other.

It would be an obvious conclusion therefore to suggest that whereas the value system proportions the value generated along it, the share available at any one transaction point is reduced where competitive intensity is highest and is moved to where it is lowest.

Thus in the example where the finished product manufacturers operate under considerable competitive intensity the value moves in three directions – to suppliers, channels of distribution and to service industries such as advertising organisations and transporters with the need to increase marketing investment and service by each manufacturer contesting to sell its products.

By drawing up an approximate model of a firm's industry value system and placing the firm at the appropriate point in the system it can be used to illustrate how the risks of change are likely to affect the firm's position. By

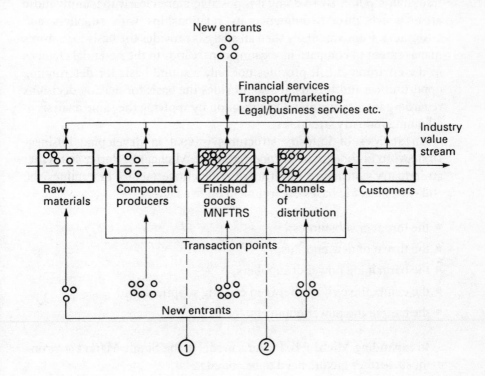

Figure 2.1 Simplified industry value system

The diagram illustrates an industry value system. As materials pass down the system towards the final consumer, the share of value is proportioned to buyers and sellers at transaction points. The greater the intensity of competing buyers and sellers at a transaction point, the lower the proportion of value shared at that point. With the creation of the Single Market, more new entrants at any industry structure surrounding a transaction point intensify competition and affect share of the value stream. The shaded areas illustrate the effects of restructuring:

1. *The effect is seen where restructuring of manufacturers changes the component producer's customer base and decreases their selling power.*
2. *The restructuring of the channels of distribution redresses the balance of seller power of the manufacturers squeezing the intensifying component structure for lower prices.*

selective analysis of those factors likely to influence critical transaction points in the system it is possible to identify those areas most likely to create risks to a firm's own position.

In analysing the value system of an industry it is important to understand the factors which influence industry structures at each transaction point. By so doing it is possible more clearly to identify those areas which directly influence its relationships with suppliers and customers. Fundamentally such an analysis provides the basis for a firm's management to compare its existing capabilities to the potential changes in the environment. It provides not only a sound basis for determining opportunities and threats, it also provides the basis for making decisions regarding integration and diversification by applying the same analysis to adjoining industry structures.

An analysis of industry structures is vital in developing business strategy. In his book, *Competitive Advantage*, Michael E. Porter states that an industry's structure in terms of competitive factors determines the ability to earn. He bases his argument on five factors:

- the threat of substitutes;
- the threat of new entrants;
- the bargaining power of suppliers;
- the competitive rivalry between existing suppliers; and
- the bargaining power of buyers.

In expanding Michael E. Porter's model to the Single Market environment six further factors need to be added:

- the removal of government support for individual competitors;
- the effect of exchange rates on relative prices;
- the problems of parallel trade;
- reduction in costs of credit;
- collaborative arrangements; and
- the consequent effect of structural changes in the entire industry value system.

By basing analysis on a competitor intensity model modified to account for the effects of the Single Market, managers can obtain a better understanding of the market in terms of its health and politics.

Furthermore, by focusing on competitive intensity we are more likely to identify both opportunities and threats more readily.

The market should be assessed from the point of view of those opportunities most likely still to afford threats from new entrants despite existing competitor rivalry. Not only should those threats be recognised, they should be seen as offering opportunities for the company itself. The competitive intensity model below (Figure 2.2) provides a very useful tool for assessing the business environment.

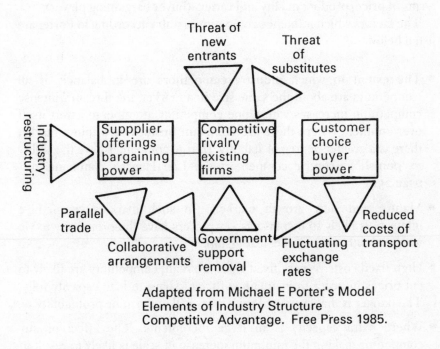

Adapted from Michael E Porter's Model
Elements of Industry Structure
Competitive Advantage. Free Press 1985.

Figure 2.2 Impact of the Single Market on industry structure

As can be seen the model focuses on competitor interactions and the effect they have on customer choice. The model can be best explained by using a monopoly example. A single supplier with no competitors to worry about would be able to control the market, meeting customer choice only to the extent that customers would refrain from seeking substitute products (supplier bargaining power). The perpetuation of the single supplier's control would be limited by factors influencing the threat of new competitors and product substitutes entering the market. These might be government protection, the small size of the market, environmental factors, the cost of technology, intellectual property such as patents and so forth. The threat to the monopolist would be some element of change which permits competitor entry. Examples are the awakening of customer aspirations of choice (television in Europe) thus creating a threat from substitutes, and the lifting of government protection (British Telecom) thus attracting new entrants and the loss of patents.

As the level of competitive intensity increases so the supplier's control of the market diminishes with the increased choices customers seek in terms of price, product quality and variety (buyer bargaining power).

The factors which influence competitive rivalry according to Porter are listed below.

- The extent to which industry competitors are in balance. If all competitors are about the same size in a market, the threat of intense competition increases where one competitor attempts to assert itself over another. Where there are dominant businesses within a market there is a greater degree of stability. (Large companies have the ability to 'punish' disruptive competitors see Len Hardy's comments on page 254).

- Mature and slow growth markets. In such markets competitive intensity is likely to increase as key players have the propensity to vie with each other for market leadership.

- High fixed costs. Where fixed costs are high, competitors are likely to cut prices in order to maintain sufficient share to load capacity fully. The danger is that sustained price wars will undermine profitability.

- Where extra capacity is in large increments. The effect of any competitor making the minimum increase in scale is likely to result in short-term over-capacity in an industry. Thus any increase in capacity by one competitor will result in the under-utilisation of capacity by others. The result will be increased price competition.

- Where there are high exit barriers. The difficulties which face companies in exiting from a market are likely to result in the persistence of excess capacity. This will result in increased competition. Exit barriers may be high where production facilities are dedicated to specific types of product, redundancy costs are high, political pressures exist, and subsidies and aid continue to make uneconomic businesses viable.

Government protection

The influence of government protection is a major factor in both stimulating competitor activity and in moderating the turbulence of the market. Government protectionist measures most commonly influencing competitive intensity are:

- protecting indigenous industry by discriminating against imports (European governments) and limiting foreign investment (Japan, India, LDCs);
- supporting indigenous industries to give them favoured status within national markets through aid and government contracts (European governments);
- supporting indigenous industries through planned government strategies to give them global advantages (Japan); and
- moderating competitor rivalry through state monopolies, price controls, VAT and duty etc.

Any change in government policy will have a major impact on the competitive intensity of a market whether it be global, regional or national by definition.

Very often companies are aware of the frustrations to business opportunities which government policies in foreign markets create but are little aware of the subtleties of their own.

Foreign exchange

Exchange rates can modify price and competitiveness where there is a large element of foreign competition in a market. Efficient firms are put at a competitive disadvantage if exchange rates adversely affect relative prices. Conversely, inefficient firms can gain price advantages where exchange rates favour them. The lack of a common currency within the Single Market means that exchange rates will play a major part in modifying cost-competitive advantages – it will also encourage parallel trade.

Parallel trade

Parallel trade is both condoned and encouraged in the European Community. It will have three major effects on an industry's ability to earn.

- Price competition is exacerbated where parallel traders buy up products where they are cheapest and sell them where they are sold most expensively in the Community.

- Products are diverted from the markets intended.

- Parallel trade can modify industry value systems because traders intervene to intercept materials, components and finished products and supply them at lower costs throughout the system.

Whilst parallel trade in the EC is most noticeable in the movement of finished foods, it occurs in the movement of both raw materials and components (through brokers largely centred in Germany). Thus parallel trade can affect the relative prices paid by producers in the value system (modifying production costs) and in intercepting and diverting finished products.

The extent to which major retail buyers will adopt parallel-buying policies on their own account remains to be seen. Those with resources and procurement dispositions within the Single Market certainly have the ability to do so, and no doubt competitive intensity within the retail sector will encourage them.

Reductions in the cost of credit

Competition intensifying in the financial services sector through the relaxation of controls will stimulate cheaper and more competitive borrowing. This will have the effect of:

- providing capital for new entrants, thus increasing competitive intensity;

- motivating companies to increase their scale of production, thus increasing the level of spare capacity at certain points along the value system (with the effect of reducing profitability at points along the system where this is damaged by price warfare or dissipated through additional marketing costs); and

- permitting external firms to enter the Community by subsidising their investments by low-cost borrowing in the Community.

Reductions in transport costs

The removal of frontier controls and relaxing transport regulations will have the effect of reducing transport costs. Cheaper transport costs combined with free movement of goods will enable companies to relocate production from their domestic market to areas where production is cheaper or where they can achieve benefits in quality and R & D in centres of excellence. This will provide them with a competitive edge in their previous domestic markets and introduce them to other markets. Furthermore, movements of this sort will upset the customer base for companies that have traditionally supplied these companies.

If costs fall significantly it will enable firms to reach markets hitherto denied them because of transport costs (companies in Spain and Portugal), once again increasing the competitive pressures within the Single Market.

Collaborative arrangements

As a response to competitive pressures or as a means of lessening the risk of entering new markets, collaborative arrangements provide a useful vehicle. Collaborative arrangements (excluding those of a trust nature) are encouraged within the Single Market, and the BC-Net and R & D projects sponsored by the Community provide 'marriage bureaux' for companies wishing to co-operate.

Even collaborative arrangements have both positive and negative effects on industry structures.

- They increase competitive rivalry by permitting new companies to enter markets at lower risk and shared costs. Because the aspirations, resources and risks are shared, exit barriers tend to be higher – because all members of a collaborative arrangement have to agree before an exit can be made. The impact on an industry structure may thus be to dissipate its profitability where collaborators are prepared to accept low or negative profits.

- Collaborative arrangements can modify value structures where the arrangement involves collaboration between sellers and buyers. Thus a component manufacturer forming an arrangement with a manufacturer on a production/R & D project, for example, may reduce the level of competition under which the component manufacturer has to operate. Similarly, collaboration between manufacturers and distribution channels reduces competitive factors in the relationship.

It can be seen, therefore, that the impact of competition created by the formation of the Single Market is far more complex than might at first be thought. The processes likely to change competition stem not only from the direct effects of firms finding new competitors in their markets but also from the changes that competitor activity will produce by changing both suppliers and customers. As firms themselves decide to expand into new markets to take up opportunities which the Single Market provides they will themselves influence the competitive features of their markets.

Understanding how competitive pressures affect industry structures is crucial in strategic planning. Once the underlying forces are revealed it allows managers to tune strategies to outperform their competitors in terms of business development and earning performance, as we will see in the next chapter.

3
Strategic Management for the Single Market

In Chapter 2 we discussed the opportunities and threats that the Single Market introduces through its impact on the business environment. The importance of understanding the intensity of competitive rivalry within industry structures and the way in which the value system of industry will evolve is crucial to developing a Single Market strategy.

The aim for all companies must be to find ways of matching their strengths to the challenges and opportunities the Single Market brings. The aim of this chapter, therefore, is to outline the processes of strategic management for the Single Market.

The outlook we will stress is the need to find competitive advantage, focusing on business development rather than straightforward growth. Above all, we emphasise the adoption of an international orientation. The strategic planning process also has to take into consideration that firms expanding into the European Community will need to increase the complexity of running their operations.

The chapter treats the Single Market as an economic union, not as a homogenous market because, compared even to the United States with its different regional and ethnic characteristics, the EC remains more complex. The Single Market, then, adds complexity to running a business. Each state in which a firm operates *multiplies* rather than simply adds to the complexity. For whilst standards and customs formalities are eventually to be harmonised, the geometric curve of complexity will still persist as companies tangle with new sets of exchange rates, contract law, employment law, taxation, VAT, language, distribution channels, advertising laws and advertising media. Even competition profiles are likely to remain very regionalised for a great number of companies for a very long period to come.

In tackling the problem of designing strategies, companies will need to recognise that generalised central issues will need to embrace the operational complexities involved in a multi-country operation. The Single Market demands of managers a general set of strategic intentions covering their overall approach but will also need subsets of operational strategies for each market. To take on the Single Market as a unitary whole ignores the advantages that its internal cultural and geographic boundaries afford in permitting firms to tackle markets piecemeal, enabling them to consolidate as they go along. It ignores, too, the difficulties of winkling out nationally entrenched competition and the differing economic cultural environments within each national boundary.

Yet for firms to exploit the full benefits of harmonised product standards, relaxed border controls and the freedoms afforded in the movement of capital and labour, a wider, all-embracing strategy will be required. That strategy must permit a firm's competitive advantages to be deployed. It must be one which enables the firm to locate its marketing and production dispositions to meet competitive levels of customer service, cost advantages and to spread risks. The aim, therefore, is to create a strategy which on the one hand deploys a company's global competitive advantages and, on the other is responsive to individual country market needs.

Strategy – reasons, aims, processes

Like it or not, most companies are going to find themselves embroiled in a fiercely contended market after 1992. Managers must be able to deploy their companies' resources and activities with a full understanding of the success requirements needed to achieve and maintain their competitive position.

Research shows that companies lacking corporate direction lose the capabilities to match their competitors' advances. The squandering of corporate strengths and competitive advantages through inaction or inappropriate adventures occurs when strategic elements in business management are lacking.

Sound development of business strategy allows management to plot the future course of business, to enable them to focus corporate advantages on marketing problems and plan for and seek resources. Furthermore, by establishing strategic intentions there are ready criteria against which managers can make decisions with the confidence that these are in keeping with the future direction of their businesses.

The aim of strategy

The aim of the Single Market strategy is to enable companies to assess their relative strengths and competitive advantages in relation to the challenges and opportunities the market affords. This will provide the foundation for a business development strategy which enables companies to plan their product market strategies, and to fuel these with resources, both physical and financial. It will help them prioritise projects and plan where to locate production.

The process of strategic planning

The logic of any planning method demands a clear statement of the mission the plan intends to achieve. This provides the basis on which to make the assessment of the mission in terms of objectives and resources. The process of strategic planning is made up from the following:

- A stated corporate mission, around which the intentions of the plan can be determined, should be defined.
- An audit of resources, strengths and weaknesses of the company's present situation should be brought out so that it can determine its future objectives and match these with additional resources.
- Objectives should be set in terms of development and performance.
- The realities of implementation should be assessed through an understanding of the challenge the company faces and the constraints under which it will have to operate.
- A plan outlining the development stages it needs to follow should be drawn up.
- An assessment of its options in terms of development stages should be undertaken to exhaust those least likely to provide the best outcomes to the strategy.
- An assessment of the alternative methods of development in terms of generic growth, acquisition and collaboration should be carried out to determine the best solutions for individual markets and businesses in which the company intends to operate.
- The evolution of an organisation to match the needs of strategy should be planned.

In this chapter we will outline the strategic planning process and in later chapters introduce the detail of options for strategic choices as well as operating activities.

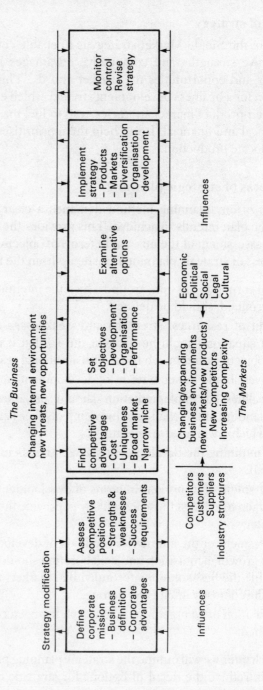

Figure 3:1 A scheme for corporate strategy development in the Single Market

Defining the corporate mission

Management must have a basis upon which to determine strategies. Mere financial performance criteria have little respect for the means of achieving them. There must be some guiding principle, some unifying force which focuses management on selecting strategic options which best favour the company – through the exploitation of that which it is best at and for which it has some innate competitive advantage.

The *corporate mission concept* is a powerful unifying force.

It is the embodiment of all corporate purposes and intentions. It is the identification of the company's business definition with due regard to its intentions, capabilities and competitive advantages.

An early exponent of 'the business definition' was Theodore Levitt who in a famous paper, *Marketing Myopia*, asked managers to be more aware of the business they are in. He attributed the demise of US railroad companies to the attitude of managers being more focused on moving rail stock rather than operating a transport business. What Levitt had to say was relevant and useful in its day. The downside, however, has been that many attempts to develop businesses around the concept of a business definition have been too broadly interpreted, leading to massive over-diversification.

Yet as a concept it provides the fundamental basis for the development of creative and objective business strategies – especially when qualified by strategic intentions.

The corporate mission adds power and direction to the business definition. By qualifying the business definition with sets of intentions it becomes not only the basis of corporate strategic thinking but enables a whole corporate culture to evolve round it. Corporate mission can be defined from a number of associations with the business definition.

Competitive advantage

How can the company's competitive advantage be brought to bear on market opportunities? For example, Sony's strength in R & D in electronics, Glaxo's strength in pharmaceutical R & D, ICI's global dispositions, Honda's developments in high performance engines . . .

Business opportunities

How can a company expand its skills into new areas of opportunity? For example, Rank's development of leisure-related industries or

W. H. Smith's developments into international communications on the one hand and other areas of retailing on the other.

Defensive and offensive competitive positioning

What position can a business take within its markets to defend its business or attack its competitors? For example, segmentation of the auto market by Jaguar both to attack competition and defend share in the upper end of the medium-priced executive car market.

Innovator positioning

Which chosen areas of technology to pursue to be 'first in and best' for example, Wellcome's domination of anti-viral technology or Boeing's development of wide-bodied aircraft.

Domination positioning

Which product or market areas can a company aim to dominate through brand promotional investment, capacity, cost and price advantages, distribution and so on to provide a secure position. This is relevant to lower-technology businesses, for example, newspaper publishing (the *Financial Times*), clothing and shoe manufacture (Levi Strauss and Bata), food and drinks manufacture (Coke, Pepsi, Nabisco Brands) and other fmcg businesses.

The corporate mission is defined from qualifying a 'what business the company is in' statement with one or more positional statements outlining the company's intentions. An example might be: 'The corporate mission is to exploit opportunities within the global leisure market by leading innovation in satellite broadcastings'.

Such a statement clearly outlines the business's mission and provides managers with the necessary parameters within which to explore marketing avenues and create strategies to exploit opportunities.

The corporate mission statement also helps guide managers back to the main issues in a business. Too often peripheral activities are embarked upon as the only areas managers feel they can influence within their organisations. Attention to the mission reduces the danger that peripheral activities are set up outside the mainstream of a company's activities, widening the cost base without adding much to the thrust of a business.

In the business play of an international organisation the corporate mission is super-ordinate to all objectives. The business can be and often is broken down to smaller units providing centres of excellence for the different strengths of the business. Each business unit should define its role within the overall corporate mission as the example below (Figure 3.2) shows:

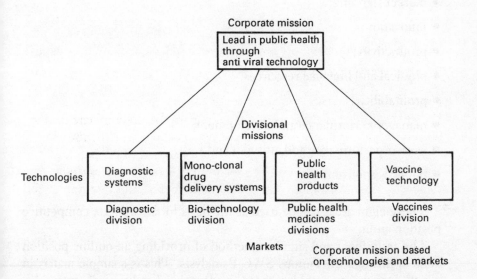

Figure 3.2 Cascade of missions for a pharmaceutical business

Analysing the company's competitive position

The ability of a company to thrive depends to a great extent on its competitive advantages in comparison to its competitors. Toyota in the US, for example, was able to exact a determined assault on Volkswagen. At the outset Volkswagen had a number of competitive advantages in terms of product, awareness, loyal customers and distribution. Yet Toyota – through painstaking research – discovered an opportunity window through which to drive into Volkswagen's share of the US auto market.

The need to assess a company's competitive position on a continuous basis is essential for two reasons. Firstly, in order to assess its own capabilities in measuring up to the success requirements needed for success in the market place. And secondly to compare itself against its competitors.

Peter Drucker named eight performance areas which are critical to the longer-term success of an enterprise. They make ideal headings under which an assessment of corporate competitiveness and capability can be assessed:

- market standing;
- innovation;
- productivity;
- physical and financial resources;
- profitability;
- manager performance and development;
- worker performance and attitude; and
- public responsibility.

These eight areas can be used as the basis for a corporate competitive position audit.

The traditional and simplest method of providing an outline position audit is through the famous SWOT analysis. This is a simple matrix in which statements can be listed under the headings of strengths, weaknesses, opportunities and threats.

The purpose of the SWOT analysis is to:

- identify those factors which contribute to the past and present success of the business;
- provide an inventory of the company's skills and resources;
- pinpoint those strength areas in the business that can be used as a foundation for a future strategy and critical weaknesses which must be shed;
- enable the company to identify its strengths and weaknesses in relation to those of its competitors; and
- identify key strengths in terms of resources and skills which are either superior or weaker than those of its principal rivals.

The SWOT analysis lends itself to the use of Peter Drucker's headings. The sample of questions below illustrates those which can be used in compiling a database for analysis.

Marketing standing

- In which of the Community's markets does the company already operate?
- What is its current market share in the total market and the major segments it occupies? Is it growing or contracting?
- Is the company in a strong position and does it enjoy a unique status in its industry?
- What are the market conditions – is the market in growth or decay? What is the rate of change?
- What position in the product life cycle are the company's principal products?
- Are prices and margins improving or decaying? How do these vary across the Community?
- How balanced is the portfolio of products in terms of innovation, growth and maturity?
- What proportion of the product range is due for divestment?
- How do the company's products compare with competition on such loyalty issues as function, reliability, quality and modernity?
- How vulnerable is the firm to exhaustion of its intellectual properties patents, licences etc? Do patents expire simultaneously across the Community?
- How effective are the company's promotion and selling activities?
- Is customer service seen as a marketing objective?
- How effective are channels of distribution?
- What is the quality of the marketing organisation and its levels of international experience?

Innovation

- Does the firm have a good marketing intelligence system to alert it against competitor innovations?
- How successful has R & D been in the past in providing commercially viable products?

- Is there an R & D programme? Is it focused on mainstream technology and product development or on short-term peripheral projects?

- Is the R & D programme directed at meeting marketing strategy goals?

- Is the R & D function internationally oriented or focused on the domestic market?

- Does the R & D function contract out its special problem areas to specialist agencies?

- How do the relative strengths and weaknesses in R & D compare to competition in terms of output, people, facilities and resources?

Productivity

- How is productivity determined and how does the firm compare to its industry and competitors?

- Is there a ceiling to volume production?

- How integrated is the production system? What is produced in-house compared to that brought in?

- How do production costs compare with competitors?

- What proportion of available capacity is fully utilised?

- Are there any restrictive trade-union practices which constrain productivity?

- Are production sites best located in relation to markets served?

- Is production located in centres of excellence?

Physical and financial resources

- Does the company have adequate resources to match its present strategies?

- What is the financial health of the company in terms of gearing, liquidity, ability to raise funds and profitability?

- How competitive is the company compared with its industry in managing its expenses as seen by its revenue-to-cost ratios?

- Does the firm have the ability to control its international funds (exchange rate, transfer pricing, dividend and repatriation of funds policies)?

- How is working capital financed and is it sufficient to meet current needs?
- Can the company raise additional funds through increasing its equity, debt financing etc?
- How well organised are the accounting systems and budgetary controls?
- Is there an effective costing system?
- Does the firm have long-term and short-term financial strategies and plans?
- Is the financial management well led, organised and controlled?

Profitability
- How profitable is the firm compared to industry competitors?
- Are earnings per share greater or less than the industry average?
- What factors, such as increasing capacity and innovation, have effects on depressing the profit stream?
- Are expense ratios in keeping with industry norms?
- What has been the pattern of profitability over the past, say, five years – is it increasing or decreasing?
- Are prices and margins increasing or decreasing?

Manager performance and attitude
- Is the company management style assertive and dynamic or passive and risk-averse?
- Is management successful in meeting its stated objectives?
- What proportion of managers have had formal management training?
- What is the age distribution of managers at the top?
- Have a significant proportion of key managers had experience outside the industry?
- Does management engage in strategic management?
- Do top management have the ability to take on the future challenges of the business in a new competitive environment?
- Have managers grasped the issues of the Single Market?

- Is there a succession plan with a depth of management to back it up?
- Are there managers with international skills?
- What proportion of managers speak foreign languages?

Worker performance and attitude

- Does the company have organised trade unions – what limitations does this place on flexibility?
- How well organised is the business to gain the best results out of its employees?
- Is there a positive corporate culture?
- Is morale high or low?
- Does the reward system retain staff and motivate performance and attitude?
- Does the organisation structure and training programme meet the needs to develop technology in production and administrative systems?
- Do employees contribute to quality programmes?
- Are employees involved in development and advancement programmes?
- Are employees aware of the Single Market and what it means to the company?

Public responsibility

- Does the company make positive contributions to win the support of its community?
- Does it have a public relations policy?
- Does it lead in such areas as personnel policy, health and safety regulation etc?
- Does it acknowledge corporate accountability?
- Has the company had any outstanding major court cases that would injure its reputation?
- How is the company seen by foreign governments?
- How active is the company in pursuing a political strategy at home, in the EC and with foreign governments etc?
- Does it have a political strategy?

The next stage is to determine the competitive position of the firm. This might well be done by soliciting questions from the model in Figure 3.3.

The model addresses the relationship between market share and a company's competitive position. It seeks to identify which success requirements need to be formulated in order for a company to maintain its present competitive position and to achieve its future market share and revenue.

In the model a company draws its present market share from the deployment of its competitive advantages. The present competitive

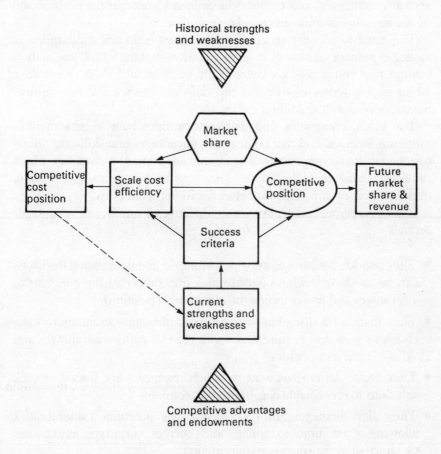

Figure 3.3 Assessment of competitive position

position is determined by the market share it holds and whether this represents a rising or falling share compared with past performance.

Strengths are determined by those factors which reinforce the company's ability to deploy its competitive advantages effectively. Weaknesses are those factors which mitigate against the deployment of competitive advantages.

The concept of success requirements which this model brings out is a positive recognition of what a company has to bring to its markets to maintain and improve its competitive position. In other words: what strengths must it draw from its competitive advantages and endowments to reinforce its position? Any shortfall to success requirements must be seen as weaknesses likely to lower the company's competitive position and hence its future market share and revenue.

The need to identify success requirements is a critical discipline in strategic management – as it is in decision-making at all levels. It is evident that companies are more likely to succeed if their competitive advantages in terms of strengths and skills match their success requirements more closely than their competitors.

Too often, companies find that opportunities have been somewhat randomly selected and that competitive advantages and skills are poorly matched against competitors. The simple adoption of a discipline which requires management to define its success requirements as a basis of decision-making can make for better decisions at all levels.

If success requirements are set as objectives a number of advantages accrue.

- They provide a basis against which strategic and operational decisions can be made (reducing opportunities for compromising competitive advantages and undermining the competitive position).

- They institute a discipline which forces managers to compare their company's success requirements with the competitive advantages and skills of their competitors.

- They create an environment in which managers are forced to seek solutions to identifiable corporate shortcomings.

- They alert managers to their company's potential vulnerabilities allowing them time to isolate and correct corporate weaknesses (ie shortfall to the success requirements).

- Probably most importantly, success criteria provide the basis of thought-out assumptions against which a common company-wide approach to the selection of alternative strategies and options can be assessed.

Such criteria will underline a company's objectives in terms of its product offerings, its markets, its deployment of resources and its marketing and production dispositions. In a nutshell, they involve reinforcing what a company is good at to give it an edge over competition. Determining success criteria means examining the following:

- the company's competitive advantages;
- resource analysis; and
- the nature of the market.

Competitive advantages

In Chapter 2 we described how the competitive intensity of industry structures determines the ability of companies to earn within them. This model is important. If managers are able to understand the structure of their industries they are better able to find strategies to outperform their competitors.

The need is to ascertain what generic competitive advantages a company can bring to the market which will enable it best to compete. The assessment of competitive advantages serves two purposes. It provides a basis upon which to compare the relative advantages a company has in terms of the competitive environment and provides a foundation upon which to build its future strategies.

It is an opportunity, therefore, to go back to basics in terms of encouraging managers to ask questions about what has made them successful in the past, what has kept them in business to date and how they can merge their past advantages with those required for the future.

The two factors most likely to yield competitive advantages are of course *cost advantages* and *uniqueness* in meeting buyer needs.

Cost advantages enable companies to extract higher margins than their competitors even when pricing close to or below industry prices. It enables them to sustain price turbulence longer than their competitors.

Uniqueness can give companies a competitive edge by enabling them to command higher prices than the industry average. It enables them to defend their products against poorly differentiated competitors as long as their tangible or psychological points of difference are perceived by customers as reasons for choosing the products.

No doubt the strongest competitive advantage a firm could achieve would be to have advantages in uniqueness and cost at the same time. Unfortunately, according to Michael E. Porter, going for both brings with it the dangers of achieving neither – thus leaving companies in the unenviable position of being 'stuck in the middle'.

Another way of determining competitive advantage is to look at how best a company focuses on its markets. Here the choice is *broad market capacity* or *narrow niche capability*.

A broad market capacity describes companies who thrive on broad markets through the scale and diversity of activities which such an approach requires. Such companies are best suited to occupying a number of large market segments seeking competitive advantages through their capacity to meet their demands.

A narrow niche capability is one which enables firms to operate in market segments which exploit and sub-optimise those firms with a broad market capacity. Such companies have a depth of narrowly defined specialisations, lower cost bases and the ability to be flexible.

Those with broad capacity often find it difficult to compete with those with a narrow niche capability. The narrowness of the field of specialisation and the relative inflexibility of larger-scale companies means that in trying to occupy narrow segments their relative costs are too high to support the depth of specialisation needed. Conversely, narrow-niche

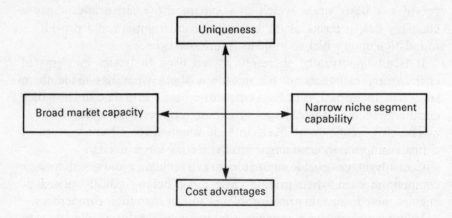

Figure 3.4 Competitive advantage compass illustrating the gap of feasibility between opposites

firms are inevitably overstretched and vulnerable to be gunned down by wide-market-scale companies if they encroach into their markets.

The options for seeking competitive advantage can be thus reduced to four. Laid out as points of a compass these give us the opportunity to illustrate the gap of feasibility between opposites.

Whilst the virtues of having unique *and* cost advantages, and to have both a broad-market capacity as well as a narrow-segment capability would be desirable, their achievement through a single business unit would be so danger-prone as to discourage an attempt. Porter gives the example of Laker Airways which began as a cost-advantaged business aimed at a narrow niche. In trying to achieve a broad-market capacity and offer uniqueness at the same time it failed as a business entity altogether.

Yet a market strategy alone fails to provide the necessary competitive advantage. Market strategies need to be either cost-based or uniqueness-based. Thus combinations of strategy can be seen as options – namely

		Cost advantages
Broad market capacity	+	or
		Uniqueness
		Cost advantages
Narrow niche capability	+	or
		Uniqueness

Competitive considerations

Whichever combination of competitive advantages companies adopt it leaves them vulnerable to the strategies of their competitors using the same strategies better or using different combinations wisely or unwisely.

For example cost advantages have to be sustainable against competitors displaying a similar strategy. Companies unable to contest cost-advantage strategies effectively are hard put to outperform their competitors. Thus companies adopting this strategy have to be cost leaders if they are to outperform their industry contenders.

Sustaining uniqueness means investing heavily in those activities which make the company or its products unique – whether they be customer service, R & D or marketing investment to create image differentiation. Companies are vulnerable to competitors who can bring more investment to their points of difference. Sustaining investment in those attributes which make for a uniqueness strategy is therefore vital.

Those companies offering cost advantages are vulnerable to their higher-priced rivals offering uniqueness – especially if the latter's R & D activities dispossess them of business through the creation of new generations of products or substitutes.

Companies offering uniqueness are always vulnerable to those with cost advantages. If the value of their differentiation is outweighed by their costs and prices they may not only lose customers but fail to sustain those attributes which have given them their advantages against equivalent generic products.

The battle between companies occupying broad and narrow markets has the potentiality not only to undermine contestants but also to damage market structures as a whole.

Narrow-niche capability allows those with the advantage to take up business uneconomic to those with broader capacity. Their strategies will encroach from time to time. The effect of broader-capacity firms to react and take up opportunities being exploited by firms with the capabilities to earn from narrow segments inevitably means that they will take up less value for the effort and resources expended.

Generic competitive advantages need to be reinforced.

Cost advantages need to be supported by demand and thus some activity in terms of keeping products up to date and meeting quality and service requirements will be necessary. Management of costs will need to take into account those needed to sustain a firm's ability to continue to offer contemporary products and meet minimum quality and service demands of customers.

Uniqueness advantages need to be reinforced by cost-competitiveness. There are two reasons.

Firstly, the lower the underlining cost base the greater the margins available for reinforcing differentiation of attributes and product development. Secondly, uniqueness may have a ceiling value in terms of price. Firms in a poor cost-competitive position are not likely to take the full benefit of their advantage. In fact poor profit performance may force managements to compromise their advantages by reducing investment in those attributes such as customer service, R & D and marketing which have hitherto provided uniqueness.

Multi-competitive advantage strategies

Whilst the plausibility of trying to achieve competitive advantages across price and uniqueness or broad and narrow market segments has been questioned it is feasible when applied to discrete business units.

For example, Nestlé uses separate sales forces to sell own-label generics of its major coffee brands. Ciba Geigi, Glaxo and Fisons have separate organisations to manufacture and sell generic pharmaceuticals. Horizontal diversification strategies could well be examined to add to business units the capability to take on market opportunities using different sets of competitive advantage. However, these business units need to be separated for two reasons.

Firstly, managerial expectations and aspirations are based on different philosophies (ie large-scale standardised product production versus highly adapted strategies to meet needs for which customers will pay higher prices). Secondly, organisational cost structures and resources are deployed differently (ie organisation to manage customers, marketing R & D and service especially where highly differential adapted products and services are involved are different from the sparser marketing and service structures of scale-oriented cost-advantage businesses).

Focus on competitive advantage is a key element in strategic management. Its success, however, is dependent upon company managers correctly identifying which competitive advantages are best for their business and then ensuring that these advantages are both emphasised and sustained. Too often advantages are compromised because managers lose sight of them. In attempts to cut costs for example, firms with highly differentiated products may sometimes cut marketing investment, cancel R & D projects or reduce customer service costs. Whilst these sorts of costs may be seen as discretionary in the short term, they represent the very activities upon which a firm's uniqueness competitive advantages depend.

On the other hand, companies which are low-cost producers may be tempted to make 'specials' for customers, adapt products for specific markets, or make special service arrangements for key customers.

Resource analysis

It is not the sum of resources which determines a company's competitive position. It is the way resources are matched and deployed to exploit a company's competitive advantages. Strategies which are tailored to resources rather than market needs are considerably weaker than those in which resources are deployed to match strategy.

Yet many of a company's resources are scarce, difficult to change and often expensive to increase. Many companies are aware of the resources they need to effect strategy but frequently find it difficult to find costing formulae to ensure that strategy needs are not overwhelmed by costs.

There is a need, therefore, to examine company resources. To assess them in terms of:

- the way they are utilised in terms of efficiency and effectiveness;
- the way in which they are controlled; and
- finding areas for the basis of competitive advantages.

One of the greatest dangers in carrying out any resource analysis stems from the propensity of analysts to attempt output measurements without relating these to the interrelationships between the various parts of a business. Such analysis may provide a considerable bank of departmental measurements yet still fail to provide any significant conclusions – other than where costs are greatest.

It is vital, therefore, to segregate elements within a business into identifiable units against which they can be examined. Whilst it is emphasised that business strategy involves directing the 'big picture' of the business it is not possible to analyse resources by looking at the business as a whole. Therefore, some form of morphological study is needed. This we will call the resource audit.

Resource audit

Traditional methods of resource auditing are usually based on some form of value analysis through which costs and benefits are assessed across company activities. The output of such an analysis provides companies with a database by which activities can be assessed for increased investment, efficiency programmes, restructuring and divestment etc.

Such methods depend on a company's ability to clearly identify the relationships between each area of activity within its structure. Where such an analysis is based wholly on a company's value-added structure it can miss a vital opportunity to assess areas of existing or potential competitive advantage. For example, a firm reducing costs by eliminating some elements of its distribution service may in fact eliminate one of its competitive advantages with a consequent effect on sales. In analysing resources, therefore, it is essential to understand the *value contribution* of each element of a company's activities. There are a number of methods by which such elements can be assessed, namely:

- value contribution analysis;
- comparative analysis; and
- redundancy analysis.

Value contribution analysis

This method of resource analysis examines each part of a company's value system in design, procurement, production, distribution, sales and marketing, customer service and the central administration. It is based on the assumptions that:

- each element of a business contributes to the value of products sold;
- some elements will contribute to competitive advantage more than others;
- the system is enhanced by 'soft values', ie those vital contributions made by people either as individuals or as groups through their individual and collective wisdom, skills, contacts, motivation and aspirations (eg the relationships between sales people and their customers, contributions by gifted R & D specialists, the skills of buyers, internal relationships and corporate culture);
- the flow of the entire business system contributes to its efficiency and effectiveness in terms of both operational costs and in customer service (eg poor procurement may influence production efficiency which in turn affects costs, stock levels and customer service); and that
- the organisation of the business is deployed both to match strategy and reinforce its competitive advantages. The way in which a business is organised has a major influence on its effectiveness and efficiency. Lines of communication and decision-making can greatly affect both the running of a business and its corporate culture.

Value contribution analysis requires management to examine each element of its entire value system in order to:

- take action to correct those elements in the value system which are sub-optimising their value contribution;

- enhance areas which contribute to competitive advantage;

- eliminate areas which make no positive contribution to the value system;

- organise the elements of the value system to improve flow and to reduce operational inefficiencies;

- focus on 'soft values' to maximise the contributions made by individuals and groups; and

- reinforce the value system through matching organisation to exploit competitive advantages and strategy.

Comparative analysis

This method assumes that the differences between the way in which competitors' value systems are deployed is a major source of competitive advantage. The purpose of comparative analysis therefore is to determine what elements competitors bring to a market which give them advantages in terms of either costs or differentiation.

Bearing in mind that making accurate estimates of competitors' cost structures is difficult, comparative analysis should be done by examining the product of its competitors' value systems rather than trying to estimate each cost element.

Methodology will, therefore, involve both market research and investigation into visible aspects of competitor activity such as company accounts, market share, marketing investment, product quality, prices and so on. Market research is used to produce evidence of customer satisfaction or dissatisfaction across parameters relevant to a firm in assessing its comparative competitive position. Investigation into those visible aspects of competitor activity should provide clues as to broad applications of cost and to their effects on competitors' revenue and market position.

The results of comparative analysis should be to provide in the first place aspects of competitor activity which are significantly superior to those of the firm in question. Secondly, aspects which show competitors as being significantly inferior are looked at.

These aspects need to be weighted. Again, research amongst customers may be necessary to pick out those activities which a firm needs to improve in order to retain competitive advantage and those which it should reinforce as superior advantages. Comparative analysis can be qualified by costing those elements of a firm's value system which need to be improved upon in order for it to be able to maximise its advantages, namely those seen by its customers as superior to its competitors. This does not mean, however, that a firm has to match costs of competitors' advantages. It only needs to do so to the extent that these do not impinge on a firm's ability to maximise its own competitive advantages.

Comparative analysis has a further value in identifying potential areas for improving efficiency and effectiveness by looking at the different ways in which competitors employ their resources. They may have found more efficient ways of doing things providing fuel for thought for management in assessing its use of its own resources. Firms should not, however, lose sight of their own competitive advantages in imitating their competitors.

Redundancy analysis

This method simply asks management to assess all the activities carried out in a business in order to find those which are duplicated or unnecessary. It is vital to balance conflicts which might otherwise compromise strategy. For example, quality criteria may reduce productivity; the need for marketing investment has to be balanced by minimum revenue objectives; procurement efficiency has to be balanced with production effectiveness. In analysing redundancy it is necessary to look at each element of the business in terms of the conflicts it imposes on others. It involves a reappraisal of objectives, practices, constraints and controls to find trade-offs which free up critical activities considered to contribute to competitive advantages. It may involve sacrifices to long-held working practices.

The nature of the market

It is important to compare the company's relative strengths and weaknesses to the market in which it operates. These change over time. It is the markets (and changes to them) which will have considerable bearing on the availability of options a company will have in determining the direction of its strategies and the success criteria it sets.

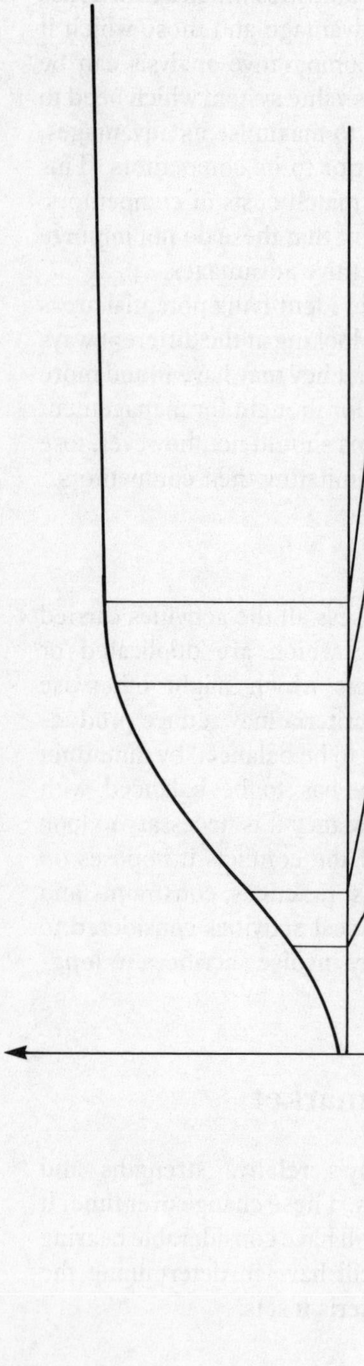

Stage	Introduction	Early growth	Massive growth	Shake out	Maturity
Technologies	Innovation	Wider application	Consumerisation or wider industrial applications	Experience effects lower cost of application	Evolving technology by leaders – development of substitute technology
Product	Unsophisticated	Development of refinements	Range stretching	Range stretching	Proliferation
Market	Narrow segments	Narrow Segments	Wider segments	Mass market	Mass market segmented
Competition	Low	Low	Intensifying (band wagon effect)	High cost producers exit market	Dominant – threat of substitutes
Prices	High	High	Lower	Lower	Low
Margins	High	High	Lower	Lower	Medium

Figure 3:5 Market development based on product life cycle

All product markets will go through stages from introduction to decline. The time-scales for different products vary considerably. The breakfast cereal industry, for example, has been in maturity for 20 years whilst the television games market has gone into visible decline. In looking at markets it is not only important to understand the processes of growth and decline but to understand the factors which influence them. Whilst the length of this book does not permit an exhaustive study it is important to outline some aspects of markets and their development.

Figure 3.5 broadly shows the typical stages of market development. Introduction commences with some basic technology adopted by a segment of the market. Through wider adoption, technological development, increased competition and collective marketing, investment growth occurs until the market take-up reaches a point beyond which major growth ceases.

During the period of rapid growth, numbers of competitors can be expected to increase. The effect of competition is to increase competitive turbulence where pricing, marketing investment and service levels reach a point where some shake-out is likely to occur. Whether by merger or withdrawal, numbers of competitors leave the market. The market will sustain a period of maturity with no growth. Firms competing for growth do so at the expense of competition. High-cost firms and those unable to maintain the pace of innovation thus become victims.

Ease of entry is greater during the early growth and massive growth stages. Once maturity follows the shake-out period, cost of entry is high. Even so the threat of new entrants is a factor which stimulates turbulence and has an effect on prices and innovative activity.

The factors which stimulate growth are technology, marketing investment, competitor intensity and adapting products to meet wider market opportunities. Factors which stimulate decline are inevitably substitutes. These may be direct substitutes such as, say, the polyunsaturated margarines which have split the butter market, or indirect, such as where personal computers have had an effect on the telegames and other hobbies markets.

Market development has its impact on strategy. It demands of managers decisions regarding investment in marketing, innovation and capacity; and diversification and integration.

A rapidly growing market will demand a pace of investment and innovation aimed at exploiting growth and widening potential. A mature market will demand market-share-sustaining strategies and begin to introduce needs to make decisions concerning diversification to create 'new legs' for a business, or decisions concerning integration to gain greater shares of the markets value.

Setting objectives

Many managers argue that they have no basis on which to set development objectives for a strategic plan. Yet it is plain that those companies which do set aggressive development targets seem to prosper better than those that do not.

Whilst corporate culture and management aspirations have considerable bearing on the relative performance of companies, one critical factor is overlooked, namely: there is a minimum below which a company's position becomes in doubt. Anzoff describes this as critical mass. It is the minimum share a company needs to support its costs and remain competitive in price. Thus any company which allows its development to decay or opens itself to be overtaken by competitors is putting its very survival on the line.

It is true that many managers argue against corporate planning. Many are complacent enough to sub-optimise performance in one financial period to attempt to show consistent growth in the next. Yet in doing so they are weakening their corporate, competitive position thus making results harder to achieve in the future.

The argument against setting development criteria is quite often the same as the reasons managers give for sub-optimising results in any single financial period – they don't know where the additional business can be found. If corporate managers singularly focused on this problem the ills of many languishing, lacklustre companies could be cured. This argument does not manifest itself in many blue chip, well-managed Japanese companies!

The roots of the problem stem from the persistence of many managers to 'force out' growth rather than focus on development. Without some longer-term thinking (which involves understanding the nature of the market, its evolution and the competitive intensity of the industrial structures in which they operate), companies will inevitably find that growth cannot continue to be 'forced out'. When this happens, re-structuring occurs.

Setting objectives calls for more than simply extrapolating performance objectives at a rate which looks consistent. It means setting a range of development objectives to provide the basis for future performance.

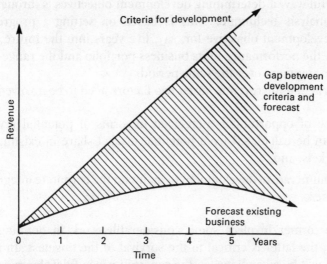

Gap analysis – showing the gap between the criteria for business development in terms of revenue and the forecast trend of existing business. Clearly the gap has to be closed if the company is not to lose its competitive position.

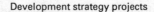

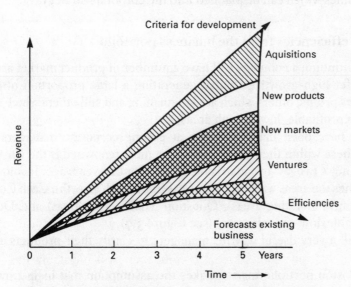

Gap analysis – shows how management can seek development strategy projects to close the gap between what it needs to achieve in terms of development and the trend of its existing business.

Figure 3.6 Illustration of the use of gap analysis to set objectives and projects

One useful way of determining development objectives is through use of a gap-analysis technique. This is based on setting a progressive revenue development objective for, say, five years into the future, then forecasting the performance of its business portfolio and the range of its revenue development over the same period.

In constructing the revenue target two factors need to be involved:

- the scope of opportunities perceived in terms of potential revenue which can be calculated from potential market share in existing and new markets; and
- the minimum rate of development to maintain the corporate integrity of the business.

Whilst the former involves some considerable work in defining opportunities, the latter is critical to the survival of the business. In many cases there will be a gap between the required pace of development and the natural evolution of the business portfolio.

Filling the gap therefore requires: finding efficiencies from the business portfolio to improve its evolution and finding projects and opportunities which can be planned into the corporate strategy.

Finding efficiencies from the business portfolio

In the continuum a company will have a number of product market areas which offer high-growth potential generating a large proportion of the companies profits, others which are languishing and still others which are frankly unprofitable, low-growth areas.

There have been many attempts at getting corporate managers to identify these within their companies. The most renowned is the Boston Consultancy's two-by-two matrix designed about 20 years ago. It colourfully defines the areas with such names as Stars (high growth), Cash Cows (high-profit-generating areas), Question Marks (grey areas) and Dogs (unprofitable, low-growth areas) (see Figure 3.7).

It is still a very useful way for managers to clarify their products and markets.

The Boston portfolio matrix makes the assumption that high growth areas (Stars) whilst contributing to the thrust of business development have a propensity to create high costs – marketing investment, R & D, facilities and other expansion costs. Yet those areas which are generating high profits (Cash Cows) are those which are showing low growth, are

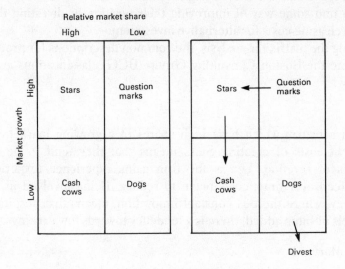

Figure 3.7 Market share

The BCG matrix is based on identifying areas of business activity falling into quadrants denoting relative market growth rate and share. It can be used to look at:

- *products (present and future);*

- *businesses within a group (present and future);*

- *customers (classification); and*

- *competitors (comparable analysis).*

mature and seek only as much investment as is needed to maintain their position. Question Marks on the other hand can either be newly launched products for which success in terms of either growth or profitability is yet to be determined, or grey areas of the portfolio which are languishing. The areas which have low market shares and contribute little in the way of profits (Dogs) are those whose continued existence needs qualification.

The idea of the Boston matrix is to use it to develop a balanced portfolio of products, businesses, customers etc. The concept involves funding sets of business activities which underpin the risks and costs of developing high-growth activities (Stars) from the revenue generated by those high-share products in stable mature markets falling into the Cash Cow quadrant. Those products which fall into the Question Mark quadrant need to be evaluated to assess their longer-term viability. Activity must be focused on them to move them into the Stars quadrant.

Those low-share activities in stagnant market areas need to be assessed either to find some way of improving their position or divesting them, thereby releasing costs for alternative investment.

In using the matrix for analysis, the common descriptions for products falling into the Boston Consulting Group (BCG) classifications are set out below.

Stars

Business activities which have high shares of a growing market. The investment costs of creating Stars means that they tend to be high absorbers of revenue. Yet as the firm gains experience (experience curve effect) over time, costs begin to reduce. Being involved in high technology, where there is constant innovation, means that despite the high levels of value added, there is a tendency towards low earnings.

Question Marks

Here the business activity, whilst taking place in a growing market, fails to achieve significant share. Where a company is spending heavily and the activity fails to gain share in a rising market, there will be a considerable drain on revenue.

Cash Cows

These activities have high market shares in mature markets. The combination of low market growth and high share means there is less need for marketing investment. High share probably indicates that the firm's experience continues to grow and thus costs are still reducing relative to competition. Cash Cows are thus the revenue generators of a business.

Dogs

These have low shares in no-growth or declining markets. They are usually a drain to revenue and absorb costs which might be better deployed in other business activities. Divestment is often the strategy of choice.

Whilst the BCG matrix has been in existence for a number of years, the basic concept is both extremely useful and adaptable to a range of problems which involve systematic evaluation of a portfolio. The approach can be extended into operational areas to include sales force projects, customer classifications and so on.

The management of the existing portfolios will therefore require:

- an assessment of the future contribution that the growth areas of the business will make to future revenue development;

- the isolation of those grey areas which are languishing and exploring activities which can make them more profitable;

- identification of those areas of the business which are a drain on profits in order to find ways of making them profitable or divesting them and re-deploying the costs into more productive development;

- assessment of the highly profitable areas of the business to determine factors which may upset their future such as substitute products or loss of patents;

- an understanding that it is from these highly profitable areas that a main share of profits may be being generated; and

- looking for opportunities to cross-subsidise contribution from these profitable areas of the business into areas which will provide future growth.

Through careful analysis of the business portfolio and through forecasting its evolution, companies can create useful computer-based models to test their strategic intentions. These provide an excellent database for budget and investment decisions.

The true value of portfolio analysis is in identifying those areas of the business where trade-offs can be achieved in financing development and covering risk. Thus, through cross-subsidisation of profits, achieving greater efficiencies in grey areas and divesting unprofitable areas, investment in new products and markets can be achieved without overly depressing the trend of the profit stream. Through portfolio planning companies not only improve their efficiency but can effectively create a congruence between growth and profitability (into longer time horizons). Companies can thus produce revenue results which are consistent with growth. This frees corporate management from the fear that market investment decisions are likely to create difficulties in justifying revenue performance in the short term.

Finding projects and opportunities

Once a company can begin to operate to longer time horizons, global orientation becomes a feasibility. It can invest in new products, new markets and facilities, redeploy resources and divest areas which do not fit. Through these activities companies can begin to evolve global marketing strategies.

Anzoff produced a useful matrix for determining options for corporate development.

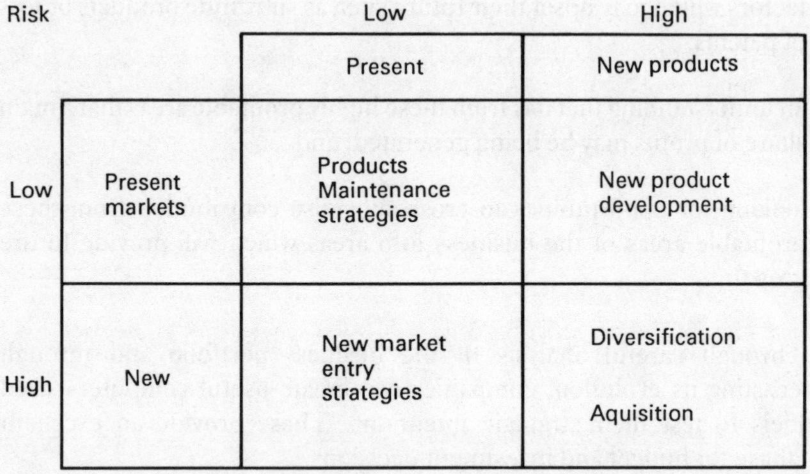

Risk		Low	High
		Present	New products
Low	Present markets	Products Maintenance strategies	New product development
High	New	New market entry strategies	Diversification / Aquisition

Figure 3.8 The diagram shows the number of different strategy options which are afforded to companies (with some conceptual attachment of risk)

Market maintenance strategies

Market maintenance strategies are those used to maintain and develop a company's competitive position in its present markets for its present products. Maintenance strategies should not be seen as merely holding the line against competitors. In a competitive environment it is vital that companies aim their market maintenance strategies at increasing market share, widening their segments and creating additional demand. The principal features of market maintenance strategies are concerned with increasing market penetration and widening market share. For example:

- high investment in marketing promotional expenditure;
- setting of competitive, market-penetrating price levels;
- widening distribution channels;
- product-range stretching (see page 198); and
- product proliferation (see page 199).

Market maintenance strategies are both offensive and defensive, maximising growth potential within markets in which companies have high levels of knowledge and understanding with products that are relatively secure and established. Market maintenance strategies are, at least conceptually, seen as having relatively less risk attached to them than any other options. The lower risks and the profit potential from high market shares should be used to balance and underpin those more risky business product and market strategy options. (This should occur before growth opportunities in existing markets or the cost of winning them becomes uneconomic.)

New product development strategies

New product development (NPD) strategies are relatively high risk but are modified by their introduction into known and familiar markets. New product development provides the basis for expanding the range of products in a market to:

- increase a company's overall market position;
- replace old and declining products;
- displace competitors through innovation (see page 200); and
- increase profit potential through obtaining higher prices on new products.

In themselves new product development strategies are not really an option – they are a necessary function of marketing. Companies with poor NPD programmes will find it more and more difficult to hold on to their existing markets. If they lose the opportunity to develop their technology through innovation they will have fewer new products to fall back on.

Risks may run high for new products but the risks of not creating an NPD strategy may be considerably higher in the longer term – even where low-cost advantages are the basis of strategy.

New market entry strategies

New market entry strategies involve selling existing products into new markets. The risks stem from the entry conditions in each new market whilst product risk is comparatively low. The advantage of market entry strategies is to provide a larger market potential for existing product, technology and production methods, thus providing a larger scale of operations through which production economies contribute to cost-competitiveness. New market entry strategies are therefore the cradle for global products.

Entering new markets is also an investment in terms of increasing company knowledge and understanding of new territories thus providing a wider opportunity for new products and larger sales potential against which to invest R & D.

New markets can be entered in several ways.

Selling standardised products

At similar prices, through the same types of distribution channel with a common approach to marketing communications to similar market segments. This strategy is appropriate for achieving market-penetration levels of economic value. It is the least costly and most efficient method of market entry for companies exploiting cost advantage. Unfortunately this approach is limited to product categories which require little differentiation between markets and rules out markets which demand highly differentiated products.

Making adaptations

Meeting customer needs in similar market segments by using different marketing channels, prices and promotional communications and adapting products are amongst the options by which companies tailor their products to secure adequate market share to justify entry.

Aim existing products at different market segments

Using any adaptations to the marketing mix which are required. For example, selling domestic garden rotavators to smallholders in markets where there is a demand for a relatively low-cost mechanical horticultural machine such as developing countries or the horticultural community in Spain, Portugal and Greece.

Diversification

Any activity which simultaneously takes a firm away from its current market and products can be described as diversification.

There are three basic forms of diversification:

- those which exploit the market value system in which a firm operates;
- those which widen its opportunities in the market value system; and
- those through which some form of synergy can be achieved.

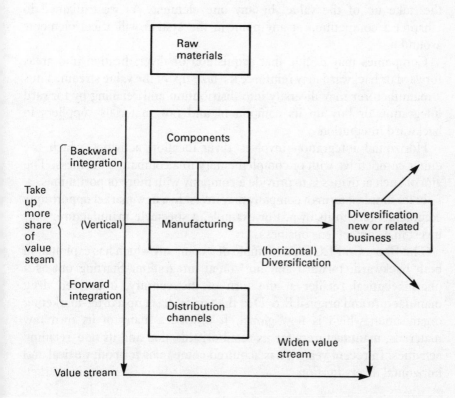

Figure 3.9 Integration and diversification in an industry value system

Market value system

As we saw in Chapter 2 the market value system can be broadly looked upon as being backward or forward with a company occupying a discrete position somewhere in the middle. A typical manufacturer's position might be as shown in Figure 3.9.

In a straight set of relationships, each part of the market value system takes and adds value. The total value of the system is the value that customers pay for goods and services. Hence each element in the system takes a share of the value by adding value from the previous element and selling it to the next. The greatest value of the total system is what the market will pay for and consume.

Each element in the system will therefore receive a share of the total value. However, the level of competition between elements determines the 'take up of the value' by any one element. As we explained in Chapter 2 competition at any point in the system will affect elements around it.

Companies may decide that acquisition or diversification into areas forward or backward may reinforce its 'take up' of the value stream. Thus a manufacturer may diversify into distribution and retailing by forward integration or buy up its component and raw materials suppliers in backward integration.

Horizontal integration involves diversification activities which are either competitive with or complementary to a company's business. The aim of such activities is to provide a company with more opportunities.

In its simplest terms a company may invest in a new market opportunity complementary to its own. For example, a spectacle manufacturer may invest in a contact lens business.

The Boots Co PLC is an example of a company which has exploited in both backward, forward and horizontal integration. Starting out as a pharmaceutical retailer at the turn of the century, it entered drug manufacture and original R & D in the 1950s. It set up a drug-marketing organisation which is now global. It produces many of its own raw materials, manufacturers for its retail organisation and its non-retailing activities. In recent years it has acquired companies for both vertical and horizontal diversification.

Unrelated diversification

The reasons for diversification into unrelated areas are often difficult to assess. They are in many instances to do with opportunism and often for power and political reasons. It is not the purpose of this book to analyse these quasi-commercial reasons. A considerable amount of corporate activity of this nature nevertheless occurs – for a variety of good (and sometimes not so good) reasons.

Investment in non-related areas of diversification may be:

- seeking synergies;
- experimenting with new areas for corporate involvement; or
- for social reasons.

The usual synergies given as examples are the acquisition of cash through acquiring cash-rich businesses, asset-stripping or acquiring tax losses.

Another reason may be the acquisition of technology which, although unrelated in the strictest senses of vertical and horizontal benefits, may have a useful purpose. For example, surface technology has many underlying common elements of science across a wide variety of unrelated industries, eg dry-freezing (coffee and detergents), metal coatings, glass manufacture and shampoo production. Thus a glass manufacture company might acquire an interest in shampoo technology to have access to knowledge otherwise trapped in a distant area of application.

Experimenting with new areas of business is again a commonly quoted reason for unrelated diversification. Small acquisitions in new business areas provide corporate management with opportunities to understand new business sectors. These not only provide vehicles for expansion but also pay their way as they go along. If the company feels it does not want to pursue a particular industry it may well acquire a capital gain on divestment.

Social reasons should not be dismissed. Altruism is costly for competitive businesses yet diversification into businesses through, say, corporate venturing or providing venture capital not only provides access to new business opportunities, it provides a social trade-off thus easing social and structural pressures on businessess wishing to divest or slimdown. This has an economic value both in the sense of returns on funds invested and in a company's social and structural manoeuvrability. It also reinforces a company's relationship with government and often shareholders as well as helping to maintain local availability of staff, managers and supporting services.

In the north west of England Pilkingtons has invested in a number of smaller businesses and in so doing contributed to its revival. However, Pilkington's Peter Sheperdsen emphasises that candidate participants in its corporate venturing schemes need to show a good return on investment.

Organisation for strategic management

Organisation of people and deployment of resources have to match the strategic intentions of the business. It is of paramount importance, therefore, that in evolving an organisational structure cognisance is taken of the following:

- dividing the business into manageable units which are highly accountable for performance and which are well led;
- creating lines of communication which permit the flows of information and direction to pass freely to target recipients and receivers;
- ensuring that an adequate decision-making structure is in place which exacts discipline and quality from decisions made, whilst at the same time providing the organisation with a sense of direction, clear criteria, flexibility and rapid response;
- providing a culture and infrastructure which facilitates creativity and makes things happen – yet which at the same time guides activity down productive avenues; and
- enabling a pool of skills and seasoned management to be created from which managers (and champions) can be summoned to manage product market projects and organisational developments (a failure of many Japanese companies).

To this end an organisation should be designed to permit the company's objectives to be focused on market opportunities. Provide for the optimum selection of new projects and opportunities. Deploy company resources to where they are strategically needed in the development and reinforcement of the company's competitive position. The organisation should be flexible allowing it to evolve to meet growth and strategic requirements.

From an operational point of view it is important to establish adequate competence centres through which company direction, product marketing and resourcing strategies, product development, production and logistics management can be co-ordinated to fulfil the corporate mission. It will be necessary to ensure that accountability and responsibility are defined at each level within the organisation to ensure that there are the minimum of conflicts, no incompatibilities in the direction of corporate effort and no waste of energy and resources through duplications of effort or poor co-ordination.

The right choice of organisation is a matter we will deal with in Chapter 15. However, it is important to emphasise that organisational structure, however well its dispositions are laid is only effective in fully exploiting a business' competitive advantages where it:

- is well-led;
- has a mission around which a committed and courageous management can aggressively maintain the corporate position against competitor forces and select and exploit new opportunities;
- inspires a corporate culture from within its ranks providing motivation for its managers and staff through challenge and self-fulfilment as well as rewards;
- facilitates the acquisition of skills, knowledge and experience from which it can learn and acquire a high standard of capability;
- provides adequate people and resources to match tasks whilst not burdening them with a mass of under-skilled unmotivated bureaucrats; and
- embraces winning as a corporate norm.

4

Domestic Firms: Threats and Opportunities

Business strategies traditionally focus on growth as the prime objective. To this end firms will pursue opportunities most likely to enable them to achieve it. The lower the risk attached and the greater the return on investment for an opportunity offer the more firms are attracted. The creation of the Single Market provides not only size and potential which few firms can ignore but a vast range of opportunities – many of which are not altogether obvious.

It will call on management's ability to concentrate on opportunities which their firms are best suited to exploiting for their competitive advantage.

Firms which fritter away their competitive advantages pursuing objectives on badly-thought-out adventures or compromising their performance with ill-fitting acquisitions are likely to become victims of the Single Market rather than its beneficiaries.

Strategies for the Single Market should therefore focus on *development* rather than on growth. Emphasis should be placed on competitive advantages rather than on size. Firms need to define sharp lines of attack rather than an amorphous cluster of businesses which can be picked off by competitors.

The reason for adopting this approach is that the domestic markets within the Single Market provide major opportunities for foreign competition – both from within the Community and from outside.

As we saw in Chapter 2 threats come not only from within the Community. The very size of the Single Market presents such potential that few external competitors could afford to ignore it. International firms have long rehearsed the practice of fighting their competitors on a global scale. Many are aware that their failure to secure a presence in Europe will not only lose them opportunities but put them at a competitive disadvantage to their global rivals. Competitive pressures, therefore, will affect domestic markets as:

- Community firms expand beyond their national borders;
- foreign, external firms incorporate in the Community and set up marketing and production centres;
- external firms recognise that the Community is no longer a group of relatively small markets and focus resources on exporting to it; and
- resultant restructuring of industries affects the traditional base of suppliers and customers for domestic firms.

Threats from international companies

Threats to Community companies then will stem largely from the competitive turbulence caused by international companies sweeping across the Single Market. Such firms have the resources, scale and dispositions to create dominant positions. They are driven as much by their need to maintain an international competitive position against their global rivals as they are in exploiting opportunities. This is true for most multinational enterprises, particularly Japanese and North American. The Community's vulnerable domestic companies are those which have either no perceptions of the threats to them or fail to find strategies to deal with them.

Threats these companies have to take into consideration are:

- the effects of change on their industry structures;
- their ability to compete in terms of cost, price and innovation against international companies once trade barriers are removed;
- incursions into their markets by a number of new competitors which will lead to fragmentation and an increase in buyer power;
- loss of independence through hostile takeovers as bigger and better-resourced companies vie for market share, brands and dispositions within the Community; and
- loss of managers and skills to those new competitors who actively compete for them.

Factors listed above present major threats to Community firms, particularly those which are largely domestically orientated. Yet at the same time they provide major opportunities for firms perceptive enough to identify them. Even moderately small firms can benefit from these if they are prepared to use their management talents to find them and dedicate resources to exploiting them. These reasons for optimism stem from the realities of the Single Market.

- It will remain for many product areas a coalition of independent markets each with its own culture and language.

- Domestic companies within individual member state markets have established end-user loyalties and dispositions.

- The psychology of governments and populations will remain nationalistic within individual member state markets for some time after the barriers are removed.

These three factors alone provide a *short-term* front-line defence for traditional domestic markets. The opportunities exist, therefore, for domestic companies to:

- create defensive business strategies based on their competitive advantages to maintain their market positions;

- seek inward opportunities to collaborate with external and internal Community firms to increase their own domestic competitive position;

- through bilateral arrangements exploit Community and external markets; and

- expand their business internationally.

Create defensive strategies

Defensive strategies should not be seen as negative, non-expansionary activities. Defensive strategy involves three elements. Firstly, finding a strong position behind which to defend the market (these will be based on a firm's competitive advantages) to force up competitors' costs of entry. Secondly, denying those segments and customers to competitors upon which their market entry strategy will depend for success. And thirdly, attacking competitor weaknesses in terms of say, service, range, marketing flexibility quality and so forth.

On all accounts avoid activities and strategies which could concede a firm's competitive capabilities or compromise its ability to sustain its competitive advantages.

- Avoid 'do-nothing' strategies. Countering competition is important from a psychological point of view (customers and internal staff) and for increasing competitors' costs of entry.

- Do not retrench activities on a broad scale as this will weaken a firm's ability to focus its competitive advantages on competition.

- Avoid strategies which involve spreading cash and resources too thinly, thus offering a number of targets to be picked off by competition. Defend in depth those areas of the business critical to survival and those critical to a competitor's success.

- Do not allow competitors to exploit disunity within the company – internal rivalry, rivalry between divisions etc. Create a unified and co-ordinated attack to harry competitors.

Defensive strategies should therefore see a concerted and unified set of missions targeted on competitors to make it expensive and difficult for them to establish a foothold. Companies will need to create plans which involve all the company's functions and exploit co-operation between divisions to act in concert to defend their corporate integrity. Areas summarised below are expanded later in the book.

Product marketing

The need to research competitors and their products, their product and marketing strengths and weaknesses is axiomatic. The benefits in formulating strategy based on good intelligence and researching the behaviour of customers in response to competitor activity need to be emphasised.

There is a need to examine a company's product offerings in terms of function, reliability, value, quality and innovation against those offered by competitors. It is important to decide what competitive advantages competitors will bring to the market (cost, uniqueness, broad market capacity or narrow niche capabilities) and find the necessary responses from the company's own armoury of competitive advantages.

It is important to review marketing promotion to establish whether a firm's promotional message is sustainable against competitor claims. It needs to review the marketing promotional tools it is using to remain competitive in terms of weight, delivery and deployment of promotional activity. It will have to ensure it has the capabilities to deploy 'hit and run' promotional activities to disconcert competitor entry strategies.

Production strategies

Production strategies will need to be evaluated against competitor advantages. They will involve finding ways to match competitor costs, quality and output.

Competitors who have the ability to put a firm at a disadvantage on all three have the capability to succeed in dominating a market. In developing defensive production strategies, firms have to ensure they do not become 'stuck in the middle' (see page 92). Often, in competing in quality, costs rise and output falls. The choice of which advantage to pursue should be trading off responses to the threats posed by competitors, ie the focus of their competitive advantage. Sacrificing an existing competitive advantage, say, quality, to meet competitor costs or output may not be the most successful option.

However, there will be a need to meet minimum competitive standards in order to enable a company to bring its competitive advantages into play against its competitors.

Quality

Improve quality (a vital aspect of creating value) through efficiency programmes and a dedication to total quality management (TQM). The imposition of TQM on production involves creating a culture and commitment to quality right through the production process. It involves commitment by line workers, involvement by engineers and R & D personnel as well as suppliers to create processes, designs and formulations which emphasise both quality and reliability and reduce defects. The effect should be to increase product competitive value in terms of how customers perceive the company's products and add to efficiency because:

- production is speeded up where suppliers defects are minimised;
- a higher level of production staff commitment is gained;
- reduced on-line defects are achieved;

- lower levels of complaints can be expected;
- there are increased product benefits for the customers in terms of reliability, design etc; and
- opportunities to add tangible unique selling points to products such as extended warranties and free service support etc are generated.

Make-or-buy decisions

Too often a company's costs are high and its capacity restricted because it does too many of its own processes. Often processes are done quite expensively 'in house' when spare capacity exists in many industries. Make-or-buy decisions need to be reviewed in order to evaluate the effect of diverting expensive processes which affect quality and presentation to specialised companies which can use their skills more effectively than the company in terms of cost and quality. Also to be considered is seeking areas of over-capacity within an industry and calculating the benefits of diverting process stages to those areas in terms of cost and released capacity.

OEM and own-label production

The competitive advantage gained through OEM and own-label production are often missed by firms. For not only are these opportunities to reduce unit costs by absorbing capacity, own-label production for major customers also:

- reduces the opportunity for competitors to develop production expertise and finance their competing capacity by manufacturing to contract without the attending costs of marketing;
- keeps production units on their toes (to produce quality at low costs);
- adds an impetus to product development and design functions;
- gives information on customer sales; and
- provides low-cost new market entry opportunities.

Whilst the disadvantages are found in competing against a company's own branded products it does contain competition. Companies such as Nestlé and Boots separate their sales functions between those responsible for securing own-label contracts and branded products. Own-label production should be subject to an objective evaluation which measures the advantages in terms of developing opportunities and maintaining a competitive position in the market against any disadvantage of opening up customer-branded or generic competition.

Manufacturing abroad

The reasons and opportunities for manufacturing abroad are covered in depth in Chapter 15. However, this option should be broadly evaluated as part of defensive manufacturing strategy.

Manufacturing abroad can help in finding cheaper sources of production to compete with competitors and breaking the production processes down to devolve those for which special adaptations or distribution costs diminish value creation in central production units (eg special packaging for foreign markets). It can also provide the opportunity to locate to centres of production excellence in countries where processing of materials, components manufacturing infrastructure and expertise exist.

Whilst manufacturing abroad may increase the complexity of managing production and increase risks of maintaining quality and giving away technological advantages, the option should be evaluated on the grounds of:

- cost advantages;
- improved quality; and
- tapping into higher levels of manufacturing excellence in centres where it is superior to that of the domestic industry.

Inward opportunities

The Single Market not only provides opportunities outside the domestic market. It provides considerable opportunity for companies to reinforce their domestic position by matching their advantages to foreign company needs. It provides opportunities for domestic companies to become international in outlook through collaboration. It enables those with the foresight to differentiate between foreign firms likely to become major competitors and those with whom they can ally themselves against other mutual competitors.

Friend, competitor, potential ally analysis

Borrowed from the political sciences, it is an analysis which can be used to differentiate other companies and potential competitors into four basic categories.

- Friends – companies which are basic allies. Where they do compete there is little internecine activity.

- Competitors – contestants in the true sense.

- Potential allies – firms which have strengths or needs through which an alliance could be of mutual benefit.

- Potential allies to foes – companies which, if they were to ally with competitors, would greatly reinforce the competitor threat.

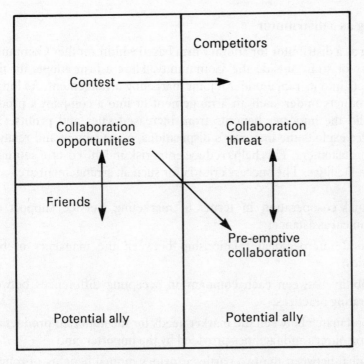

Figure 4.1 Division of potential competitors into friends, contestants into allies

The purpose of this analysis is first to identify firms it would be beneficial to collaborate with to reinforce strengths and – through combining competitive advantages – add to the competitive capabilities of both. For example, a firm in Britain with an effective marketing and distribution system might join with a West German firm with a high-technology product advantage to market its products in the UK.

Secondly it seeks to identify firms whose alliance with competitors would create a formidable threat. In a political situation, competitiveness in wooing a foe's potential allies involves high levels of diplomacy (and the activities upon which spy thrillers are based!). In the business environment it involves inter-company diplomacy at the highest level.

By carefully assessing the mutual needs of both parties, firms can find best matches from their competitive advantages for forming alliances. The criterion for success should be that they can both see a mutual benefit from an alliance in respect of using the other's strengths. The following are examples of possible areas for investigation permissible under EC law.

Acting as a distributor

Acting as a distributor for another firm based within another Community country or from outside the Community. Here a firm adopts its ally's products into its range under a joint marketing arrangement. As long as the products under such an arrangement fit into a company's product portfolio the importer benefits from increased sales and profits. The exporter exploits the importer's dispositions, management and relations with its customers. This helps reduce entry risk and the costs of setting up its own facilities. The success criteria for such an arrangement are:

- mutual co-operation in terms of marketing, service support and technical assistance;
- a good interpersonal relationship between the managers of both parties;
- flexibility between each company in accepting differences between operating practices;
- a good match between the market needs for the imported product and the resources and facilities provided by the importer; and
- the deal between the two parties provides mutual benefits of roughly equal value. The venture is profitable to both parties.

Bilateral marketing agreements

Considerable strengths can be gained from bilateral marketing agreements. Such an agreement expands the benefits of joint marketing arrangements to both parties involved. In its simplest form this would involve firms agreeing to sell each other's products in markets where they have relative strengths. Taking the example of the British firm and the West German, the British firm may offer more than just the UK market, it might include Commonwealth markets for its German partner's products. The German company may offer a market to the British partners in Switzerland and Austria. Such a relationship tends to evolve as companies involved in such agreements find more and more opportunities of mutual advantage. Again, the key to success is the ability of two firms to get on with each other and work to each other's advantage.

A good example of a bilateral arrangement is quoted in *The Economist*'s survey of the internal market in July 1988 which describes the agreement between the private Dutch company BV Safari and the French company Continentale de Conserves – both companies being roughly the same size and both operating in the pet food and animal feeds market. Their plan for the Single Market makes an ideal example as *The Economist* survey illustrates:

- Each will take a stake of about one-third in the other.
- Each will have the exclusive right to market its own products, and the products of the other, in its own country.
- They will jointly own a marketing subsidiary which will sell the products of both firms across the rest of the European Community.
- They will jointly run and finance a research and development unit.

The virtues of the plan? There is a good fit between the products of the two companies, within a clearly identified business. Each partner will go on playing to its existing strengths in the country that it understands, but with a wider range of products to sell. The effort, emotion and cost of a takeover are avoided. Relatively little day-to-day collaboration is required. On the other hand, the cross-shareholdings make sure that both companies gain from the success of the whole adventure.

Europe must be full of companies that have a fine market or brand position at home, and that want to 'Europeanise' themselves rapidly without losing their independence. For them, a 'twinning' formula of this sort would seem to have much going for it.

Contract production

Here a company uses its production advantages to the benefit of its foreign ally. This reduces the foreign firm's need to set up its own production facilities by providing production close to its markets. The contracting manufacturer benefits from the production volume from non-competing lines (see page 309).

Licensing-in

By 'licensing-in' products from foreign firms a company enjoys the benefits of additional products, sales and production without the expense of R & D. Licensing-in may of course be used strategically where a firm finds difficulty in matching its R & D output to its development and competitiveness objectives. The benefits accruing to the licensor are described on page 175.

Cross-licensing

Cross-licensing implies a bilateral arrangement through which firms swap licences between themselves. These may form part of a specific one-for-one arrangement, ie firm A agrees to allow a licence to firm B to make and market a product in its markets in return for firm B's licence for its own. Longer-term arrangements may provide that two companies offer each other access to their respective licences over a period of time in the future. This enables firms with a ready development to negotiate with firms with developments still in the future.

The great benefit of long-term bilateral agreements is that firms have access to continuous R & D output. They avoid duplicating each other's activities. As long as the agreements are mutually beneficial firms can develop products with a reasonable assurance they can find a licensee ready to take up a licence. The downside to such arrangements comes where one or other of the parties enters at a time when it is unable to exploit its development other than by a licence arrangement. If subsequently a firm wished to set up its own facilities in a market, a long-term bilateral agreement might well mean that it could not access its own R & D output upon which to base its business.

Mergers

Increasingly, firms which find they cannot provide a competitive edge on their own, seek to combine their strengths with those of others through mergers. Many also see the benefits of surrendering themselves for acquisitions by larger firms which have the necessary capital resources and skills to enable them to bring enhanced competitiveness to the market place. This sort of voluntary restructuring mitigates the traumas of hostile acquisition and enables the integrity of businesses to remain very much in place even after synergies have been exploited.

Mergers should be considered on the basis of the benefits which are likely to accrue. Within the Single Market there are basically three options:

- combine with a domestic company;
- combine with a community company; or
- combine with a foreign external company.

Combine with a domestic company

The advantages are of course that language and culture allow domestic firms to integrate more successfully. The choices of partners will depend upon the objectives the merger aims to achieve. These may be to provide a stronger defence of the domestic market, provide a stronger international presence or have technology or production advantages. The disadvantages often arise from emphasis on domestic marketing where synergies – whilst strengthening domestic capabilities – have no international advantages. Consequently, the merger reinforces the domestic position without providing significant European or global benefits. Ideal mergers would be between companies where at least one had significant international dispositions – where the aim is to provide a competitive basis for business in the Single Market and beyond.

Combine with a Community company

Where a strongly positioned domestic company merges with another from a different Community country there is a great commercial advantage – once both parties get along together. The benefit for the merged business is the access to markets for the production from the two halves of the business, particularly where neither had a significant presence before. It may mean that the two business organisations can keep their own structures and individual cultures largely intact, thus minimising the traumas of integration – except in overall management, financial and reporting procedures. The synergies will be reflected in increasing marketing opportunities rather than through rationalisation.

Combine with a foreign external company

The creation of a Single Market has made Europe an even more attractive place for foreign external firms. Through acquisitions they are able to incorporate within the Community. The advantages of merging with or being acquired by a foreign external company are somewhat harder to define than for the preceding combinations. Where a combination is to create a bridge into the Community market as a whole there are major opportunities to exploit the combined strengths and resources to enter and develop in the Single Market.

Where the combination provides for a two-way opportunity for products to the Community from the foreign company and the acquired company to the foreign company's markets, considerable commercial advantage is achieved.

As in all voluntary mergers and acquisitions where maintaining the integrity of both businesses is an objective, both parties involved need to work to the advantages.

Voluntary mergers based on maintaining the integrity of a business reinforce its opportunities in terms of development. The product market opportunities which the merger affords need to be carefully thought through. The ideal commercial advantage is to provide wider product market opportunities for both rather than becoming a marketing vehicle for the dominant firm in a merger.

Expand internationally

Despite the number of international companies which have long learned to match their foreign competitors by establishing strong competitive positions at home and abroad little of what has been written focuses on this need for competitive position as a reason for international business. Too many books are concerned with opportunity-seeking and anecdotes about how to skim foreign markets on the cheap. It is a fact of business life that companies which do not become internationally orientated will find themselves at a severe competitive disadvantage. For the success of foreign firms in becoming dominant in different national markets is a result of their becoming competitive in cost, price, innovation and marketing through scale generated by their global activities. Swiss firms for example have a tiny home market yet companies such as Nestlé, Roche and Ciba Geigy have become industry giants by growing in the wider world market. They have not enjoyed the innate advantage of large home markets which have so endowed US and Japanese companies.

Each individual market in the Community is large enough to encourage foreign competition yet is too small for many companies to reach the levels of scale by which to remain competitive against larger foreign companies. The creation of the Single Internal Market within the EC is a recognition by the governments of member states that global survival for much of their domestic industry will be dependent upon the existence of a large home market which permits companies the opportunities to increase in scale.

Community companies therefore need to become internationally orientated for three basic reasons:

- to create a large enough scale of operations to compete with foreign competitors by being competitive in costs, prices, innovation and marketing;
- to provide a portfolio of markets in which offensive and defensive strategies against foreign competitors can be fought; and
- to provide opportunites for international collaboration in terms of R & D, marketing channels, production etc.

Corporate management will therefore need to examine the international option in defining future success requirements – if they are to continue to thrive in an increasingly hostile competitive environment.

Yet many corporate managers live in genuine fear that investment into new markets will run down short-term profits and reduce earnings-per-share ratios. These, together with the increased risks which attend such ventures, are justifiably seen as making their companies vulnerable to corporate predators. Adding a few per cent to growth through low-cost foreign adventures without rocking the financial boat is about as far as many corporate officials are prepared to go in considering the international option. Risk aversion is not merely a strategy for personal survival but a perceived strategy in ensuring corporate independence.

This is a genuine problem for companies whose equity value is based on the fickleness of the stock market and the second-hand value of their shares. Even so, the stock market is unlikely to become less unsympathetic and the impact of investors dissatisfaction with capital gains prospects for their holdings are conditions under which corporate management has to work.

Yet any alternative systems for the supply of capital proffered as a solution to the ills of industry are not only 'pie in the sky' but ignore the tremendous benefits of the present one. Whilst many applaud the benefits of cheap bank-capital afforded to Japanese companies it has to be remembered that only about 20 per cent of Japanese industry are true beneficiaries. Some 19,000 major liquidations occur every year. Only as long as Japan is awash with capital and the Yen value affords low interest rates will blue chip Japanese companies remain the beneficiaries of their system.

Despite the fickleness of the stock market and its present volatility, the stability of ownership is based more on the competence of its corporate managers and the success they create for their business. Companies which lose ground and squander their competitive advantages are just as vulnerable whether they are financed by equity as in the UK or are highly geared as in Japan.

The belief that corporate managers have to work to meet short-term performance outcomes is not altogether well founded. The stock market measures companies by its expectations and consistent performance. Whilst annual results provide snapshots of performance they say little about the way managements are adapting and creating new strategies to meet future threats and opportunities. Many analysts today look for the vulnerabilities in terms of a company's competitive position, its spread of markets and the deployment of its resources. Consistent growth, successful new products and balanced product market portfolios tend to have a greater influence on their perceptions of company worth than mere appraisal of short-term returns. Sluggish growth despite high returns on net assets probably makes a company more vulnerable to acquisition than those which are aggressive, competitive and showing consistent growth in earnings per share.

The idea that international competitiveness is limited by the structure and workings of the capital markets is of doubtful origin. Managements which have the wisdom and courage to plan their strategies to provide for sufficient cross-substitution from present revenue for investments into new products and markets will provide a steady and consistent perform-ance over the longer term.

Business strategy only becomes short term if managers permit it to be so. The working of the stock market may exacerbate short-term thinking but it does not create it.

The international option therefore should not be ignored. The opportunities provided by the Single Market offer a basis for expansion into Europe and beyond it into the wider global market. Orientation of business from domestic to European should be but one step towards the global market place.

The rest of this book is dedicated to the internationalisation of business. The principal point of focus is the Single Market but it draws important points of reference to a more global orientation.

5
Marketing Research for Business Strategies

Marketing research is an important marketing tool. For it is used in both assessing new markets for products and evaluating new products for markets. It also plays a vital role in continually testing management assumptions about its on-going competitive position.

If there is no systematic selection of markets and no end-user assessment of product requirements, promotional communications, pricing, distribution, customer service criteria then the necessary marketing strategies cannot be designed to build permanent market positions. Where there is no assessment of competitor strengths and weaknesses in satisfying a market there is little opportunity for companies realistically to set and up date their success criteria.

Marketing research should be used to assist management in determining marketing priorities and in making and testing assumptions made in regard to those priorities. Marketing research is described by the American Marketing Association as 'the systematic gathering, recording, analysis and interpretation of data or problems relating to the market for and the marketing of goods and services'. This description is probably the most universally accepted.

The roles assigned to marketing research in relatively sophisticated marketing organisations are:

- prioritising market opportunities;
- substantiating rationale for marketing and investment decisions;
- mapping markets;
- selecting market entry modes;
- supporting planning decisions for market maintenance strategies;

- providing a knowledge and understanding of customer needs against which new product development programmes can be shaped and targeted;
- finding criteria against which to adapt products to meet end-user needs;
- defining market segments;
- setting criteria for designing, planning and executing advertising, sales activity and promotional communications objectives;
- monitoring operational effectiveness;
- testing the results of marketing activities;
- testing and assessing service levels;
- defining public relations missions through assessing target interest group attitudes towards the company, its objectives and product offerings; and
- seeking and identifying potential distributors.

Marketing research activities can be viewed at two levels. Firstly, *strategic* aiding, selecting and prioritising marketing missions; and secondly, *operational* monitoring and testing marketing effectiveness in how well the company satisfies market needs in relation to competitors.

In this chapter we will discuss the following:

- methods of marketing research;
- prioritising markets;
- mapping markets;
- identification of competitor weaknesses and strengths;
- determining success criteria for marketing operations;
- testing individual components of the strategy;
- assessing public attitudes to products and the company;
- practical application of marketing research;
- setting and executing research projects;
- methodology for desk research;
- organising a system for marketing information;

Methods of marketing research

Marketing research involves collecting and analysing information from which assumptions can be drawn. Traditionally market research is divided into two methods.

Desk research is the collection and analysis of published data which is relevant to the research project.

Field research involves the collection of specific information by scientifically based methods usually involving questioning a statistically based sample of respondents.

Both types of research are involved in the marketing research process. They are frequently differentiated in terms of relative cost with the assumption that desk research is cheaper than field research. This differentiation, however, misses the point as neither type of research can substitute for the other: both are complementary.

Desk research should be used to provide an overall database from which market opportunities can be prioritised and general information about the marketing environment can be gathered for mapping markets. Marketing research through field activities or by commissioned projects is used to research specific questions about the market.

Prioritising markets

Future viability of scope for growth can be put into serious jeopardy if the initial selection of market opportunities is wrong. Furthermore, if modes of entry are inappropriate a company may be forced to withdraw from a market – with the attending financial losses, missed opportunities, embarrassment and loss of competitive position.

Market opportunities therefore need to be prioritised as part of the strategic business plan so that dispositions, resources and facilities can be planned for and marketing planning can begin to set outline objectives.

Prioritisation decisions need to be made on the basis of good marketing information which can initially be done largely by desk research. All markets should be evaluated in sufficient depth from which a shortlist of market candidates can be selected for further, in depth, evaluation. At the first stage the following is a minimum of information required:

• assessment of market potential;
• limits of accessibility (ie barriers to trade);

- recommendations for most suitable mode of entry (export, licensing, joint marketing arrangement etc);
- description of competitors;
- brief evaluation of competitors products; and
- outlining of trade channels and any restrictions which their structure imposes (lack of self-service outlets, controlled distribution for products recommended for introduction etc).

This initial overview allows managers to compare marketing opportunities on the basis of:

- marketing potential;
- mode of entry;
- competitive intensity;
- possible segment opportunities; and
- marketing channel limitations.

Mapping markets

The map or – as often referred to – its marketing profile for each market selected will include all relevant information about the market and the environment. These will help determine the success requirements for entry and the strategies most likely to meet them.

The market map includes all those items in Figure 5.1 which are the minimum requirements of the mapping exercise. Again, almost all the information required for mapping can be obtained through desk research.

Identification of competitor weaknesses and strengths

One of the most relevant aspects of many Japanese strategies is to remind us that the best place to attack competitors is where they are *weakest*. Through commissioned research, competitors' product weaknesses can be assessed in terms of:

- quality;
- functionality;
- reliability;

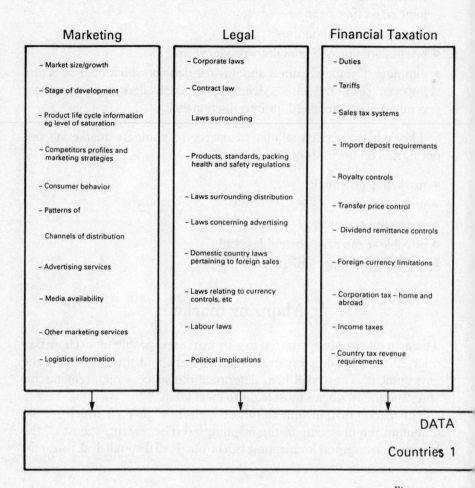

Marketing	Legal	Financial Taxation
– Market size/growth	– Corporate laws	– Duties
– Stage of development	– Contract law	– Tariffs
– Product life cycle information eg level of saturation	Laws surrounding	– Sales tax systems
– Competitors profiles and marketing strategies	– Products, standards, packing health and safety regulations	– Import deposit requirements
– Consumer behavior		– Royalty controls
– Patterns of	– Laws surrounding distribution	– Transfer price control
Channels of distribution	– Laws concerning advertising	– Dividend remittance controls
	– Domestic country laws pertaining to foreign sales	– Foreign currency limitations
– Advertising services		
– Media availability	– Laws relating to currency controls, etc	– Corporation tax – home and abroad
– Other marketing services	– Labour laws	– Income taxes
– Logistics information	– Political implications	– Country tax revenue requirements

DATA

Countries 1

Figure 5.1

- price;
- image; and
- distribution.

Attitudes and perceptions towards competitors' products should be assessed in relation to consumers' desires and habits, and distribution channels – their structure and trading requirements.

As well as competitors' weaknesses, their strengths need to be assessed. Their ability to respond to attack; their expected reaction to competition;

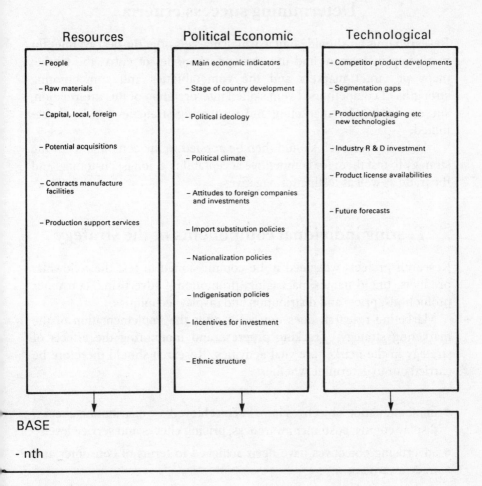

Resources	Political Economic	Technological
– People	– Main economic indicators	– Competitor product developments
– Raw materials	– Stage of country development	– Segmentation gaps
– Capital, local, foreign	– Political ideology	– Production/packaging etc new technologies
– Potential acquisitions	– Political climate	– Industry R & D investment
– Contracts manufacture facilities	– Attitudes to foreign companies and investments	– Product license availabilities
– Production support services	– Import substitution policies	– Future forecasts
	– Nationalization policies	
	– Indigenisation policies	
	– Incentives for investment	
	– Ethnic structure	

BASE

- nth

Mapping the market

their size, resources and financial strength; whether they are beneficiaries of state aid and protection – all need to be researched. This can be done largely through forms of desk research. Some commissioned research may be necessary for trade channels to find their views about competitors and their habitual responses to competition.

It also goes without saying that the same commissioned research which is used to find competitor weakness can also show strengths in terms of customer perceptions towards products, prices and service levels. An important question is why are customers loyal to their suppliers?

Determining success criteria

Research thus far should point to which markets offer the best avenues for marketing investment and the appropriate modes of entry, the market maps of target markets and the vulnerabilities and compensating strengths of competitors. From skilled interpretation of this information, success criteria for marketing and resourcing strategies can be determined.

Marketing research should then be applied to the components of the strategy to test them for competitive acceptability amongst customers and the trade as well as testing for negatives.

Testing individual components of the strategy

Research projects will need to be commissioned to test the following: products; brand names; packaging; promotion – advertising, consumer promotions; price; and distribution and display techniques.

Marketing research does not cease after the implementation of the marketing strategy. Tracking progress and monitoring the effects of strategy in the market are vital activities. Research should therefore be carried out to determine whether:

* implementation objectives have been achieved, eg distribution checks, display counts, customer awareness, pricing checks and service levels;
* advertising objectives have been achieved in terms of consumer and trade awarness;
* the creative strategy is effective in influencing buyer behaviour;
* customers have responded in terms of changes to their purchasing habits, ie trial, gain and loss analysis to assess the quality of initial conversion in terms of whether it signifies adoption;
* distribution channels have responded in terms of satisfaction with sales, service and handling of complaints received about the company's products; and
* competitors' responses have been effective.

Activity tracking provides managers with operational information against which to measure the outcomes of activity. This allows them to intervene where activities fall short in performance or where well-executed activities are not achieving objectives demanded of them.

Assessing public attitudes to products and the company

Public attitudes result from personal experience, opinion influencers (eg journalists, specifiers, doctors etc) and most importantly 'word-of-mouth' communication between adopters and non-adopters. The effect of information flowing positively or negatively about the company or its products affects the diffusion of adoption. Negative factors can adversely affect adoption whilst positive factors speed up the diffusion process. Testing attitudes is therefore vital. Early warnings of negative reactions can be countered quickly through changing elements of the marketing mix and through PR activities. Positive attitudes can be reinforced.

Assessing public attitudes should be a continuous element of research, particularly amongst specifiers in industrial or medical markets.

Ad hoc attitude surveys should be conducted as an immediate response to either a major competitor entry to test for loyalty or a major public relations disaster such as a food-poisoning scare which incurs severe adverse media comment. Companies need a clear understanding of consumer and trade channel attitudes in formulating response strategies.

Practical applications of marketing research

The length of this book does not permit an exhaustive treatise on the techniques of marketing research, but some review of basic approaches and aspects of research in a multi-market company is necessary. We will therefore focus briefly on the following:

- the need for comparability;
- setting and executing research projects;
- finding information for desk research;
- commissioning field research;
- cultural and social restraints; and
- comparability.

Obviously, there are considerable differences between countries. Whether they be linguistic, cultural, economic or whatever, they make it difficult to achieve a level of comparability of research between different markets. The achievement of comparability is nevertheless important. The reasons are obvious.

- Management must be able to compare markets.
- Comparability not only allows differences in market needs, expectations and so forth to be identified but also and more importantly allows similarities to be identified.
- Experience records of new product introductions, new marketing developments and promotional activities can be maintained across several markets to compare their relative application and effectiveness.
- Strategically, corporate management needs to see the 'big picture' of global activities, competitor threats and economic trends. Comparability is therefore necessary in producing a consolidated global picture.

The principal areas to watch in creating a database and commissioning field research can be summarised as follows.

Statistical sources

These may be difficult to compare between countries because they are collected over different time-frames; data classifications may not be standard and data may misrepresent the truth (see page 147).

Language

This is a major constraint in field research. Considerable skill is necessary in wording questionnaires to ensure comparability in meaning. Even so, culture values lead to semantic differences and these are likely to creep in. It may be necessary to try and identify these early in research projects so that weighting factors can be ascribed to respective markets thus enabling responses to be adjusted against a benchmark. Marketing research has statistical techniques to set weighting factors.

Consumption patterns

These can lead to confusion amongst the unwary. For cultural, historical and economic reasons consumption patterns may seem to have apparent differences between countries. Drug-prescribing traditions, for example, between, say, the UK and Belgium may seem to indicate low usage of particular types of drugs. Yet detailed analysis may show that doctors in

Belgium tend to prescribe much lower doses of particular drugs whilst having a tendency to prescribe several drugs at the same time. Thus where the relative size of the drug market in proportion to the population size may be directly comparable, individual product categories may seem to be less frequently prescribed.

Until the prescribing habits of doctors are understood it would be an easy mistake to assume that fewer patients are prescribed particular categories of drugs. The number of patients receiving prescriptions may in fact be comparable, but the doses they receive, lower.

Market segments

These require a clear and consistent definition across all countries under study. Failure to do this will make it virtually impossible for management to understand and value its potential opportunities.

Social and economic conditions

These will also affect comparability. The complex issues of income, family size, religion, social class and family structures, education and occupation make it difficult to define comparable target audiences. Weighting factors may be introduced in an attempt to achieve comparability yet where there are vast socio-economic differences between, say, rich, developed and lesser-developed areas it is usually necessary to divide markets into clusters so that comparability can be achieved between each market within its own cluster.

Clusters of markets should be defined as the largest group of countries or areas which can be directly comparable across a number of key factors. Such cluster groups may defy attempts at geographical clustering although for management purposes markets with similar comparable factors may be broken down to fit into geographical patterns.

Setting and executing research projects

The setting and execution of all research projects must be based on a logical sequence of activity. Otherwise, the outcome may not provide the answers to the questions posed.

The sequence of a research project should follow the lines prescribed below.

Define the problem

What is it that marketing research activity is asked to find out? Is marketing research the right tool to use in contributing to finding a solution?

Define the objectives

Define the parameters of the research. This step is crucial to ensuring that in preparing the research brief and planning activities a clear goal is communicated. Too often research projects come to grief because managers lose sight of the intentions and scope of what they are trying to achieve. The objective needs to be reiterated at each stage of the research as a reminder of what the project is about.

Develop the research plan

This is based on setting work targets and evaluating options in terms of methodology and assignments. The development of the research plan will be concerned with:

- the information which needs to be collected;
- the assignment of organisations and people to the collection;
- the methods by which the data should be collected; and
- a timetable of activities including the finish date.

Interpretation of information

This is achieved through analysis. Here the skill of interpretation comes to bear. For no matter how well the research is carried out, the quality of interpretation will ultimately put the value on the project. The analyst needs to be sure that the data collected is statistically acceptable. He or she should have ensured this either by using a pilot study or testing the quality of the sample selected by examining data collected fairly early on in the research project. The assumptions underlying data-interpretation need to be noted to identify the rationale around which conclusions are drawn.

Research report and conclusions

These should be published and presented to managers. The report should present conclusions against the original objective but may of course highlight any useful information which comes to light during the research. It is also vital that conclusions which are based on statistically inconclusive data be noted as such. This is particularly important when dealing with small numbers (say 1 per cent to 5 per cent within a large universe).

The report should also recommend areas where further research activity is needed to refine knowledge in some of the 'query areas' of the findings.

Methodology for desk research

Where experienced desk researchers are not available, desk research often falls upon managers.

Such projects are time-consuming and a bind for those who find it boring to work their way through endless piles of statistical information. Many desk research projects fail because people assigned to them are neither motivated nor cognisant of methodology.

From experience, methods found to be both motivating and productive are those which use the exercise both to amass information from which a general understanding of the market can be obtained and at the same time meet the research brief. Divide the work into three parts.

- List the information required.
- Plan the data collection process.
- Collect and analyse data.

Then write the report.

The model worksheet illustrated below is a useful tool. It acts as a work

Information required	Sources	File number	Completion date

Figure 5.2 Model worksheet for finding information

sheet, it adds to the information-source database which can be referred to in the future and it provides a basis for filing and retrieval of relevant information.

The data collection process begins with locating sources of information, ie: company information sources – either from within the amassed databank or from records held within the company; and information guides held in specialist libraries such as the Department of Industry Statistics and Marketing Intelligence Library, business libraries, Embassies, etc.

Government information services

Most governments provide information or market intelligence services within the relevant trade departments. Other ministries provide published statistical data and reports. Much information about individual countries can be obtained through embassies or visits to the relevant trade departments within countries.

The Department of Trade and Industry (DTI) in Britain for example, through the British Overseas Trade Board (BOTB) provides a very comprehensive list of services to companies.

US embassies also have highly efficient trade departments and extensive libraries. Again, this can save considerable time and effort for many projects.

Other information sources

Banks

Banks are particularly active in providing information on countries and markets. Major banks have an international network of continental banks, branches and representatives. Some actually have specialist divisions to further client relations. One of the best examples is the Banque Nationale de Paris which has a special division called Banexi that specialises in using its 2,000 branches in France to provide information for foreign business.

Company staff

Company staff based abroad or who travel frequently to assigned areas are a valuable source of information. The most important human source of external information is company executives based abroad in company subsidiaries, affiliates, and branches. Many modern international company executives living or travelling abroad should be a major source of market and environmental information. By being on the spot, specific questions can be asked of company staff.

Distributors, customers and suppliers

There is no doubting the value of distributors and customers as a source of information. It is often biased in their favour and not altogether reliable in quantitative terms but does often provide valuable qualitative data. The trade's views and level of confidence in a company's own or a competitor's marketing activity is useful feedback. Such problems as poor trade liquidity, parallel importing or dumping are first noticed by the trade because they are at the rockface of the market.

Suppliers are often forgotten as sources of information. Packaging suppliers make useful contacts in that their business is demand-derived. The ups and downs of demand are reflected in their order books. An investigator can find out exactly the market size for a particular product from suppliers' information.

United Nations

The United Nations publishes masses of data and statistics with central reference points in key centres. In Europe, for example, the UN has its own Economic Commission for Europe that produces a flow of data in published form for general consumption.

European Commission

The Commission in Brussels employs thousands of researchers, statisticians and clerks who compile data on all forms of economic indices. The data ranges from GNP comparative performance to investment in railways and consumer spending curves. EC offices in major centres provide booklets of diverse subject headings at relatively low cost.

Non-governmental services and bureaux

Non-governmental services and bureaux from which data can be obtained can be divided into two categories. Firstly, those institutions and associations which provide information for clients and members as an additional service to their main purpose and secondly, those which specialise in providing information.

In the former category we have the chambers of commerce of foreign trade associations, which provide and exchange information. In the second are companies such as The Economist Intelligence Unit and AC Nielson which market reports and research back-data.

- The media for example, particularly *The Economist* and the *Financial Times*, have information published on the markets and products.

- Advertising agencies have a wealth of information which may have already been put into reprint formats.

- Competitors' catalogues, company reports, stockbrokers reports and reports from credit agreement agencies provide insights into competitors' activities.

- Indexing and abstracting services can save considerable time by locating and obtaining information.

- Trade and technical magazines not only have a wealth of qualitative data but may have produced reports on the very aspects of information being sought. Foreign trade magazines within the targeted territories may be extremely useful sources of information.

- Visit countries under study and make use of national statistical offices, visit packaging suppliers, distribution channels and talk to buyers as well as visiting exhibitions, trade outlets, banks and so on.

Process data

Processing data requires two main activities: verifying the quality of data and drawing conclusions from it.

Verifying the quality of data is a major problem as much published data is already out of date and, if provided by governments, may be tendentious, misleading or too general. Verification of data can however be achieved by comparability analysis or cross-referencing.

Comparability analysis, means taking known information from similar countries and testing the data against that from the subject market. This exercise may show the data to be comparable and hence probably reliable, or it may show significant variations against which further research will be necessary.

Cross referencing is done by checking several sources. Government statistics may well be skewed for political reasons or even suspect if based on tax information. Editorial sources are often tendentious for marketing or promotional reasons.

Information can also be compared against competitor company reports, stockbrokers' reports and credit status reports as these will provide some idea of their trading capacity which can be used to test market-size assumptions.

Drawing conclusions

The drawing of conclusions from verified data requires more than simply setting down a list of relevant statistics. It requires finding patterns in the information and applying the qualitative feel gained from an understanding of the market. So, apart from the data collection, the researcher must read as much background information as possible, visit the market and discuss aspects of it with people qualified to provide information and anecdotal commentary.

The conclusions of the research will rely considerably on the assumptions made about it. These should be noted so that discussion can be centred upon them. Assumptions may need to be tested by commissioned research if they are crucial to the validity of the conclusions.

Assessing market size where specific information does not exist

This is one of the most difficult problems for researchers.

The first problem is deciding whether the existing or potential market size should be assessed. The existing size might well be assessed using the system below.

- Analysis of domestic capacity of target market from:
  – company reports, stockbroker reports, credit standing reports;
  – government production statistics;
  – packaging suppliers;
  – production machinery statistics.
- Analysis of imports by the target market for relevant product classifications.
- Analysis of exports of the relevant product classifications from the target market.

These three pieces of information will provide clues as to the size of the market by assessing the domestic production capacity plus imports less exports.

The import and export analysis is not only useful in trying to determine the production capacity but also provides further clues. High imports may mean that there is a large domestic consumption not met by local production. Hence local production capacity (less exports) is fully utilised for the local market. Low exports may verify the above assumption. High exports indicate either a relatively small domestic market or, more likely, considerable competitive advantages by domestic producers.

Estimates from national income statistics

An estimate of market size can be determined from the assumption that a proportion of income is spent on a particular market. The method seeks to relate national income to:

- population total;
- demographic analysis;
- wage scales across the demographic profile of the country;
- relative prices;
- consumption statistics;
- retail sales statistics;
- health statistics; and
- level of education.

Here the assumptions require skill in using comparative data and qualitative argument such as in areas of education and sophistication of the population. Items such as health statistics can point to potential for drugs and health-care products but also indicate ideas of lifestyle particularly through analysis of reasons for mortality.

This method is probably better for indicating potential market size than actual market size, and the validation of comparability assumptions will need testing.

If prices are comparatively low it indicates high demand and high penetration of potential users (given an absence of price control) in a competitive market. High prices indicate low penetration from which the propensity for potential users to enter the market at lower prices may be estimated.

Neither of the two methods indicated will provide an accurate answer, but if both methods are carried out and similar answers are obtained then an approximate market size is probably indicated. This figure can be tested against commissioned research projects designed to provide ratification of the key assumptions.

Commissioning field research

There can be few exceptions where the execution of field research projects, particularly those requiring a large and established field-interview force, are not contracted out to marketing research companies. The process of commissioning a research project is divided into three parts:

- selecting the market research organisation;
- briefing the selected organisation; and
- receiving the research report.

There are four types of organisation that might be employed.

National research agencies

These are located within the target country and can be usefully employed where they are known to local advertising agencies, distributors or subsidiary company managers. For projects conceived at headquarters – particularly where no management structure exists in the target country – the employment of national research companies may create a number of difficulties.

- The need to visit several candidate agencies and select one from a list of unknowns is risky and time-consuming.
- Personal briefing will be necessary and will involve travel expenses.
- Communication and supervision of activities may be difficult and involve considerable time and travel.
- Comparability of results with other countries may be difficult to achieve.

International market research agencies

Those with a branch or head office in each European centre provide a number of advantages to clients. The most important is that relationships can be established over a number of projects so that both client and agency gain a mutual understanding of each other through working together. The central choice of agency means that local agencies are automatically determined and that briefings can be made centrally. Any communication problems ̇are of an internal nature between the co-ordinating echelons of the agency, which need not bother the client. The only concern the client need have is whether the competence and quality standards of the agency head office are universal within the agency's international network.

Confederations of marketing research agencies

These provide services similar to those of international agencies. It has to be remembered that the confederation is made up of a number of single companies, each with its own independent management and financial structure. The ease with which the client can select and brief the agency is the same as for the international agency. However, a prudent client would be well advised to investigate the closeness of the confederation before commissioning. Again the question of universal competence and quality standards is raised.

Central marketing research agency

These sub-contract work to foreign companies especially where agencies have a close relationship with their clients and act more or less as commissioning agents. Only experience can tell whether the central research organisation has the ability to select, brief, control and exact quality standards from its sub-contractors. Such a relationship, whilst offering the convenience of both international and confederations of marketing research agencies, relies much on the competence of the central agency in managing the sub-contracting work.

It must be made clear that the agency's lack of international status is not a reason for claiming excessive set-up costs in commissioning work from foreign companies. This method can only be recommended where the central agency acts more or less as the client's marketing research adviser and where considerable contact has been established.

A local agency with centralised staff to do research abroad

This is only viable for certain types of projects – ones highly specific in nature such as in industrial research or desk research projects.

Finding the right marketing research organisation

As with any contracted service function, candidates need to be sought and selected. The most common route for finding candidates for companies inexperienced in selection is through their advertising agencies.

Other sources of information are:

- The International Directory of Market Research Organisations (Market Research Society, London);

- Bradfords Directory of marketing research agencies and management consultants in the US and the world (Ernest Bradford, Middleburg, Virginia);

- International Directory of Marketing Research Houses and Services (American Marketing Association, Chicago).

Methodology in overseas markets

Methods of carrying out marketing research may have to be varied to cope with the different social and cultural conditions as well as the fact that each market has its familiar methods of doing things. For example, in the USA telephone interviewing is a familiar technique which expertise, the high distribution of telephones within homes and social and cultural tolerance towards the technique have allowed to become a major method of collecting information. Yet it is not a technique easily transposed to countries where telephones are not highly distributed and where expertise in this method of data collection does not exist.

There are a number of local cultural problems that may be encountered. In many Latin and Muslim countries it is difficult to employ female researchers to carry out field research; at the same time women respondents may be reluctant to talk with men unchaperoned.

In many states, political imputation and fear of tax investigation makes it difficult to carry out certain types of questionnaire-based research. There are also social taboos and traditions which may exclude certain topics except under very controlled conditions – this occurs as much in Europe as in less developed countries.

Thus even in the area of information gathering the cultural, social and practical constraints of carrying out activities quite normally acceptable at home may have to be adapted and tailored to the norms which exist in foreign countries. Local advice is needed. Methods which are considered as stepping outside the norm should be tested before application in foreign markets.

Organising a system for marketing information

As a company expands into more markets the complexity of management increases. The need for good information upon which to make decisions is axiomatic.

An information system provides management with relevant informative material from which they can gain knowledge and reduce uncertainties in their decision-making. Such a system should be able to seek, buy and gather data, and synthesise results into usable information.

A system set up to provide a company's management with information can work in several ways. It can merely watch markets, monitor events and produce regular updates on the company's markets, competitor activities, legal changes and so on. The system might also be assigned specific tasks of investigation, research and building econometric models to provide the company with a 'crystal-ball facility'. In many information systems, the elements of surveillance, investigation and research are usually combined.

As a system, it should provide a continuous flow of information. It

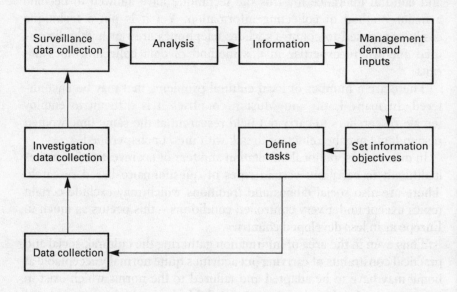

Figure 5.3 Marketing information system

should not be closed but should permit management the facility of making information demands and carrying out specific investigative and research projects either on a continuous or ad hoc basis. Furthermore, the system should provide information which is comparative on a market-by-market or a market-cluster-by-cluster basis.

The marketing information system has to be accessible to all levels of management and thus meet both strategic and operational needs. There has to be a means by which management throughout the organisation can gain a knowledge of what information exists and also be informed of a new and pertinent knowledge.

Management of the information system

Much is made of the arguments as to whether to centralise or decentralise the management of the information system. Very often corporate managers want to have their research or information managers close to them in order to provide information at a moment's notice and to control costs. Line managers would in most cases prefer to have their research facilities at market level in order that projects can be undertaken to meet operating requirements quickly and unencumbered by headquarters bureaucracy.

The centralised export company will no doubt have access to research and marketing information at the centre, very often under the charge of a line manager or, as often is the case, contracted out. The global multinational on the other hand will require facilities or functions throughout its global organisation.

The marketing information system has to be organised in such a way as to match the needs of the marketing organisation and conform to its structure. There should, however, be a central function which can amass and diffuse information upwards and downwards within the company as well as across functions. The central function acts to co-ordinate the system, demand information and supply information on request. However, the control of the central function must be ordered to ensure the marketing information facility conforms to the needs of corporate strategy. And, whilst it may be charged with setting up a marketing-research strategy for global issues, does so on the basis of corporate management intentions and organisational needs: not on what the marketing information function decides the organisation needs.

The system for information gathering and diffusion should be co-ordinated for strategic reasons but should not inhibit projects from being carried out in the operational areas of the business. It may be necessary for the co-ordinating function to exercise a quality-control duty to ensure that work is carried out to a sufficiently high standard and that resulting data is used to update corporate knowledge.

The central co-ordinating function should be accountable for supplying a 'competitor watch' facility within the organisation, providing briefings and information about targeted and new competitors around the world and drawing attention to threats and opportunities.

Many centralised marketing information services fall down because they fail to:

- provide a marketing research service in terms of knowledge, skills and quality of interpretation to meet needs at all levels of the marketing structure;

- ensure a continuous database against which marketing performance objectives and competitor activity can be monitored to provide a basis for line management decisions in, say, product distribution, promotional activity and countermeasures to competition;

- provide facilities for specific and ad hoc projects for individual markets such as market segment analysis, target audience perception and habits, customer dissatisfaction analysis, product, brand name and advertising testing;

- provide an internal information service database from which managers within the total global organisation can find and retrieve data about past research activities, general market information, political and economic technological information;

- use the information coming in from whatever sources to alert management about new threats and opportunities which appear anywhere in their international markets;

- form good interpersonal and working relationships with line management to provide a service rather than attempt to control the whole international marketing research and information system from the centre which will only lead to frustration of those working at the 'rockface'; and

- organise its information retrieval system to permit the flow of information.

From experience, it is probably not a good idea for marketing research people employed abroad to report to the central marketing research function. Rather they should be under the control of line management within the marketing function but with open communication lines to the co-ordinating function to allow for the information flow to take place.

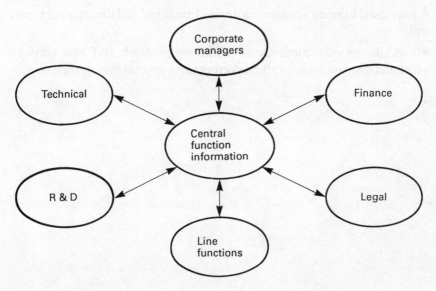

Figure 5.4 Co-ordinated information flows within a company

Figure 5.4 shows the way in which information support should be co-ordinated in the centre providing for information-flow both upward and downward and across functions.

The centralised co-ordinating function can usefully add the following to its *modus operandi*:

- a data retrieval system which must be computer based (this is not difficult given appropriate hardware);
- an information service system which will meet the demands of the organisation;
- services for carrying out centrally-conceived projects, whether desk research or commissioned field research;

- negotiation with international data collection agencies and marketing research companies for special corporate rates;

- negotiation with government agencies for grants and contributions to marketing research projects;

- a periodical update of new projects completed for distribution throughout the management organisation;

- marketing alerts based on threats and opportunities from competitors, new legislation etc;

- periodical briefing sessions for senior functional and line management; and

- bulletins on new methods of marketing research and new services which become available to all marketing units around the organisation.

6

Organising for Europe

In reality, marketing on an international scale involves overlays of activities in terms of products, markets and corporate ventures in many foreign countries. Many companies will have lots of activities in a number of differing markets, each with their own peculiarities. Flexibility is imperative. Yet the key to success internationally is to find those areas of business and opportunities through which a major corporate thrust can be directed. The overriding objective must be the focusing of business activities into profit streams where the company has the right product offerings and success requirements fully to exploit the opportunities offered. Having occupied positions in its markets the company will need skills, resources and commitment to defend them.

Business theory tells us that a firm should focus its competitive advantages on markets and segments where it is most likely to compete effectively. Yet in a dynamic environment market opportunities have a tendency to shift around and customers, competitors and technology change. At any point a company can look at its operations and find some in the wrong place, some under-exploiting opportunities, some doing well and others doing badly. Furthermore, most companies have neither the skills nor the resources to make rapid changes to the deployment of their commercial dispositions.

In understanding the strategic issues for a foreign business it is necessary for managers to appreciate that structure and operations evolve. Evolution occurs through the processes of development and diversification. And yet, because of environmental changes, difficulties in controlling the evolutionary process and mistakes made along the way, it is no easy matter to make a plan for the process. At best, strategic sets of intentions can be created, control systems can be implemented, and opportunities targeted. Even so, much of the evolutionary process will advance under its own momentum. It is therefore the direction of this momentum which is so important if a company's main competitive advantages are at the same time pointed at the most profitable opportunities and deployed in defensive dispositions against competition.

Phases of international evolution

Observers have noted five phases in the international evolution of firms.

Introductory

The introductory phase begins with demand for a company's products being received in the form of orders. The diffusion of Coca Cola in Europe, for example, had much to do with its introduction to countries by US armed forces resulting in demand by local nationals. It is now more often the case that companies becoming aware of the potential for their products abroad begin by selling surplus production, or their technology through exporting or licencing.

Colonisation

This second phase occurs when companies begin to establish a presence in foreign markets, initially through distributors and then through corporate dispositions such as branch offices or subsidiary companies in their most profitable markets.

Many of the resultant *colonies* may find it difficult to grow and develop entirely from the products sourced from the parent company. At this stage local initiatives in terms of local production, entrepreneurial activities such as designing, launching and acquiring local products take place.

Unification

The unification phase begins to occur when the parent organisation realises that it needs standard control procedures to manage its foreign business. Management systems and central staff functions are brought in at the centre to administer and control the business. The feature of the unification phase is the tightening of central control and the introduction of global objectives.

Rationalisation

The effect of unification is often to slow down and emasculate local initiatives. The rationalisation phase is usually awakened by a slowdown in growth and revenue. Management realises that it has a conglomeration of businesses which have developed separately and are difficult to control. Management then has to sort out which parts of its business are mainstream and which are peripheral. Furthermore, corporate managers may have to redeploy their activities from poorer areas of potential to richer but more competitive ones.

The rationalisation phase is completed when either the business is restructured to provide manageable groups of business units or where divestment of peripheral or uneconomic areas of the business takes place.

Strategy maintenance

The final phase of the evolutionary process and the basis for running a permanent business. The strategy-maintenance phase is based on directing the resources and strengths of the business in order to keep its competitive advantages deployed in such a way that it benefits most from maintaining and developing its competitive position. Strategy mainten-ance involves regular assessment of a company's success criteria and the acquisition and deployment of corporate strengths to meet them.

In the following pages we will examine the principal methods through which the EC's markets can be accessed. Whether each of the options presented offers a different mode of entry or a means of maintaining a corporate competitive position depends entirely on its suitability in application and management's own perceptions.

Exporting

There are few companies which do not use exporting to at least some degree in marketing their products internationally. For many, exporting is their only means of distributing products to foreign markets. Export management involves all the aspects of marketing, namely product policies, promotional strategy, pricing and distribution. The main function of the organisation needed for exporting is to support the marketing of goods and services in export markets. A considerable burden is placed on all exporting firms to manage the movement of goods and documents through export channels and into the buyer's importation channels.

The organisational requirements, therefore, are concerned with:

• providing a marketing and distribution structure in each foreign territory;

- setting up a management team to handle exports; and
- organising to handle documentation and logistics.

Marketing and distribution structures

Exporters have a number of options in structuring their marketing and distribution activities and we will explore several of these. Before doing so it is important to emphasise that the chosen structure must match the exporter's customer's requirements competitively. Structures chosen must be entirely compatible with the type of customers, the distribution channels and at the same time provide a competitive edge.

The following present a number of options which exporters commonly use:

- home-based sales staff to visit foreign customers;
- export houses and buying agencies;
- agents;
- distributors; and
- joint marketing arrangements.

Home-based sales staff

Many companies, particularly those supplying industrial customers, employ sales staff based either at the company's head office or dispersed through regional offices around the world. These staff visit customers and take orders and provide a communications channel between the customer and the exporter's service echelons.

The principal feature of this approach is that it is highly sales-orientated. In many cases it requires the back-up of centralised promotional support to provide leads through direct advertising, exhibition organisation and so forth. This type of activity is suitable where:

- there are a limited number of customers;
- costs do not outweigh the economies of not using intermediaries or locally based marketing and sales organisations; and
- central support services are available to supply promotion, technical support, logistics and other services.

This method is, therefore, quite suitable for supplies of raw materials – for example, Givandan, the Swiss based chemical and perfumery company sends home-based sales representatives to call directly on manufacturers in several countries in the world.

Direct calling on foreign customers can also be extended to calling on retail customers where such customers are large and dominate their markets and the markets are proximate enough to permit good communications and frequency of visits. It is also usual for customers to hold stock directly imported through the exporter.

Boots, for example, market their No. 7 range exclusively through chosen retail chains in Europe, and these are serviced by a headquarters-based staff of sales managers. Supplies of own-label products to foreign store chains will often use the same method.

The advantages of this method of serving customers are:

- the exporter has control over negotiations, service standards, company image and the building of customer relationships;

- the exporter's products do not have to compete for an intermediary's time in competition with other exporters' products; and

- costs can be more competitive and profits higher when an intermediary's margin or commission is not added to production costs, thus allowing the supplier to compete for business where price is the major factor in the buying decision.

The main disadvantages of using home-based sales staff are perceived to be:

- the method is highly sales-orientated and is thus only suitable for certain types of customer-and-seller situations;

- local competition or exporting competitors with a greater depth of marketing and service support may make this method of selling highly vulnerable;

- sales staff are required to acquire considerable customer and market knowledge as well as linguistic skills – there is obviously a difficulty in finding people with the necessary abilities; and

- customer relations may be interrupted when sales staff leave, are moved or promoted.

There is a limit to the number of customers that a team of centrally-based staff can reach effectively. New business may therefore be foregone when a team is already stretched in meeting service levels required for existing customers.

In conclusion, therefore, using home-based sales staff has a great number of advantages for specific types of operation. It would, though, be totally unsuitable for consumer products requiring high levels of retail distribution or products requiring a competitive level of service or logistics support.

This method of servicing customers can, however, be progressive. As business expands, staff could be dispersed to regional centres and branch offices set up in key markets in order to provide a greater competitive level of customer service.

Export houses and buying agencies

Export management through companies created by their owners to buy and sell and provide financing for export shipments offers a broad range of services. Export management companies (EMCs) are a feature of North American business, probably accounting for about one-third of US exports. In Europe the term 'export house' is more familiar, and, although similar to the EMC, it plays a lesser part in export management. In Britain for example, export houses account for only about 15 per cent of export volume.

Although the export trade carried out by export houses has gradually fallen, these organisations offer a broad range of services which includes sales and limited marketing back-up, finance and the shipment details with the foreign purchaser. Specialisation is a feature of the export house – this may be by geographical region or type of goods handled.

Such companies offer a number of advantages for the exporter in that they handle a great amount of the complicated procedures and have many long-standing contacts overseas. This is of great value to the small exporter in that the export house can act as its staff. The major disadvantages are that the export house relies heavily on having a number of clients or principals and thus cannot offer more than an economic proportion of its time to any one principal. The export house thus imposes limitations on the export and its contacts with customers and their control over marketing.

Export houses are a useful means of exporting where the company's product is easily saleable. However, many export management companies, through a need to ensure their own survival, have extended their services to include such activities as setting up licence arrangements and contract manufacturing arrangements for their principals.

Government buying agencies

Typical of a government buying agency is Crown Agents, a British institution created to acquire goods and services for colonial administration of the British Empire. Its services are still in demand by the British Commonwealth and other governments in the seeking of goods, services and a variety of other functions such as technical assistance and recruitment of personnel. Crown Agents will publish tenders in Britain for foreign governments or process purchase orders for specific goods and services from weapons systems to cutlery.

In dealing with government buying agencies most business is generated through tenders. Exporters will therefore need skills in handling tenders competitively. Many large companies, or those reliant on tender business, employ a manager to seek tenders and make recommendations to management as to how best to handle individual tenders. Price is usually the key element for a tender and few governments will pay a premium for products that exceed their quality specifications. Governments will, however, blacklist companies which fail on delivery or whose products fail to meet specifications. Exporting companies win tenders based on making to specification at a competitive cost and meeting service requirements. Few win by offering higher quality substitutes and seeking uncompetitive prices.

Selling through government buying agencies is often a reactive process, particularly for commodity items. Yet in sophisticated areas of marketing defence systems, telecommunications and major construction works, companies will need to seek out and influence ministers and civil servants involved in the decision-making process. A major supplier of a defence system, for example, would need to find several hundreds of thousands of pounds in producing presentations, literature and models just to compete for a single contract from a single government.

Agents

An agent is a person who is contractually entitled to act on behalf of a principal. In strict legal terms agents can totally commit their principals to contracts. The use of agents in exporting goes back at least a couple of hundred years where both buyers and sellers would appoint representatives residing in each other's countries to carry out business on their behalf.

Agents today sell an exporter's products and act as intermediaries in setting up such agreements as licensing, local production and so on, for their principals. For these activities agents will collect commissions or fees. Agents, however, do not carry stock on behalf of their principals, nor are they usually responsible for credit risks on business they have transacted. Agents described as 'Del Credere', though, cover principal credit risks but take higher commission to cover their own risks.

Other than carrying out negotiations with customers, agents do little in the way of promotional marketing – although they will often despatch catalogues and mail shots.

Agents are particularly useful in dealing with government contracts – particularly in sensitive areas outside Europe such as the Middle East where their ability to make and sustain contact is the basis of their livelihoods. Agents can also be used in the same way as direct sales staff. The criteria for their viability is the same, and many of the advantages apply. However, few agents act solely for a single principal, thus each principal competes for their agent's time. The disadvantages are legion, the main ones being that:

- agents are concerned with earning commission regardless of the quality of customers, and their methods may not be entirely compatible with their principals' desired image;
- few agents provide any promotional or service support and so their effectiveness is limited to specific types of customer–seller relationships;
- in many regions some agents have a virtual monopoly of influence, particularly with government buying organisations and consequently may act for competing principals, taking commission on all goods supplied for very little work; and
- in certain European markets, eg Western Germany, if it is proved that an intermediary is an agent, considerable damages may be secured through the courts on termination of the agent's contract.

Agents, then, are useful in specific situations and often essential for capital goods bought by many government buying agencies. Agents are unsuitable where stockholding, distribution, promotional activity and service support are required in an export territory.

Distributors

Using distributors is the most commonly employed method of distributing consumer products in export markets. Distributors buy goods on their own account and re-sell them through the distribution channels in their markets. The principal difference between a distributor and an agent is that the former takes 'title' for the goods sold to him, which an agent does not.

Distributors will, however, attempt to weld their inventory into a family of items which can be sold in combination as a packaged assortment to individual customers. In many cases distributors' efforts are directed primarily at obtaining orders for the assortment rather than for individual products.

A full service distributor will offer the following to exporters:

- stockholding (which agents do not);
- physical distribution including bulk stock breaking, repackaging and so forth;
- promotional support;
- customer service and after-sales care;
- sales reporting;
- sales forecasting and market information; and
- sales force activity.

The main advantages of using distributors are:

- exporters can enter markets using distributors' infrastructures and thus be concerned only with production and promotional costs;
- distributors will have considerable trade and customer knowledge which enables the exporter to compete on equal terms as regards local knowledge;
- continuity of the business relationship between the exporter and distributors motivates distributors to build business to increase sales and profits on their own account and at the same time please their principals;
- because of their presence and size of inventory offered, distributors may have access to major customers otherwise unavailable to the

exporter whose products may seem to be of little importance or relevance when presented on their own; and

- distributors carry a high proportion of risk for a product-launch failure in that the exporter will lose only marketing promotional costs whilst the distributor will have to carry trade debtors, stock losses, overhead costs and possible redundancies.

The principal disadvantages to using distributors are:

- an exporter's products will compete for time and attention with the distributor's own priorities and projects; and

- distributors have a large appetite for acquiring large, established and profitable brands and are often reluctant to commit resources to the risks of new and untried products.

Joint marketing arrangements

Joint marketing arrangements are in many ways the same as a normal distributor–exporter relationship. The difference is that the distributor is not a normal marketing importer but a mainstream company selling its own products in its particular field. Thus the exporter is not merely finding a distributor but entering into a marketing partnership.

The term 'piggy back' is often used to describe such arrangements where a small company enters into an agreement with a large dominant company.

The main difference between using a normal distributor and having a joint marketing arrangement is that where they are most effective the importing partner takes the exporter's products into its own range and treats it as if it were one of its own. In many cases the importer is taking in a product to both increase its own sales and to reinforce its position in the market.

Many companies have been reluctant in the past to act as importers merely to extend their sales. Yet with increased competition and higher R & D costs, finding products which fit well into a company's existing range is becoming increasingly more important.

Thus, whilst offering all the benefits of a normal distributor arrangement, joint marketing offers a number of superior advantages.

- The importing partner is seen by its customer as a primary supplier rather than a middle man.

- The motives for joining the arrangement by the importer are ones associated with reinforcing its market position rather than merely expanding its product assortment. For example, Astra markets Boots anti-arthritic drug Brufen in Denmark and other Nordic markets to give it leadership in one of the largest therapeutic market sectors.

- Such arrangements are limited to a small number of principals and therefore each principal's product competes on equal terms with other brands sold by the importing partner.

- Large sophisticated companies will tend to have a depth of marketing, selling and logistics skills that can be focused on making the principal's products a major success.

- Very often the reputation and market position of the importing company will add credibility to products newly introduced through this type of joint marketing relationship.

Success in this type of relationship is based almost entirely on the ability of both parties to agree on how products are to be marketed and positioned. This is unlike conventional distributors who tend to rely heavily upon their principals for marketing support. Major companies selling an imported product as one of their own brands tend to seek a degree of marketing freedom.

Too heavy a hand on the promotional plan by the exporter will often demotivate the importing company's product managers and sales staff.

Distribution agreements of this nature have to be negotiated on the basis of ensuring that the imported brands meet both the importer's desire to meet specific company market-position objectives and at the same time meet the exporter's specific positioning aspirations. Choice of partner and the compatibility of mutual objectives will therefore be keys to success. It should be emphasised, therefore, that negotiations should be entered into from the point of view of a partnership and not from the middle man arrangement which typifies the conventional distributor–principal relationship.

Certain aspects of these agreements will need to be carefully considered.

- The right choice of partner from which the superior advantages of such a method of marketing and distribution are exploited is crucial.

- The corporate goals, management system and methods of marketing practised by the importing partner must be understood. Any proposed methods of marketing which fall outside the importer's normal skills and capabilities will reduce the benefits of the arrangement.

- Prices and gross margins will need to be negotiated on the basis that the importing partner will have a profit contribution criteria for all his products. If the exporter's products fall short of this criteria the negotiations will either fail or there will be subsequent problems when management reviews the profitability of the arrangement.

- Promotional policy will need to be negotiated within the exporter's global plan and the need for local flexibility. Here a broad policy should be agreed, leaving the importer's marketing team to use its expertise to manage on a day-to-day basis.

- Stockholdings and supply logistics will need to be agreed to meet the importer's general company stockholding criteria. Again there will be a difference in attitude between a company importing under a partner-ship relationship and the conventional distributor. The stockholding will be controlled as if the product were one of the company's own. Supply will have to meet the importer's requirements.

The disadvantages however, need to be noted in evaluating this option.

- Conflicts between the exporter and importer often arise, usually in the area of who controls promotional policy. Here two companies with differing internal and cultural pressures have to evolve methods of resolving problems without compromising a product's chances in the market.

- Short-term costs may be greater than in using conventional distributors as the exporter will have to ensure that margins meet the importer's cost criteria. Distributors tend to have to compete with other distributors for choice brands and tend therefore to work to fairly tight margins.

- The exporter will be very much in the hands of its partner with regard to time allocated to products. An arrangement negotiated at a time when the partner is short of new products or feels vulnerable in a certain market sector may change when the importer's R & D function provides new products. Consequently the partners brands may have to take second place when the importing company has to allocate a large proportion of its time to ensuring success of its own innovations.

- Changes to the importer's corporate position, or directions in its activities may make the joint marketing arrangement an unnecessary aspect of the importer's corporate plans. Such changes are rare with distributors, but with companies for which acting as distributor is an exception rather than a rule, divestment of such activities may become a priority during rationalisation.

- Adding further new products to the agreement may incur fresh difficulties. The importer may be very happy to take a key product to meet its own needs in the market but additional lines may be a poor fit in the importer's product portfolio.

Branch offices and subsidiary companies

The principal reasons for setting up a corporate presence in foreign markets are to:

- focus a greater level of corporate commitment on to a company's major market;
- provide a commercial vehicle to attract and employ local nationals;
- increase profitability through taking over distributor's share of the profit stream;
- widen the range of activities undertaken in a market which are either beyond the distributor's capabilities or which are of little interest to them;
- achieve better control of marketing strategy, providing more effective competitive response and facilitating the introduction of new products and range extensions;
- provide the infrastructure for managing local procurement, production, contract manufacturing etc;
- set up a corporate company within a market to overcome barriers to trade;
- create a financial vehicle for raising finance, taxation reasons or to simplify acquisition of local companies; and
- appear national in the minds of customers.

The difference between a branch office and subsidiary company is in its legal status. A subsidiary company is incorporated with its own board of directors whilst a branch is an extension of the parent company.

The principal advantages of branch offices and subsidiary companies are:

- there is an accountable team of local staff committed to building the company's business in a national market;

- unlike a distributor's organisation, local management dedicate their entire efforts and resources on the company's business without the distractions of other principal's products;

- the parent company can exact standards and quality in terms of marketing, PR, distribution, customer service and so forth;

- the parent company can influence local activities by greater control of people and resources;

- standards of reporting, marketing information and control of stocks etc can be set to meet the parent company's methods and standards; and

- through good management and motivation of local staff greater performance is a likely outcome.

The disadvantages of setting up a local corporate presence are those which involve investment costs, personnel management problems, the presence of fixed costs regardless of revenue achieved, and exposure to local taxation as well as political and financial risks. To these can be added the costs of creating administration and line-management structures to run foreign-based structures within the parent company.

Corporate management should also be aware of the dangers of *exposure to legal liability* for the parent company from activities of subsidiary companies and branch offices. Structures should be created to avoid any adverse impact on the total company.

The main points in establishing a local subsidiary or branch office can be considered as follows.

- Define the level of business required to ensure long-term viability. *Critical mass* is the minimum share of a market needed to permit a business to thrive competitively in terms of its costs (product costs, facilities, marketing costs, sales force, administration, distribution etc) and at the same time be competitive in price.

- Determine the initial purpose for setting up corporate presence and ensure that the resultant structure and organisation reflects the purpose.

- Selection recruitment, training and managing local staff is a vital ingredient in the success of a new branch or subsidiary. The importance of making the right personnel decisions at the outset cannot be overstated.

- The handover of business from distributor to the company's own marketing structure needs care to avoid turbulence and minimise disruption in the market.

- There is an obvious need to begin to create a local corporate identity and to ensure that all relevant directories, trade associations, customers and so on are aware of the existence of the branch or subsidiary.

Shared ownership

That there are advantages in owning all the equity in a foreign subsidiary is beyond doubt. But, for a number of reasons, there has been a trend to part-ownership or shared ownership over the last decade. The reasons for this are centred around four factors.

- The risk involved in the venture.

- The need to raise sufficient finance or to overcome constraints on capital investment by foreign exchange regulations or the constraints in the company itself.

- Environmental pressures such as governmental regulations controlling the level of ownership by foreign firms. While these are slowly being abolished within the Community, they persist in the outside world. For example, Nigeria demands up to 60 per cent local ownership. Mexico has similar requirements.

- A willingness by head office executives to accept shared ownership arrangements both to mitigate risks in turbulent environments and to comply with local regulations.

Through shared ownership arrangements, many companies have been able to expand. In the last ten years a number of companies have taken the plunge in setting up foreign operations to pre-empt competitors and to maximise sales potential.

Shared equity also enables a company to become local rather than be perceived as foreign. This not only helps safeguard subsidiaries from adverse public and governmental attitudes, but also makes it easier to operate. In Italy, for example, the local bureaucracy has tended to be anti-foreign.

In Europe there are a number of problems in language, local culture and regulations affecting the operations of a company. A certain degree of local participation helps to establish the company in a foreign and otherwise alien environment. The company also gains assistance from local investors in orientating to a new cultural, social, legal and economic environment.

Joint ventures

Peter Drucker describes the joint venture as being 'the most flexible instrument for making fits out of misfits'. In international business it is of key importance as a method of operation. However, it is both a difficult and demanding alternative to direct ownership.

There are three basic types of joint venture.

Mutual benefit
These pool the strengths of participating partners. For example, a leading pharmaceutical company working on anti-cancer products created a joint venture with a bio-technology company to produce a monoclonal drug delivery system which targets anti-cancer substances at specific cancerous cells. Here both parties were able to bring together their unique skills and provide a new drug system that neither could have developed on their own.

Multi-party
Joint ventures which bring together a number of organisations which when joined together create a large enough size to become viable entities in terms of finance, facilities and skills. These may be temporary consortia, like those found in the construction industries, or permanent institutions such as those involved in satellite broadcasting systems. (For example, News International, D C Thompson, Ladbroke Group, Ferranti and Equity and Law.)

Dual-nationality
The last relevant form of joint venture in this area of business is founded

primarily to 'harmonise political or cultural obstacles'. Examples are to be found in trading with the USSR, for example.

Drucker illustrates examples of joint ventures working well between Western and Japanese Corporations. The rationale for such ventures is the harmonisation of the Japanese company's technical and product knowledge with a European company's knowledge of its market, language and culture.

Many of the same arguments in favour or otherwise of shared ownership can be used in discussing the joint venture as a viable form of ownership. However, there is a tendency for joint ventures to dissolve over a period of time. This may occur because the joint venture is designed to fulfil a specific purpose (such as with a construction consortium) or simply because partners cannot get on with each other. Studies have shown that companies with high tolerance to joint ventures include those that are fairly new to foreign operations and those which have a decentralised decision-making structure.

Minority control

Very often companies are unable to own all their equity. Sometimes they cannot even own a controlling interest. Why should a company accept or embark upon a foreign investment for less than a controlling interest?

Firstly, a company may have been forced into relinquishing its control through governmental intervention. In such a case, the company is concerned with maintaining its corporate presence and protecting its markets. The only alternative would be to sell off its own equity or put up with the situation for as long as it is economic to do so. Secondly, ownership may have second place to a company's desire for a base over which it has some control. The scope of the business is controlled through its company articles which endeavour to maximise its earnings from the subsidiary through product transfers, licence fees, management technical fees, and its portion of dividends. Thirdly, even as a minority owner, the company may see such a compromise as being the only viable way of staying in a market and reaping some reward from it through ensuring that it owns the biggest block of voting shares. This it achieves through selling limited amounts of shares to members of the public rather than to institutions.

Another method of control available to the minority owner is having some command over the sources of raw materials by owning the patent rights, or by having a dominating access to the markets for the company's products.

Management and turnkey contracts

Two other forms of foreign involvement both fall into the broader context of international business. Management contracts involve the company in a contract to supply management to a foreign company on an annual fee basis. Such contracts are mostly found in the state-owned companies of lesser-developed countries. The extent to which such arrangements offer an outlet for the company's products through direct export or other forms is dependent upon the contract agreement. Companies, however, do benefit from the earnings from the contract.

Setting up operations for third parties under what can be described as a turnkey contract involves the sale of technology. Sometimes a licence or franchise agreement is part of the contract. Britain's major glassware company Pilkington has set up a number of such projects, as has Firestone in the USA.

Licensing

A licence agreement is one where the company, the licensor, grants rights to another company, the licensee, to manufacture, assemble, or otherwise use a product's registered name or patents or both. Such rights are usually, but not always, exclusive. Under such arrangements the licensee is usually asked to pay a licence fee and an annual commission or royalty for the use of the licence each year. This is either a fixed sum predetermined by contract or based upon a percentage of volume or value of sales.

Licences can be based upon any saleable know-how and can be applied to any of the following cases.

- Intellectual property such as patents, registered copyrights and brand names.
- Technical, production and marketing know-how which, although not protected intellectual property, provides the licensee with expertise it could not otherwise obtain.

- Existing business and goodwill surrounding a product where a company may wish for whatever reason to change its present method of operations.
- A subsidiary arrangement in reinforcing contract manufacturing or distribution agreements.

Licencing as a mode of entry to a new market is often used in the following situations.

- Where cost of entry by other means is too great. British companies launching new products into larger European markets have frequently found that marketing investments are too great in terms of cost and risk exposure.
- Where high rates of duty, import quotas, prohibitions or technical barriers limit market access. Licensing may be chosen as a mode of entry in place of investment in local production for practical or economic reasons (or to reinforce local production contracts).
- Costs and practicalities involved in transport of finished goods or components often mean it is not economically viable for exporting.
- The marketing advantages of licensing to a major manufacturing and marketing organisation are superior in terms of gaining market share and competitive positioning.
- The company may have no other international capability through which to exploit its opportunities abroad. Licensing provides access to foreign markets without the investment needed to set up an international structure.
- In rapidly innovating areas of technology licensing may offer the most rapid means by which new inventions and modifications can be brought to the market either to pre-empt competition or to exploit revenue opportunities within the short life-cycle of the product.

Licencing to protect patents and other intellectual property is another important role.

In certain parts of the world increased competition is coming from companies prepared to risk litigation through pre-empting or ignoring trade mark and patent rights of companies. This is one major reason a company might attempt to establish its patent rights quickly and effectively in all its markets. Western Electrics in the USA overcomes this problem by marketing licences to avoid patent litigation.

There is also the problem of gearing up international distribution and production to meet patent deadlines in some countries. Most countries acknowledge and accept international patent agreements but some put a time limit on patent and trade mark exploitation. Certain countries will demand the exploitation of a patent or will compulsorily enforce a local licensing arrangement. In other countries, trade marks will lapse if not commercially exploited in periods of between three and five years. Hence, to meet time limits, licensing may be usefully employed to protect a company's intellectual property.

Political reasons are often given, since licensing of products provides some protection against the political risks of expropriation and national-isation – if only as a negotiating tool at the time of expropriation.

Licensing and cross-licensing agreements may offer opportunities for companies to trade off markets and technology in order to gain superior advantages from each other. Where two companies agree to give each other first refusal on new products or processes in their respective markets there is potentially a superior trade-off between using other modes of marketing and the access to new products and technology at home.

Nationalism and most-favoured status amongst companies supplying government contracts may limit access to those valuable markets. Through licensing, national government supplier access may thus be achieved. This reason may provide opportunities for Community companies to take on licences from external companies to compete for tenders across the entire Community.

Licensing is a means of providing outlets for a company's technology and expertise which it may itself not wish to develop but sees advantages in exploiting through licensed partners.

There are also disadvantages to licence agreements.

- The licensee becomes a major competitor, as can be seen by a large number of Japanese companies who began by using US licences.

- Licensees may not use the licence to full advantage, thus under-exploiting the market opportunity. This not only loses revenue from missed opportunities but, more importantly, opens the market to competition.

- Control of marketing, production and quality control are difficult to maintain once an agreement has been finalised. Even if costly and time-consuming litigation is effected the disruption to the market and the ill-feeling between partners may severely hamper the development of the market.

- Licence fees, it is often said, go directly to profit and thus provide no contribution to production overheads. They therefore serve little in reducing costs through scale of production. They do, however, contribute to the return of R & D investment which, for many companies in the high-technology business, may be more important than scales of production.

- Remittance of fees may be difficult in many less developed countries and may be subject to special taxes. This is not however seen as a major constraint in the EC, USA or Japan.

Licencing offers a great many opportunities for exploiting marketable expertise. For many companies aiming to become globally competitive the licensing-out and licensing-in of products and processes can contribute to their competitive position and development.

The main issues which potential licensors should consider are set out below.

Selection of the licensee

As with any third-party arrangement, capability, reliability, trust and interpersonal relationships are absolutely critical. If a licensee has neither the financial capability, skills nor structure to exploit the licence, then major marketing opportunities will be foregone.

Agreements

These must be carefully put together. The main issues are ensuring that the interests of both parties are mutually covered and that cancellation clauses have teeth. The ownership of the process, product or brand name should revert to the licensor at the end of the agreement.

Control and monitoring

These activities should be an integral part of managing licensees. Agreements should provide access to production and marketing activities as well as means through which sales and production can be audited.

Shared benefits

These are a key to success. No matter how strong the agreements between the licensor and licensee, it will be the relationship and the gain of mutual benefits which accrue which will go a long way to ensuring the success of the arrangement. The licensor must be prepared to go well beyond the minimum agreements in the contract to maintain frequent contact, production assistance and advice on marketing.

Franchising

A franchise is basically a form of licence arrangement. The main differences between a franchise and a standard licence are that the franchisor provides a number of components which are essential to the arrangement. The components may be ingredients, marketing packages or marketing and management services. The franchisee is expected to provide a contribution to capital, financial and other resources involved in running the franchise. The franchisee is normally expected to conform to conditions of the franchise in terms of image, promotion and quality standards.

Many of the international soft drinks companies have such arrangements and provide dry or wet mixes which are diluted and carbonated by franchisee bottling companies all over the world. Holiday Inn, Kentucky Fried Chicken, MacDonalds and a number of other catering companies offer their name, goodwill and back-up services in terms of staff training, reservations and so forth to promote their franchisees.

Franchising involves both a direct export component and licence fees in obtaining remuneration from franchisees. The advantages are increased total earnings from the two methods of obtaining payment and a greater control over end-production quantities. In pure licensing agreements the licensor is paid retrospectively on the basis of audited sales or production output. This means that licensors tend to have to wait some time for their money as well as having to rely heavily on the licensee's honesty in reporting sales. Furthermore, in some countries, exchange control delays may mean that companies have to wait considerably longer than the contracted period before receiving payment.

Most international franchises are set up in foreign countries through a local holding company which then recruits franchisees and maintains a supervisory role over their activities.

7

Product Strategies for International Markets

This chapter aims to help the reader focus on the principal issues of constructing an international business. Products are what business is about. Yet many managers find it difficult to see the 'big picture' of an international product strategy. There is too much confusion between the micro aspects of brand management issues, such as whether to standardise or adapt products for their markets. Too often the commentators do not really clarify what international product strategies are about and tend to dwell on trivial differences between domestic and foreign strategy requirements.

Product strategies in an international environment are based on the philosophy of making businesses globally competitive whilst remaining nationally responsive. In whatever field a business operates it needs to assess its product strategy against the market share it requires internationally to provide a competitive base. At the same time it must evolve product strategies at national levels to develop and defend its individual market positions. Development and market share criteria at a minimum are dictated at the strategic level by that which is required to maintain critical mass (see page 102) and at the local level by that which is required to maintain a competitive position.

The issues which attend the Single European Act are critical to the way corporate management has to plan its international product strategies. As we have already noted, the Single Internal Market not only provides a huge home market upon which companies can grow to become globally competitive but also provides increased opportunities for foreign competitors both inside and outside the Community to sweep across the EC and undermine uncompetitive rivals.

This chapter, then, attempts to address the problems of creating an internationally competitive position for a business through its product strategies. It will examine and review the following issues:

- corporate style;

- global orientation; and

- specific products for specific markets.

Corporate style

The direction in which companies' product strategies evolve is largely in response to the orientation of corporate management: its vision, skills and application. Yet it is clear that many companies do not view the world with the same enthusiasm as Alan Sugar at Amstrad or Tony Berry at Blue Arrow. Many plod complacently on with limited vision until displaced by predators or competitors. If the Single European Act achieves nothing else it will at least force managers to shape up and lead their organisations more courageously.

Domestic orientation

When companies concentrate on putting their home markets first in terms of marketing and product design, with little thought to making major modifications for overseas markets, then we are looking at companies with *domestic orientation*. Such a style should not be confused with that employed by companies standardising products internationally under common brand names, eg Walkman or Coca Cola. The difference is that in the former case a company is trying to standardise on its home market offering and in the second it is exploiting globally orientated brands.

Companies like Bovril, before it was acquired by Beecham, found ex-British-colonial markets for their brands of Bovril and Marmite. Yet only a relatively small proportion of total Bovril and Marmite sales was to export markets – the home business was substantially higher than global sales. It is this characteristic – the inverse proportion of sales turnover in a smaller domestic market to that of a much enlarged global market opportunity – which is a key indicator of the more parochial domestic orientation.

The problem for many companies is that management is often unaware of the damage that domestic orientation can create for a company. Not only does such an orientation deny the company opportunities for exploiting the global opportunity, it also reduces the company's ability to compete against global competitors at home. It ignores the fact that many so-called domestic customers shop from the world market. The Single Market will make it even easier for them to do so.

The invitation for foreign competition through the Single European Act will force Community companies to be more international in outlook either in response to foreign competitor activity or as a result of being overtaken by them.

This style may be seen as being quite appropriate for the smaller company. Yet companies like Amstrad in the UK, which have grown rapidly in recent years, went for a global product offering from the outset by using its technology to satisfy global needs. It is often forgotten that Akio Morita did not build up Sony's international fame and fortune by selling the rice cookers upon which he had founded his business, but on US transistor technology which he adapted for global appeal.

Geographic domination

A number of large international companies have a proliferation of national markets within which a number of products are sold virtually exclusively in each market. In many cases there is barely no cross-national marketing. Their strength lies in dominating large areas of geography by having major shares of national markets.

The reasons for this arise from the roots of the business. Often companies offering highly differentiated products between their markets do so because taste and culture demand different products. Others have arisen because during the company's colonial stage of development local markets were built by the entrepreneurial initiatives of local managers.

Obviously, companies expanding by acquisition will also acquire numbers of local brands.

The weaknesses of this multi-product position are that:

- it becomes difficult to focus resources behind particular products to provide thrust and momentum to the business;

- even competition with cohesive international strategies has largely to be fought on a country-by-country basis;

- evolution of the business tends to unfold around markets and subsidiary companies that make the most of their local opportunities and this does not always mean that resources and marketing investment are focused on the most strategically important markets; and

- global planning of the marketing attack is not a practical proposition.

The strengths of the multi-product approach are often found in the security to the business of having a portfolio of products and markets that ensure risks are widely dispersed. Many companies that fall into this category tend to have a sluggish growth record but at the same time often show reasonable returns on capital employed.

Such companies have a ready-made global infrastructure to launch global brands. A number have begun to divest some of their peripheral activities and are now concentrating more on their international brands.

Glaxo, for example, following massive success with their anti-ulcer drug Zantac, were able to divest some of their non-mainstream businesses to concentrate on the global application of medical research.

Global orientation

Global orientation bases its success on building business on similarities. Too many companies try to look for differences in culture and nationality. The discovery that nearly 800 million people in the free world's sophisticated markets have a lot of similar needs and aspirations has enabled companies with vision to build mighty markets for their products.

Nina Ricci fashions, Levi jeans and Swatch watches are worn by certain types of people, most commonly younger city dwellers, television watchers, Walkman owners from reasonably well-off families. They drink Coke and eat at MacDonalds. From San Francisco to Tokyo, similarities show in these young-person groups across both cultural and national boundaries.

Global segments can be found across a wide range of products in consumer and durable product areas, in both industrial and service fields. It is up to managers to identify them and assess their potential. It is this orientation by management to seek out large, global applications for their technology which differentiates their outlook from the two previously discussed styles of management. The aim of global orientation is to make companies globally competitive yet, in so doing, responsive to national environments.

Advantages of global orientation

Companies which focus their product strategies through the development of globally orientated products enjoy a number of benefits.

- They acquire large international markets for individual products with the attending advantages of cost and production efficiencies.
- R & D costs are invested against the global potential for sales.
- The marketing attack can be globally played and targeted against international and local competitors alike.
- The experience, skills and orientation of the whole global organisation are collectively dedicated to the success of individual products.
- The mobility of management and transfer of marketing and production skills between markets facilitated more easily where managers have developed a depth of product knowledge.
- Organisationally the business structure can be simplified to administer and direct global operations for a range of international products more easily than for a proliferation of brands and markets.

Global orientation has too many advantages for it not to be seen as the most superior of the three options for management style presented. For high-technology businesses it provides the potential sales to fund R & D activities. For low-technology businesses it provides large markets to enable them to compete in cost and price as well as funding competitive levels of marketing expenditure.

For many firms the practicality of true global orientation of companies such as achieved by Coca Cola, Seiko and Glaxo may be constrained through faults of history and the highly differentiated quality of certain product market relationships. Yet the closer companies can align themselves to this orientation on key areas of technology, developing future brands as global candidates, the more its competitive advantages can be focused on to its markets. Such a strategy in the long term will involve redeployment of resources and facilities to those markets offering the greatest potential, as well as improving and adapting existing products for global development and divesting areas of the business which fail to fit profitably into a global structure.

There are basically two ways in which companies can become globally competitive. Firstly, they can build business for key company products across a large area of international geography. This we might describe as the *global product route*. Secondly they can export technology, know-how and skills through collaboration with third parties with capabilities or matching technology to exploit opportunities within national markets and regions. This we might call the *collaborative route*.

Global product route

The global product has evolved from companies with particular competitive advantages exporting their best products to foreign markets. The strength of the approach is to create large market shares which provide a global security against competitors. Such products, which can be easily branded, fall into the fast-moving consumer product description and sustain their market share through intensive and expensive promotion. Yet such a strategy is more difficult for low-technology, poorly differentiated products such as tile edges and shelving systems.

A global brand is a product sold under the same name in the major markets of the world which has approximately the same customer satisfaction attributes and would be recognised as such by consumers the world over. A global brand presents one of the most efficient uses of resources and is a powerful marketing tool. The principal benefits that global brands bring to a business are those associated with global orientation: production rationalisation; focusing of organisational skills and experience; global direction of the marketing attack; transnational mobility of management; simple organisation structure and the amortisation of R & D costs across larger, global sales potentials.

In the fast-moving consumer goods markets brand names like Coca Cola, Camel Cigarettes and Maggi Cubes stand out. Global brands take years to build. Despite the billions of pounds and dollars spent on potential candidates, probably less than 4 per cent of such brands successfully mature. Yet there are literally thousands of recognised brand names carried on global products which range from filing systems to pharmaceuticals, fast-food retailing to childrens dolls, industrial dyes to forklift trucks.

The two principal investments on products which are potential global brand candidates are promotional investment and high distribution (and customer service). This means that marketing promotional costs will be high throughout the product's life, initially to build awareness and trial and later to maintain market share. Distribution will also need considerable investment and will probably involve acquisition of production bases and service support organisations in all principal markets.

Brand name or product

There are two basic elements of the global brand:

- products which are similar in each market; and
- brand name which is common.

Global orientation exploits both elements where it is the most appropriate way of maximising marketing efficiency and where it is practical. It is not always possible, however, to register the same brand name around the world. For example, Elastoplast is Tensoplast in most of the world and Nurofen is Nerofen in Europe.

There is also the international name, which, whilst serving a family of products may be slightly different from market to market. Japanese companies such as Seiko and Casio are exponents of brand-proliferation techniques (see page 199) with the same name branded on each of up to two thousand different products within the same line.

Problems of creating global brand names in Europe

The inheritance of a fragmented European market has meant that many companies have been frustrated from creating global brands within the Community.

The lack of a common trade mark authority has meant individual countries have set their own criteria for trade marks, making it difficult for firms to find trade marks acceptable to all countries across Europe. At the same time, the diversity of languages has meant that it is difficult to find common names which have universal acceptability across Europe.

Post-war reparations between Germany and the rest of Europe, the US and Canada involved the loss of many pre-war names to companies outside Germany. This means that many well-known names are held by differing companies in their national markets.

Pre-emptive registrations of brand names by companies in the Community has led to a situation where competing companies hold registrations for each other's brand names.

Lastly, past restructuring and mergers of European companies have left brand names with residual owners.

Whereas these difficulties have led to inconsistencies in the past (and will no doubt contribute to future problems), there are moves within the

Community to harmonise trade-mark registration. This will enable firms to register new names across the Community providing that they do not impinge on existing trade marks. There are no provisions to permit legitimate trade mark holders of conflicting marks to sell their products under the same or similar names in each other's markets.

Criteria for global brands

A product destined for globalisation needs many qualities.

- An identifiable and sufficiently large market segment is required, where needs are universal and significant cultural differences will not impinge on the general acceptability of the product concept.

- A product or service needs technology or key elements which can be protected either through patents, secret formulae or registered copyright. Marketing investment must be sustained long enough for the product to become established.

- There must be an organisation with sufficient resources and direction capable of conceiving, developing and furnishing the size of marketing investment required to establish an international brand.

- A suitable communications structure is needed through which markets can be informed of the product and through which the diffusion process can be maintained.

- A product, pricing or organisational competitive edge will ensure that the product is not stifled by competitors during its launch period. This means:
  - a product which has unique or technical features which good marketing can make superior to competing brands;
  - pricing strategies aimed at securing market share;
  - an established, well-resourced organisation which has command of the distribution channels and can provide customer service support.

- A product must have the potential for an extended or extendable life-cycle which will exist long enough for it to be come profitable as a global brand.

- A product must be based on core technology which allows the company to become and remain competitive in innovation, output, quality, reliability, cost and price.

- Access is required to production facilities in key territories to ensure availability, price competitiveness and to overcome tariff and non-tariff barriers in each market (where these apply).

Finding product candidates

Finding products which have a potential for the marketing criteria may present considerable difficulties. If the global brand route is to be pursued the product candidates have to be suitable. There will be considerable marketing investment and many years of market building even after the brand is successfully launched. There may need to be investment in facilities to support the brand as it develops.

Products existing within the company

These are an obvious choice. Not only are production facilities already in place (and probably considerable marketing experience within the company), there is also an established market at home upon which production risks can be taken. Ideally, products should already have achieved some measure of success and have economies of scale in production which allow them to be competitive in cost and price.

In taking existing products into a wider global market companies have potentially two options. Firstly, they can extend the product unaltered to the global market thus benefiting from economies in scale of production. Or they can adapt products to meet local needs more closely, thus widening market opportunities and making products more competitive.

The former strategy frequently falls down in that it does not offer a wide enough set of opportunities upon which large market shares can be built around the world. Even where broad similarities between markets exist, competitors may meet consumer choice criteria more closely. Distribution channel buyers will be reluctant to stock foreign products which obviously need a certain amount of adaptation – even if companies have identified market niches in which their products have a high chance of success.

There are practical difficulties in meeting the host of product norms and standards regulations in each country which have hitherto bedevilled the EC's markets. There can be few products which will not need some degree of adaptation if they are to be universally acceptable.

Expansion of universal acceptability

Products may be adapted, even in a small way, in order to broaden their extension potential. The substitution of pork fat in many food products have opened up Middle East potential for many food companies yet has not affected domestic markets. Hence the company still benefits from international standardisation. Johnsons Wax in the USA has adapted internationally to the use of butane gas in its aerosol cans in the face of adverse publicity to fluoro-carbon gases in some of its markets. Yet in meeting the requirements for these markets it has widened the potential for its products internationally – as well as making them less expensive to produce. Adaptations need not, however, be permanent.

Temporary adaptations

Making a temporary adaptation may sometimes be necessary to gain initial understanding of the product concept by consumers or to overcome, say, an initial taste shock amongst trialists. Kenichi Ohmae in his book, *Triad Power*, gives two examples of temporary adaptations to food products in Japan.

Firstly, when Mister Donut was being introduced into Japan, consumer research showed some adverse reaction to the cinnamon taste. The company reduced the cinnamon considerably for the launch but over the next five or six years the cinnamon level was gradually increased back to the level used in the USA.

MacDonald's hamburgers tell a similar story. Japanese consumers have a preference for fat to be mixed with beef – that is the Japanese idea of a hamburger. Thus when MacDonald entered Japan it had to alter the red meat content. In the last ten years it has reached almost the same level as in the USA.

Permanent adaptations

There are instances where a company markets fairly standard products throughout the world yet makes special adaptations for major markets. The Barbie doll for instance is marketed universally except in Japan where special adaptations were found to be necessary following extensive consumer research carried out amongst Japanese children. Takara, Barbie's licensees, redesigned the Barbie making it smaller, substituting blond for darker hair, and giving it smaller breasts. The resultant product made a major impact on the Japanese market.

Adaptations for cost

In some markets there may be a potentially high demand for products such as semi-luxury consumer durables like wrist watches or cassette players, but prices are out of reach of the populace. Many Japanese companies, for example, have made special cost adaptations to offer their branded products (although somewhat inferior) to Third World markets. The danger of this strategy, of course, is if the goods are re-exported to higher-priced markets they will affect the company's quality image.

Restraints of universal acceptability

The two fundamental restraints on creating universal acceptability (other than total dissimilarity between markets) are the legal factors surrounding product standards and the duty and import restrictions and taxation.

Legal factors

Despite a firm's attempts at creating products with universal consumer acceptance, legal factors within individual countries may so distort design features that it becomes impossible to produce a common, if not standard, product.

Europe is – and will remain until standard regulations are harmonised around 1992 and 1993 – one of the most complicated areas for product standards. This will change, and, along with the opportunities, a new set of problems about how to re-educate users will arise when new harmonised standards to familiar products come into effect.

Standards regulations are introduced for three reasons:

- protection of the consumer (food and drug, health and safety consumer protection);
- protection of the environment including both physical and cultural aspects such as religion, social taboos etc; and
- protection of local industries, ie non-tariff barriers to trade.

Whilst these persist adaptations will be necessary if market entry is to be achieved.

In the European Community the objective for standards-regulations harmonisation are to allow companies discretion in design whilst setting common standards for health and safety, consumer protection and environment protection. Even so, as was pointed out in Chapter 1, it will be difficult to market products outside the standard norms accepted in individual markets because of usage and practice factors.

Duty and import restrictions and taxation

Where duty and import restrictions and taxation are based on such concepts as the material content or usages of products this can affect the way products are made or marketed. For example, in Sweden products using alcohol as an ingredient are taxed more highly than those without, even where it is not consumable as alcohol. In some countries items discriminate between usage. Baby Powder for example was charged at lower duty rates than other talcum powders because it was primarily seen by the authorities as a baby product, although it has a high adult usage.

Furthermore, duty and VAT varies between countries making a common marketing positioning difficult.

Adaptations made to alter the material content of products not only make production-rationalisation extremely difficult but lead effectively to different products often with different attributes. Where the adaptation of marketing and product positioning becomes necessary the products may need further adaptation to meet the needs of different marketing segments. Obviously the greater the difference (caused by both standards regulations and import duties, restrictions and taxation) between products and marketing in different countries for non-marketing reasons, the fewer the benefits a global product will bring to the company.

However, it will be a fact of life for many companies that global orientation will involve both global brands and local-market-specific products.

Specific products for specific markets

Once a company has made a breakthrough in R & D it is incumbent on it to exploit its technology to the full and innovate around it. Smaller companies or companies whose brands are not leaders can increase both output and market share in individual markets through expanding their product lines. Such additional share and output may help them to compete with market leaders in terms of cost, price and relative costs of production.

Specific products for specific markets still go some way to exploiting the synergies of global orientation where:

- the specific products increase the standing of local companies in terms of market share and retail dominance;
- specific market opportunities offer themselves and enable the business to steal a march on its competitors (for example, Beecham launched a chewable analgesic for regions where potable water was scarce);
- the highly differentiated nature of markets makes it difficult to sustain local activities on global brands alone;
- additional outlets for technology contribute to either or both returns on R & D investment and increments to production volume; and
- historical development has made a particular local or regional brand a significant 'cash cow' from which revenue can be earned for cross subsidising other activities either within the market concerned or at the centre.

However, this orientation will need to be qualified to ensure a congruence between the longer-term global benefits and the need to remain nationally responsive, spread risk and provide for financial performance criteria.

Specific products for specific markets are therefore justified in the global operations providing they are supportive of the longer-term globalisation of products and company structure (where this is a practical option) and where they contribute to the overall competitive position within each territory. They are to be discouraged where:

- they lead local operations away from the overall direction of the strategic intention (ie local operations go their own way);
- the demands of R & D and NPD programmes are so great in meeting myriad local needs that they exclude activity on products with global potential;
- the overall cost of commercialising a mass of local products impinges on a company's ability to finance the introduction of global brands without creating the same benefits; and

- they involve investment in facilities and production for products and activities which add little to the thrust of the business yet widen the cost base.

Collaborative route

This route is becoming increasingly more important as smaller companies collaborate to become large enough or skilled enough to compete. Examples are joint ventures between companies where, for example, one has technological expertise and the other has a marketing infrastructure. Such routes can reduce cost of entry to new markets whilst providing a firm competitive base against competition. By the joining together of two or more firms' activities it becomes possible by combining resources to achieve more than they could do as separate entities. The collaborative route involves not only joint ventures but licensing of technology and the franchising or marketing of skills.

The collaborative route offers considerably better scope for survival in the larger, tougher markets of the world. It should be evaluated as an option where companies cannot achieve the levels of investment needed to enter a foreign market. Whilst finding the right partners may be difficult, the routes offer considerably better prospects in the main than trying to enter foreign markets with weakly conceived unsupported sales strategies.

The European Community's Business Co-operation Centre provides a service for seeking a business partner. The new B-C Net will help put smaller companies in touch with each other. Transnational co-operation is also made possible between firms especially in the area of innovation and new technology through the centre's SPRINT programme.

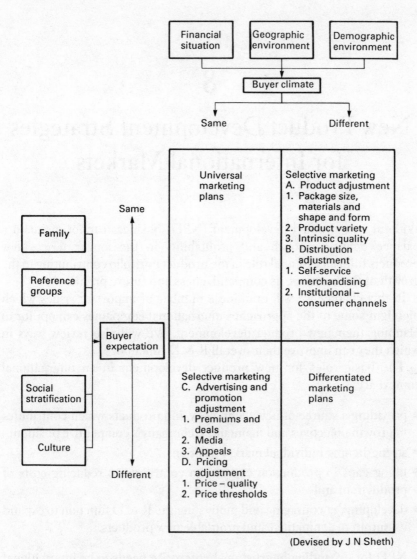

(Devised by J N Sheth)

Figure 7.1 A scheme for differentiated marketing programmes
By kind permission of European Research (UK)

The scheme devised by J N Sheth provides a way of evaluating the need for differentiating marketing programmes. Using the two by two matrix he explains how to determine similarities between 'buyer expectations' and 'buyer climates'. Where these are pretty much the same, then universal marketing plans are probably the most economic. As the levels of difference increase, then so does the level of differentiation. The scheme, however, presents a demanding market research programme to determine its 'buyer climate' and 'buyer expectation' co-ordinates and for testing the resultant marketing programmes.

8

New Product Development Strategies for International Markets

Without new product development (NPD) business cannot maintain a balance between growth and profitability in the longer term. New products fulfil an essential role in the product portfolio contributing to the growth of the business, its competitiveness and future profits.

In this chapter we will examine a number of important issues which highlight some of the approaches international companies can opt for in planning their new product development. We will also review ways in which they can improve their overall R & D function.

The basic roles for new product development in an international context are:

- providing a source of new technology and products which contributes to growth objectives and maintains a company's competitive position;
- strengthening individual market positions;
- filling gaps in production capacity to contribute to reducing costs of production; and
- developing, encouraging and motivating the R & D function to expand its output of competitive and profitable new products.

NPD for expanding international enterprise needs to be international in outlook but at the same time responsive to individual markets. It is too easy to say that all new product-development work should be for the international market but if market-maintenance requirements for individual territories are ignored then the global activities may suffer as a result. Furthermore, such dogmatism may result in high cost capacity being under-utilised, thus affecting the cost-competitiveness of the business.

The argument may simply reduce to the two basic options for companies to concentrate their product development resources on creating new international products or use their technologies to develop products specifically for individual markets.

These arguments fail to distinguish between NPD for breaking new thresholds in developing and applying technology to the global market and developing and maintaining individual markets. The fundamental basis for organic growth into new markets is the development of strong markets. In the continuum, a business company will at most times find that there is a need for individual-market NPD activity as well as activity directed at global applications of technology. The key issues which we will examine are therefore:

- the direction of activities aimed at global development and application of technology;
- market maintenance requirements for NPD;
- corporate application of technology to utilise production capacity; and
- creating a competitive R & D function.

Global development and the application of technology

It goes without saying that the greater the market potential for a new product the greater is the return on investment for R & D expenditure. In fact many companies in the high-technology field would be unable to finance their R & D were it not for the global market. For example, it costs at least £30 million to bring a new pharmaceutical substance to the market. Glaxo's Zantac or Wellcome's Zorvirax could not have afforded such investment were these two drugs designed for their domestic UK market alone.

Focusing on key areas of technology and their application on to the wider world market provides a company with a number of principal benefits.

- Greater returns from R & D investment from a greater potential market than the domestic market.
- Areas of discovery, technology and excellence from which further new products, product adaptations and line extensions can be developed for international and local application.

- Opportunities for exploiting technology through the marketing of expertise and intellectual property.

Aiming R & D activity at the global market should provide a company with the capabilities and components from which it can select product market options most suitable for each of its national markets.

Obviously, approaches will vary with the type of business individual companies operate. Yet the principles remain very much the same. In highly differentiated product areas, key technology suitable for global application can be developed from which NPD can design products suitable for local application. For example, the development of superior technology in freeze-drying of coffee offers opportunities for companies to select flavours and textures with competitive advantages over existing brands for individual markets (Nestlé).

Where companies operate in less differentiated markets a unique formula may be suitable with few adaptations for a global product (Coca Cola). A company may find that its technology offers opportunities both to create international products and ones specifically designed for its major markets (Canon). A further, more complicated, strategy may involve even greater levels of technology exploitation which include both international products, individual products tailored for individual markets and the marketing of technology and intellectual rights to provide additional revenue from OEMs and own brands (Toshiba).

Thus the exploitation of technology development aimed at global opportunities can:

- provide a basis upon which to develop individual new products offering competitive advantage in individual national markets;
- introduce truly international new products;
- provide the basis for both international and local products; and
- exploit a basketful of global opportunities through international products, local products and marketing technology and intellectual rights.

Developing specific products for specific markets

Purists argue that such a strategy under-utilises the R & D function, yet there are genuine reasons for devoting part of the NPD process to specific markets. To do so strengthens a company's position in key markets by developing products which meet unique market needs, for example specific pharmaceutical or agrochemical products for specific diseases in specific markets (anti-malarial products, agrochemical products for sugar cane etc). It also provides products for major national markets which are large enough to warrant specific new products eg the USA and Japan.

Directing R & D at specific markets can also provide products for identified product niches in the company's domestic market where it has a strong base, existing knowledge, customer loyalty and an established presence in its channels of distribution.

Collaborating with other companies to develop products specifically for their markets is feasible if the collaboration leads to new areas of knowledge or as a means of market entry.

The trade-offs between devoting R & D efforts to international and local markets are obviously related to the cost of the benefits achieved. Low-technology companies will tend to apply NPD more nationalistically, especially where there is considerable product differentiation as in the food industry. High-technology companies, where R & D is very expensive, will need to seek larger international opportunities for their product and technology developments.

The three dangers to be avoided are:

- starving individual country markets of new products because R & D is focused entirely on global opportunities;

- proliferating NPD activity on a mass of individual country projects which diverts R & D from finding key areas of technological application to reinforce a company's competitive advantages; and

- focusing the main thrust of R & D on the domestic market thus denying a company the opportunity to develop a wider global market.

NPD in market-maintenance strategies

Much of the published discussion on NPD is concerned with the creation of new product opportunities. Yet NPD plays an important role in maintaining a company's competitive position.

Len Hardy, former Chairman of Lever Brothers points out the role for R & D in regard to existing brands. He prescribes a continuous flow of developments for existing products as follows:

- improvements in the performance of existing ingredients;
- improvements in the processing of the product, which enhances performance; and
- improvements in either the product formulation or in its processing which brings about a reduction in cost.

In many companies breakthrough innovations may occur quite infrequently. The dependence on existing brands in many companies for both market dominance and as candidates for geographic expansion is a real fact of life. Within the portfolio of options there are four areas of activity on which marketing strategies and R & D functions can focus. These strategic options should be evaluated for inclusion in a company's competitive armoury. They are, according to Kotler el al:

- product-range stretching;
- product proliferation;
- product innovation; and
- quality improvement.

Product-range stretching

The idea of product-range stretching is to widen the range of products available in order to spread a product line out of one segment to embrace several. Stretching can be used as a defensive strategy by closing opportunity windows to competition trying to penetrate a company's market by launching into adjacent market segments. Conversely, stretching can be employed offensively to widen a product range across a number of segments for invasions into competitors' market segments.

Product-range stretching is a strategy commonly employed by leading pharmaceutical companies. Here the strategy might be horizontal, vertical or two-way. If we take the example shown in Figures 8.1 and 8.2 the concept of stretching might be more easily understood.

In Figure 8.1 we see a matrix of market segments chosen by pain indication and drug-delivery system (for the sake of simplicity). Drug A is a tablet suitable for mild to moderate pain. By stretching horizontally, higher-dose tablets could be introduced to extend the product's usage in higher-pain segments. By stretching vertically, the product may occupy more segments through presenting different drug-delivery systems. A two-way stretch would involve movements towards

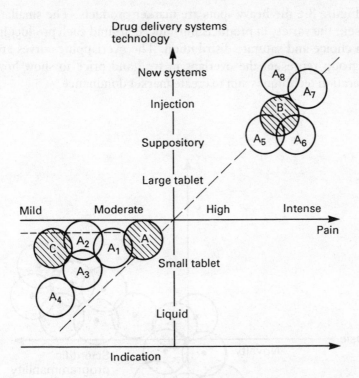

Figure 8.1 Product stretching strategies drug indications/drug-delivery systems
Pharmaceutical products in a market shown by indication and drug-delivery system.

higher dosages and by developing new drug-delivery systems. In a real example higher doses can be given by suppository or injection to avoid side-effects involving the stomach, and lower doses, say for paediatric use, by liquid. This attacks products B and C's position.

Product proliferation

Product proliferation involves the introduction of a wide range of similar products or models around each product line in order to open up a large number of market niches simultaneously and at the same time dominate the channels of distribution.

Take for example the hand-held-calculator market. Casio and Sharp have launched a whole range of high-priced and low-priced calculators with different functions from programmability to music, with prices from a few pounds to hundreds.

In Figure 8.2 the heavy spots are marker products. The smaller dots represent the variety of products introduced around each product line to widen choice and saturate distribution. The overlapping curves around each group represent the overlaps in type and price to show how the proliferation techniques aim to create market dominance.

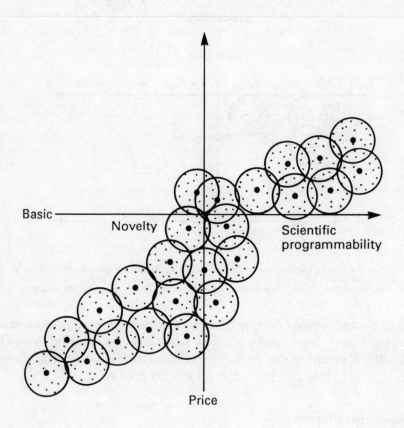

Figure 8.2 Product proliferation calculators

Product innovation

Product innovation involves the acceleration of R & D deliberately designed to shorten competitors' product life-cycles and to make a major leap in technology so as to render competitors' products obsolete. For example, when Bell Laboratories introduced the transistor, the radio valve became obsolete. Today, huge leaps in technology can have the same effect in the computer, electronics, pharmaceuticals and biotechnology market, for example. The difference today is that it takes months rather than years for innovation leaps to occur.

The example shows (*a*) the traditional view of a product life-cycle and (*b*) the shortening effect of life-cycles as each new product is introduced.

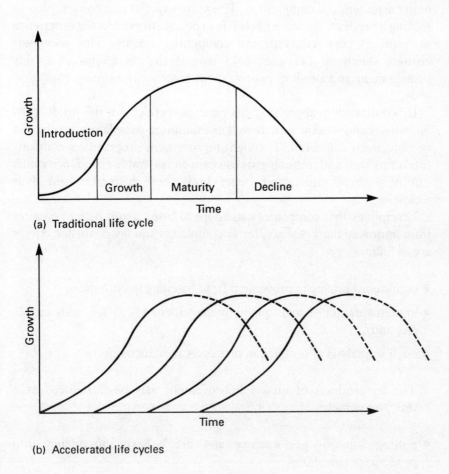

(a) Traditional life cycle

(b) Accelerated life cycles

Figure 8.3 Contrast of traditional view of a product life cycle and the shortening life cycles for high technology products

The successful company which can keep ahead of its competitors in this way can achieve a savaging effect on its competitors. Once it can generate sufficient market share to fund its R & D expenditure it can keep ahead of the race, often forcing its competitors out of the market.

However, companies wishing to follow this strategy may have to modify the way they treat R & D in their costings.

Quality improvement

To suggest that the quality of a product cannot be improved is to ignore both customers and competition. The more experience a company has in making a product, the more likely it is to be able to express the experience in terms of cost reduction and competitive quality. This seemingly obvious statement can only hold true if the disciplines of quality management and product improvement targets can become company-wide.

By continually reappraising customer perceptions of the product, its limitations and weaknesses, as well as examining complaints, quality can be objectively improved. Through improvement programmes company marketing staff and technologists can gain considerable experience which can help them understand better both their customers and their technology.

Disciplines that companies can adopt to bring about better revenues from improved market share, fewer complaints and fewer on-line rejects are as follows:

- continuous quality improvement from listening to customers;
- implementation of total quality management (TQM), quality circles etc; and
- on-line analysis of production processes to reduce rejects.

The by-products of quality improvement may be introduced as a *product plus* namely:

- putting superior performance and break-down infrequency into product specifications;
- extending warranties and guarantees;
- offering free parts and maintenance services; and

- re-allocating expensive resources hitherto handling complaints into more productive service functions.

Technology to utilise production capacity

A controversial issue amongst marketing purists surrounds the area of applying company technology and production capacity to product opportunities which are not branded and over which companies have little control over marketing. Such areas include own brands, OEMs and contract production.

Many companies have a psychological aversion to such areas and dismiss opportunities without a great deal of thought as to their advantages. The facts are:

- R & D is becoming ever more risky and expensive, thus the more applications that can be provided, the greater the return on funds invested;

- under-utilised production, particularly where new state-of-the-art facilities exist, increases unit costs of production, reducing a company's cost competitiveness;

- markets, particularly larger ones, are expensive to enter and require considerable entry costs in terms of promotion; and

- channels of distribution are increasingly seeking to provide own-label products (up to 27 per cent in the USA and UK for many fmcg product categories).

Thus bypassing opportunities for exploiting product technology in the ways suggested ignores three critical issues. Firstly, the need to acquire market share which the marketing of technology provides – but may be beyond the capabilities of a company's marketing structure alone. For example, where Matsushita achieved 60 per cent of the US VCR market, 45 per cent was as an OEM supplier. Secondly, the activities of competitors can undermine a leader's market share through acting as either an OEM supplier or supplying own-label. Toshiba took a major share of the US television market by supplying key multiples with own-label televisions. Lastly, the need to achieve critical mass to enable a company to compete competitively in terms of cost, price and innovation can be jeopardised by such a policy.

Thus in developing applications for a company's technology and production capacity the areas suggested should be rigorously evaluated in order to find opportunities which enable a company to reinforce its competitive position. Decisions relating to these activities should not be delegated to the lower echelons of an organisation but should be part of the overall strategy of the company.

A well-known British pharmaceutical company denied a European company the opportunity to form a joint marketing arrangement for one of its medical substances. Its patent had expired but the company still had the lead in technology. The European company joined with another to develop the technology and consequently became a major competitor.

Making research and development more competitive

In a competitive environment, R & D is the major weapon a business has in its armoury. Without an effective R & D programme any business will suffer on three counts.

- It will be unable to bring new and viable products to the market to meet development performance criteria through organic growth.

- It will be vulnerable to loss of market share in terms of volume, prices and margins to competitor products.

- It will suffer the gradual loss of its R & D people and winding down of its R & D resources, funding and facilities.

Few companies do not have an R & D organisation – whether it be the entrepreneur in his laboratory, marketing and systems groups producing new service products or major laboratory facilities spread across the world's centres of scientific excellence. Yet not all companies have mastered the direction of the R & D function. In too many companies today R & D is not involved in key strategic decisions regarding meeting future development criteria, reinforcing the competitive position or finding areas upon which to focus core technologies. Too often, R & D either works in isolation to marketing functions producing products for the company to sell or is a subordinate service function prioritising developments for the marketing groups which shout loudest – more often than not the company's domestic marketing groups.

Where R & D output is measured on the number of product projects undertaken rather than on the quality of its output in terms of fulfilling strategic goals it is difficult to assess its contribution to corporate profits. R & D functions working on a mass of low-priority peripheral projects without the guiding hand of a corporate strategy find that they often become one of the first areas in a business to lose funds when discretionary expenditure is reviewed.

The role which R & D has to play in maintaining and reinforcing a company's competitive position is strategic. It is one based upon harnessing core technologies to work in unison with the marketing direction which the company pursues and match R & D activities to corporate growth criteria objectives. It also provides facilities to meet R & D and product adaptation requirements throughout the marketing structure and provides an information base for corporate direction to assess its competitive technological capabilities against those of competitors.

In the continuum, R & D will also be responsible for seeking, evaluating and proposing new areas of technology to develop.

The essence of good R & D activity management, then, is in concentrating its expensive resources on priorities which will reinforce the company's competitive position – not on hosts of peripheral projects. This ensures that R & D's contribution to business is resourced and financed to provide a competitive thrust to the business. It is this contribution by which R & D investment should be measured.

As with all business activities it is the skills of people and the way they are directed which sets good companies apart. Returning once more to Len Hardy, I cite his list of the criteria for a successful R & D function.

- Get good people.
- Use skilful direction, ie concentrate efforts over a limited number of carefully selected projects.
- Motivate R & D people by involvement in strategic thinking and successes.
- Know when to close down a project.
- Back projects with people who believe in them (or as Tom Peters describes such people *champions*).

R & D – a major cost centre

R & D is potentially one of the biggest cost centres in a company. Few of the projects being worked on will produce short-term contributions to profits. All R & D activity, therefore, is devoted to future profits. This leads invariably to the notion that R & D is a major drain on current profits.

Companies have gone to extreme lengths to find ways of isolating R & D costs. Two common examples are firstly, setting up the R & D function as a separate division or subsidiary with its own profit and loss accountability. This unfortunately divorces the R & D function from the mainstream of marketing direction and often stifles lower-level innovation (say at brand-group level) where work is charged back to the initiators. Furthermore, it focuses all areas of R & D, including conceptual work, into the R & D function making R & D the special preserve of the division or subsidiary.

The second example involves costing R & D into each individual project so that organisations can calculate the return on investment for R & D activity against the future revenue returned on sales of the new product. This has two advantages: namely, excluding low-return unprofitable projects and providing ease of accounting. However, it is not a sound method of measuring R & D activity where overheads involved in the project are charged to the project costs; no account is taken of the value of discovery, experience and new leads into other areas from which the R & D function and the company as a whole can benefit; and major breakthrough projects may be discarded on the basis that the R & D cost cannot be recovered in a targeted period of time.

R & D activities are essentially *sunk costs*. This means they are costs which are borne as revenue expenses during measurable accounting periods. Therefore R & D expenses incurred this year are set against this year's company profits; they are not carried forward.

So why should they be added to the future costs of a new product? Nobody in their right minds adds up all the past advertising for a product and adds them to future profit plans. This is not to say that R & D activity should have free reign, unrestrained by costs and freedom to pursue projects regardless of contribution to the business. It is the freeing of constraints on the most important areas of R & D focus and not merely those which offer rapid payouts which is the point at issue. Thus any method by which R & D is funded and activity costed has to be constructed internally to ensure that essential work is done to meet strategy needs.

New products should reach the market unencumbered by past costs. Such costs in any one financial period have to be cross-subsidised from revenue generated by activities in previous ones. Any attempt to encumber the future with past costs or the present with restraints garnered from narrowly defined future returns on an individual product's direct payback calculations are too inhibiting. They do not match those methods used by aggressive competitors such as the Japanese, West Germans and Italians.

Many successful Japanese companies are masters at cross-subsidisation of R & D costs. The basis of their success stems in investing heavily to crack a major area of innovation which provides them with a competitive advantage, and then exhaustively innovating around the area. The investment is based more on securing a competitive position in the first place and reinvesting their knowledge and discoveries into a rapid series of new products, few of which would reach the market if R & D were costed against each product. The costs of R & D are paid for out of current revenue, and because of the pace of innovation they are able to command high global market shares from which to provide greater and greater R & D appropriations.

If taken on a project-by-project basis, Japanese R & D management would give many European corporate financial officials apoplexy. Yet the Japanese do not plan their R & D piecemeal. Once a high revenue base is achieved they are more concerned with maintaining a competitive position. Rather than discouraging expenses, R & D is charged with earning its keep through a high output of profitable new products.

All the same, R & D in high technology is becoming ever riskier and more expensive. So it is vital that where a danger exists that R & D activity will fail to keep up with the need for new and profitable products, that the organisation is prepared to use outside sources.

Central and decentralised R & D

There are obviously a number of different methods of organising for NPD which by their very nature involve marketing, technical, production and finance people. In NPD, teams are put together to work on projects and are co-ordinated by a senior NPD or marketing official. In a centrally controlled company which relies mostly on centrally based management and production there can be a clear-cut decision to centralise the NPD function. For multinational companies however, the problem of central control may prove to be inefficient in coping with data and developing and adapting products for the global market.

Decentralisation of R & D

In some multinationals, extensive NPD and R & D work is carried out by foreign subsidiary management teams. Innovation based overseas may be of advantage where:

- pools of technological talent exist in centres of excellence, for example, in the US Silicon Valley;

- staffing is relatively inexpensive (another example from the pharmaceutical industry is the use of centres in India where there exists a large pool of relatively inexpensive, technically qualified staff);

- subsidies and tax relief are given to companies setting up R & D facilities in particular countries, eg Spain and Italy; and

- large potential markets exist and it is seen as necessary to situate R & D as close to the market as possible. For example, Glaxo, Intel and Analog Devices are some of the many high-technology companies to locate in Japan. Apple recently opened in Paris to get closer to the EC.

The decentralisation of R & D is a major sign that a company is becoming truly global in outlook. Providing that there is a guiding of strategic direction there are a number of important advantages in decentralisation.

An international pool of technologists and scientists is brought into the business adding not only a wider range of technical skills but adding an international flavour to the function. Also, project work requiring specific skills in greater abundance than at home can be attracted to the business more easily than recruiting expatriates. At the same time, projects requiring the focus of R & D activity on specific markets can be devolved to subsidiary operations where there is innately a greater sympathy and understanding for the market than might be the case at the centre.

Global project work can be syndicated throughout the international R & D function (this is now commonly done in large pharmaceutical companies) to bring an international dimension to each project and at the same time cope with local adaptation needs as they occur.

The downsides to decentralisation come with those aspects of R & D direction which fail to ensure co-ordination and harmonisation of international projects and a tendency for local R & D organisations to tread their own path.

Devolution of R & D

There is an increasing danger that R & D activity, regardless of how well it is funded, will fail to keep up its output of new and profitable products. Companies which fall behind in innovation face a great risk of discontinuation.

In meeting the challenge for greater output of innovation, a number of major companies have penetrated the psychological barriers which R & D functions erect to protect their preserve.

Venture teams

A number of well-known British and American companies are users of venture teams, including Dow, Westinghouse, Unilever, Monsanto and General Mills. Mark Hanan sees Venture Teams as a reawakening of entrepreneurial inventiveness: 'By incorporating a small business-minded group of zealous men around a common objective, venture teaming reproduces in spirit and substance what is largely a more modern version of the founding fathers' bicycle shop'.

Venture teams are groups of managers from the various disciplines of the organisation formed to explore opportunities, conceive ideas and bring new product candidates to the market place.

'Skunk works'

This American expression brought to parlance by Thomas J. Peters and Robert H. Waterman in their book *In Search of Excellence* describes the practice of companies who, like Hewlett-Packard and 3M, provide time and resources for individuals and groups to pursue their own innovations for their companies. Projects may be undertaken by anyone with an idea, thus providing a major source of inventiveness unconstrained by the bureaucracy of a formal R & D structure.

External devolution

The antipathy of many R & D functions to external sources of R & D work is being broken down far too slowly. The difficulties which face so many inventors of breakthrough ideas in attracting companies to take them up illustrates the point.

External devolution of R & D provides a company with an inexhaustible supply of new product ideas and access to patentable property. It allows it to delegate certain areas of activity to enable internal resources to be focused on the main strategic projects the firm is engaged upon.

The main reasons for supplementing R & D activity with external sources are to:

- delegate certain activities to specialist areas of research found outside the company to complete tasks beyond the short-term scope of the company;
- bring projects to fruition more quickly than internal resources can achieve;
- spread the costs of major projects through collaboration;
- tap into new areas of technological breakthrough whilst they are in their infancy to provide new, future areas of accessible technology;
- fill short-term gaps in the product inventory;
- seize serendipity opportunities which fit into the company's business portfolio; and
- deny competitors access to a new invention or process which might influence their overall competitive position or which might be directed against the company.

The principal sources of external R & D which a company might access are set out below.

- Specialist research centres and centres of excellence. These may be specialist private companies or commercially based functions within universities. Such organisations might be employed to undertake specific parts of a project for which the company does not have expertise in-house; take on work to bring a project to fruition more quickly; or work on a project jointly which the centre of research has devised.
- Research grants to universities and polytechnics can be awarded to set up research in centres of excellence to study the underlying science for a particular area of R & D work.
- Collaboration with other companies to share the costs of R & D; or two or more R & D groups together, each with their own area of expertise to work on a project requiring each other's expertise. In the EC a great number of pre-commercial R & D programmes are actively sponsored (see page 213).
- Buy in or license technology or inventions to provide products essential to either the company's strategic objectives or to strengthen the inventory.

The last area for accessing technology and new products is through corporate venturing. A product of the enterprise culture, it is a comparatively new concept. As such we have chosen to explain it at length.

Corporate venturing – a new opportunity

Corporate venturing implies the acquisition of a minority holding in a small company by a large company to enable the small company to achieve an agreed objective of mutual benefit to both organisations.

The cash injection from the larger organisation enables the smaller organisation to achieve the larger's objective whilst achieving a number of its own. A typical deal would be for a large company to tap into the smaller company's R & D activities whilst financing its worldwide sales activities.

Companies such as Monsanto in the USA and Pilkington in the UK use corporate venturing as a means of:

- advancing their technology base by investing in highly innovative companies;

- keeping their options open in the direction of technological development by investing in companies which are looking at new ways of applying technology;

- allowing themselves to participate in peripheral activities without diverting internal resources away from their mainstream activities;

- investing in potentially lucrative opportunities as a means of using otherwise unutilised funds to generate additional revenue with considerable tax advantages;

- mitigating the impact of local plant closures on the social environment and thereby being seen to be good citizens; and

- enhancing their company's reputation as supporters of business opportunity development through the advancement of technology.

The advantages which accrue to the smaller company are also great.

- Funds are acquired which can be used to develop their R & D and marketing resources.

- Opportunities are presented to tap into the large company's worldwide marketing infrastructure.
- The credibility and support that the association with a large company offers.

At present, Europe lags behind the USA in corporate venturing for many reasons.

Many large European companies are unaware of the opportunities which corporate venturing can bring to their businesses. European accountants are reluctant to consider minority holdings within their corporate structures as they complicate financial control and reporting. Many European companies lack the management resources to find and co-operate with small entrepreneurial businesses.

There is a strange reluctance in Europe to accept that ideas created outside the company's own R & D function have any commercial viability. At the same time, managers of large companies seem to feel that their companies should get more out of a deal than the smaller company. As a result, negotiations often break down.

Many small companies are ignorant of the potential sources of co-operation, and struggle on with their developments using their own limited resources. Lastly, entrepreneurs, often people who have left large companies, do not want to return to the frustrations, bureaucracy and long decision-making times inherent in big companies.

The whole field of corporate venturing is new, and, whilst some companies have been involved for more than 15 years, it has only really taken off in the USA in the last six or seven. Corporate venturing should become an option to be evaluated by the international business as its offers opportunities for technological advancement, new products and markets as well as a basket of financial and intangible benefits.

Companies should, however, ensure that they gear themselves up to the management of such activities. They must find the right type of managers, capable of working with entrepreneurs (many of whom will become millionaires whilst managers will remain on their salaries).

Advice given in forming corporate venturing agreements between partners is to begin a relationship through some other form of activity such as a joint venture on a project, distribution agreements or licensing arrangements. Then, as mutual trust and personal relationships mature, make a formal investment commitment.

Corporate venturing is an opportunity for the future which if European companies are reluctant to exploit, foreign ones will. For corporate venturing is not limited by national or EC boundaries. European companies can also find venture partners in foreign lands as a means of both tapping into R & D and as a means of entry into those markets.

Yet before the corporate venturing opportunity can take off to the advantage of European companies, many will have to overcome the myriad of internal psychological barriers.

EC-sponsored research and development

The European Community is heavily involved in R & D funding. Roughly half of the Community's research budget is spent on commercial application research programmes. The basic aim has been to bring company R & D, university and government research organisations together. Half the funding is usually found from Community funds.

About $6bn is allocated to pre-competitive industry-related R & D, such as automotive design and development. Over half the budget is devoted to the EUREKA project although this is not controlled by the Community.

In 1987, the Framework Programme was agreed to cover a whole range of market sectors and technologies. The principal areas of focus are information technology and telecommunications. However, considerable sums are allocated to research into manufacturing processes, process technologies, materials and biotechnology.

By far the biggest project is ESPRIT, concerned with microelectronics and software technology. $1.6bn has been allocated to this programme which aims to enable European firms to compete with the Japanese and North Americans.

Many companies entering Community schemes, however, have found large chunks of their budgets are absorbed by Community administration. Many companies, having been introduced to collaborative projects through Community projects, have decided to continue to work together without Community sponsorship. They find this gives them more freedom and flexibility and, after taking away the costs of Community overheads, is sometimes just as cost-effective.

R & D should seek the opportunities for Community-funded projects which will help subsidise the costs of their activities. The Community's BC-Net is also available to find marriage partners for companies seeking collaboration and licence opportunities between small and large companies. This can be accessed through appropriate consultants who are recognised by the BC-Net.

Participation and compliance – product standards directives

The formulation of directives on common standards will need considerable attention. The various standards organisations (BSI (UK), DIN (FDR), AFNOR (France), and so on) represent national interests on the European standards bodies, CEN and CENELEC.* Companies will need to participate if they are not just to react to standards being handed down. Presently, Germany holds the secretariat of some 40 per cent of the 80-odd technical committees, France some 20 per cent and Britain 12 per cent.

Directive 83/189 EEC

Under Directive 83/189 EEC member states are required to notify the Commission in advance of any proposals for new technical regulations. This allows the Commission to freeze activity on implementation for three months giving the Commission and other member states the opportunity to take action if a regulation is seen as a barrier to trade. This is then extended for up to twelve months if the Commission decides to propose Community-wide measures. Directive 83/189 is now being extended to agricultural products, foodstuffs, pharmaceuticals and cosmetics.

New approach to technical harmonisation

In order to expedite common standards throughout the Community, directives covering essential health and safety requirements will provide the criteria for the various European standards bodies to issue an EC market. This means that products cannot be refused entry for technical

*CEN Comité Européen de Normalisation (European Standardisation Committee)
CENELEC Comité Européen de Normalisation de Eléctro-technique (European Standardisation Committee for Electrical Products)
(includes the national standards bodies of the EC Member States and all the EFTA Countries except Ireland).

reasons. So far the machinery for creating standards has only achieved directives on toys and pressure vessels.

Eighty-one other standards projects are presently under way. It is important therefore that companies get themselves involved either through direct participation or through their national standards organisations.

Compliance

Once directives are issued, companies will have to comply in order to gain the EC mark for their products. Pre-emptive R & D activity will, therefore, be vital if new standards are to be adopted. Competitively, the first companies to meet the new standards will have an advantage over those laggards who are slow to comply.

Yet, from a marketing point of view, simply adopting new standards will not in itself provide sales opportunities.

- Whilst products may not be refused entry on the basis of technical specifications, countries have usage regulations and norms. These need to be understood on a country-by-country basis in developing and adapting products to meet country norms. Here considerable industry activity should be involved to break down hidden restrictions and provide an open market place for products.

- Whilst conforming to minimum regulations, products have to be designed with the customer in mind. Conforming to directives should not override the firm's responsibilities in providing marketable products.

- Competition will operate under the same rules, and nationally entrenched competitors will (in many industries) continue the practice of subverting the environment in their favour through such activities as lobbying insurance organisations and local standards authorities to maintain non-technical barriers.

Product Liability Directive

There is an ever-increasing concern for people and companies injured by products to obtain compensation. The Product Liability Directive makes both manufacturers and importers strictly liable for any injuries caused by defective products. The R & D and quality-control functions, therefore, need to work very closely in designing products which are less likely to inherit faults due to manufacture or materials used. Testing products thoroughly to find potential faults will be essential, as will designing production processes to eliminate faults likely to occur through the process itself. Quality control (QC) procedures will have to ensure that defects are not introduced through materials and defective products are not passed on for sale. Also, complaints and defect reports will need to be recorded and analysed by the QC function in order that common occurrences can be isolated and dealt with.

It is worth pointing out that the free movement of goods within the Community permits unauthorised dealers to handle products. Parallel traders may well divert products to distribution channels and export markets for which they are unsuitable. Whilst this in itself may not be a direct problem for the R & D function, the probability that the company may not have complete control over the movement of its products may be a consideration for some sensitive products.

9
Concept Development for New Products

One of the most difficult problems in marketing is developing concepts for new products. Innovative companies can normally thank quite a small number of people for coming up with the ideas for their major products.

Concept development is normally centred in a company's marketing and R & D areas. Yet there is frequently an abundance of ideas which can be harvested from employees working outside these two areas. The problem is that very few companies provide a way that ideas can be communicated internally. Even those flickers of inspiration that do arise are extinguished because of the psychological barriers the marketing and R & D functions erect around themselves.

Staff schemes and other methods

Every company should listen to its people's ideas. It creates a motivational environment and provides an abundant source of concept-triggers, if not viable concepts in their own right. What is needed is a clearing house to bring ideas in from employees and use them as raw material for product concepts. Such a clearing system should not be based on sorting ideas into piles, ie those worth investigation and reject. It should instead be based on sifting through each idea painstakingly and using each idea submitted to trigger feasible concepts.

Everyone who submits an idea in company does so with at least one of three thoughts in mind:

- the desire to be noticed;
- the desire to contribute to the business; and

- the recognition that if the idea is adopted it could help his or her department, eg a production area, a sales opportunity, a transport opportunity.

Whilst the first thought should be treated as a way of recognising the individual and the second as reinforcing commitment, the third is the one that is most likely to yield the most value. If Joe Snooks recognises that his production line needs more work and proposes a solution through a new product idea he should be listened to. Ideas often highlight the under-utilisation of spare capacity in a sector of the business. Why build a new facility for one new product when capacity exists for another!

The dangers with staff schemes are that:

- they tend to be run by the wrong people – the personnel department;
- they are evaluated by the wrong people;
- ideas are not vigorously examined; and
- once the rejection slips start being distributed, people's enthusiasm wains and contributors become demotivated.

Staff schemes should be corporately intitiated and vigorously supervised. People with ideas should have the opportunity to discuss them. In some companies, people are actually given the resources and corporate support to develop their ideas further (Hewlitt Packard and 3M).

There are more formal methods of finding new product concepts.

Targeting

This involves focusing on specific market needs to set the parameters for a new product and then developing a range of concepts to fit the target. Targeting is applicable in high technology areas such as pharmaceuticals, electronics, defence systems and so forth. It is the basis of brand stretching and brand-proliferation strategies. It lends itself to most fast-moving consumer product areas and to services such as financial, training and IT.

Scanning

This involves painstakingly searching for discoveries, technology or engineering breakthroughs which may lead to new inventions. This is a favourite strategy of pharmaceutical companies who between them screen and test millions of new substances every year to seek their therapeutic values. Now and again a new substance offers itself as a drug or at least as a model against which analogues can be designed.

Opportunity windows and competitor weakness

Opportunity windows are gaps in the market into which the right product would provide the company with an entry vehicle. The idea is to identify the window and set product criteria around which NPD can be focused. The Walkman was an example of such a strategy when Sony recognised a niche for a portable, personal stereo player.

Leading on from this approach is the identification of competitor weaknesses. We have enlarged this topic because not only is it a means of finding opportunity windows it is a favourite tactic of companies seeking to enter and dislodge the market leader. Such companies may well be the targets of such a strategy as well as its instigators.

Identification of competitor weaknesses is a favourite strategy for Japanese companies to find the weaknesses amongst competitor product offerings and to design tightly competitive substitutes.

The principal areas of analysis are functionality, quality and reliability.

Functionality analysis is the breaking down and investigation of customer needs and dissatisfactions in relation to what is on offer and providing a superior substitute for which the customer is happy to pay. There are five basic approaches.

Add features

Existing products can be enhanced to widen the functions they can fulfil. For example, both Casio and Sharp added features to their pocket calculators at low cost yet were able to command higher prices.

Reduce products to basic functions

This is done by re-analysing the functions that customers require of the product. Eliminate sophisticated and costly 'add-ons' and produce a low-priced product which will meet the customer's needs.

Invent or adapt

This is done to produce products that perform the exact function at a price required by the customer. Examples are the Walkman, portable televisions, compact copiers, SLR cameras. Here companies have defined exactly what the need is and then produced products which match the function required at the price required.

Quality analysis

This involves both the physical assessment of competitors' product quality and a study of consumer psychological needs and perceptions in finding what quality attributes should be introduced to a product in terms of design, packaging, physical feel, appearance and price.

Reliability analysis

The study of competitors' products and service offerings in relation to customer needs and attitudes. Through product-testing and customer investigation it is often possible to define critical dissatisfactions which customers have or perceive in products they use.

A strategy based on improved product reliability offerings might be based on freedom from breakdown (Ford), extended warranties (Toshiba), superior service support (IBM), and compatibility of spare parts (Amstrad).

Reliability strategies however, need to be heavily and ruthlessly promoted against the critical dissatisfactions customers have or perceive for their existing products. The key to the strategy is to win product adoption whilst leaving adopters with a long-lasting residual dissatisfaction with products to which they were previously loyal: a problem British Airways laboured under for many years in the 1970s and early 1980s when hit by foreign competition.

Lateral thinking

A useful means by which new product ideas can be generated either against targets or to pursue ideas harvested from staff or from scanning. Lateral thinking juxtaposes concepts (either randomly selected or generated using well known methods such as brainstorming or Synectics) against the product idea problem. Such exercises should be led by a lateral thinking expert or by someone trained within the company.

Outside NPD consultants

A viable option in many areas of business. Such consultants prosper by being successful. The expenses involved may well shorten the NPD process for inexperienced companies or where there are not sufficient resources to focus adequately on the problem. Strangely enough many of the blue chip consultants boast major international clients on their list.

Collaboration and corporate venturing

These provide myriad opportunities for developing and exploiting technology. This is described on page 211.

Independent inventors and centres of excellence such as universities and polytechnics (see page 209) provide an abundance of new ideas and inventions which need the resources of larger companies in order to exploit them. Inventors should not be turned away because even if their idea is not what the company is looking for, intrinsic elements of the invention may be useful.

Screening new product ideas

Most discussions on screening begin with the idea of reducing product concept candidates to a manageable few. Yet this ignores the question of who should do the screening and who should permit valuable ideas to be discarded.

It is absolutely amazing that major product concepts should be so easily discarded. Many organisations bite their lips when they see competitors making profits from concepts or inventors they turned away. Unless organisations recognise that every idea proffered is potentially worth millions in revenue until exhaustively excluded on the basis of sound judgement they will not only discourage invention and miss opportunities but will also create competitors. When one sees the detailed rationale for proceeding with an NPD project, one wonders why in so many cases such a detailed rationale was not produced for failed concept evaluations – probably because it is easier to say no!

It must surely be a duty of management to handle and evaluate product ideas as a source of potential value and to be accountable as much for opportunity losses as they are for new product successes. Corporate management must ensure that it is not being denied access to ideas. If they are to be involved with approving proposed projects they must too be involved with proposed rejections.

Screening stages

Having regard to what has been said in the preceding paragraphs, we can now turn to the process of screening.

The screening process is divided into four main stages, the idea being to reduce the number of non-viable concepts before too much cost, time and effort are expended.

The first stage is preliminary screening, an initial evaluation of the product concept which eliminates product ideas which are obviously impractical or otherwise unacceptable.

Stage two involves a patent search in all target markets to establish who controls patents and licences and which areas are unprotected by patents.

The third stage of the screening process is the business analysis. Here the screening process should seek to assess the general practicality of the product, the nature and size of the market in broad terms and any changes that will be required in distribution, sales methods, organisation and manufacturing. The business analysis should be carried out in a number of markets to provide a general idea of the product concept's worth for further development (see market research).

The fourth stage we can call a final screening for it is at this stage that the product concept should be either accepted for development or screened out. Here the company's key marketing and technical people must be in a position to review the product concept and assess it against data collected in the previous three stages. A product candidate will obviously be ruled out where market potential is limited, production is not feasible, or where profit expectations are too low.

The ultimate test for screening a product out is an evaluation of the impact on the business or the market should a competitor launch a similar product.

Turning an idea into a product concept

In this second phase of concept development, we have to change what is a relatively crude idea into a tangible and marketable product concept. The product concept, therefore, has to be developed in terms of engineering, production and manufacturing methods and in terms of being totally *packaged* as a proposition for customers through branding, packaging, promotion and pricing. During this phase the product concept is refined and tested from the point of view of its functional performance and is adapted and retested depending upon successive test outcomes.

It is during this stage that field trials should take place in target markets to establish functional performance capabilities under different market and usage conditions. This phase will require a considerable amount of work in refining the product design. A certain amount of consumer research will be necessary to test for and establish consumer preferences for certain aspects of the design and the range of functional capabilities offered by the product.

When the technical and marketing personnel involved in the project are satisfied with their interpretation of the product concept a number of pre-test market activities will take place. Keegan suggests that

'whenever a product interacts with human, mechanical or chemical elements there is the potential for a surprising and unexpected incompatibility. Since every product is involved with one or more interactions it is important whenever any significant investment of money or manpower is involved to test a product under actual market conditions *before proceeding* with full scale test marketing effort.'

It is absolutely necessary to iron out 'any bugs' in a new product, its production, logistics systems and above all to test consumer acceptability.

Tests to verify logistics, handling and product robustness should also be carried out. These usually include transit tests in various markets under different transport and climatic conditions. Physical handling tests should also be carried out by organisation-and-methods personnel to assess both the company's own handling problems and also those likely to arise within the channels of distribution. Pre-testing of advertising appeals and packaging will take place at this stage so that when a test-market proposal is finally put together the product will be tested with the best interpretation of what the company believes will influence the consumer in stimulating product trial.

Patent applications

It is essential that before any new product is exposed to the world at large (even in prototype trials) international patent applications should be lodged.

If products are not patentable in themselves, copyright or design should be registered and processes examined to find patentable aspects.

Intellectual property rights are complex issues and can only be effectively handled by law firms specialised in this field.

It is necessary to seek advice early on in the product development process and apply for registration for as many areas as possible. Even if the company ultimately decides not to commercialise its property it has the option to license it or to prohibit competitors from exploiting the idea once it has become public knowledge. Care has to be taken in certain markets where non-exploitation of a patent may lead to its expiry.

Furthermore, whereas patent regulations are fairly common throughout the world, copyright is not. Copyright registration may require considerably more investigation than patent registration.

European Patent Convention

The European Patent Office is located in Munich. It was created out of the 1978 European Patent Convention. Whilst this originated from a European Community initiative, it is not a Community body. It includes a number of non-member countries – Austria, Switzerland and Sweden – but does not include Denmark, Ireland or Portugal.

The benefit of the European Patent Office is that it allows firms to file patents in the contracting countries through a single application. However, once a European patent is granted it is really a set of independent national patents. This means that the enforcement and validity are determined at each country level through their national laws and courts.

The Community is undertaking to bring national patent laws into conformity – with rules applicable to European patents. The member states within the Community have almost concluded a Community patent convention under which a European Patent will become a European Community Patent within the EC. The convention will also harmonise rules and establish a common body of law. Member states would then designate courts as Community Patent Courts – whose jurisdictions would extend across the entire Community. There will also be a common appeal court to guarantee consistency between the decisions of different courts.

Whilst many of the provisions of the Convention have been agreed, there are still a number of difficulties to be overcome. There is still no agreement on either how or when the Convention is to be brought into force. However, the ratification of the Community Patent Convention is on the agenda for the Single Market programme. It is likely that it will be in place by 1992.

From concept to new product

Having developed a product concept the next stage is to bring the product to life. This involves the assembly of physical and psychological benefits into a complete product package around which promotional communications can be brought to bear. Experienced marketing people will understand that the physical aspects and function of a product are only part of its customer appeal. Other magical attributes determined from research or good knowledge of the target customer groups need to be added.

Whilst pricing strategies and advertising are dealt with separately in this book, they are necessary ingredients in bringing the product concept into life as a commercial entity. The key issues we will focus on at present, however, are:

- product function;

- styling and design;

- brand names;

- packaging; and

- reliability and service support.

These are critical aspects for development of a product. Yet in the international context they are often the most difficult to transfer geographically.

Product function

Whilst function may be defined in broad terms, customer psychology and culture often lead to wide variations in their perceptions of what a product is and what it is used for. A car may be a mode of transport but it is also a status symbol, a runabout, a 'second' car etc. Function therefore needs to be defined both across customer segments and across countries.

Cost of function should be carefully taken into consideration. North American cars have never really penetrated foreign markets because they consume petrol very heavily. The cost of function for industrial products is very often the *second* buying consideration though – after initial outlay price – and very often the deciding factor after weighing up competitors for price and service.

Market research will invariably be necessary to identify function criteria in terms of physical use, psychological and cultural perceptions and attitudes towards the cost of function.

Styling and design

These two aspects are what give a product its physical attributes both in terms of the function it has to satisfy and in terms of appeal and quality. Again customer studies will need to be carried out to test for similarities and differentiating factors across markets. This will indicate the extent to which design features and colour etc will need to be adapted for individual markets.

Design features may be greatly affected by standard regulations. The EC and the Worlds Standards Organisation are advancing harmonisation of standards so that regulations affecting customer and environmental safety become common whilst permitting producers freedom in terms of styling. Yet there still prevails an anarchy of regulations, prohibitions and restrictions around which product designers will have to work in producing acceptable products.

International function capability is a major factor in the design criterion for an international product. When a consumer in a distant country buys a product it has to function without too great an additional outlay in 'getting it adapted'.

Electrical gadgets are a major point in question. For whereas European and Japanese companies provide adaptors (for example, some international electric razors by Philips have voltage adaptors built in) many US companies do not – thus consumers buying American equipment find they have to buy them before the product will function.

Climate and even altitude affect product performance, as do local supplies of, say, petrol and water as well as road conditions, port handling and so forth. International products, therefore, need to be designed either to meet a wide variation of environmental condi-tions or have specific adaptations made. It is also important that where climatic extremes are felt such as in parts of Europe, North America, African countries, Asia and South America, products be tested in each territory.

As well as functional capability there should also be compatibility in measuring systems. For example, those products, the specification of which are in DIN or BSI, that are sold in countries using other systems are at a competitive disadvantage – if not already frustrated by local standards regulations. In examining the most important aspects of design and styling in the context of international marketing we are concerned about producing a product which is acceptable in terms of meeting consumer preference, being relatively economic in terms of its cost of function, complying to laws, standards and other regulations, being compatible to local measuring systems and having an international function capability.

Product designs may win awards or gain publicity but even so commercial success may not always be the outcome. Research and rigorous testing is obviously needed to reduce the probabilities of failure.

Brand names

The brand name identifies the product for a buyer and gives the supplier the opportunity to create a reliable franchise of repeat users. A brand is a 'name, term or sign or symbol or combination of them which is intended to identify the goods and services of one seller or group of sellers and to differentiate them from competitors'.

The use of a brand name enables the marketing company to encapsulate all the product's physical and psychological benefits into a single identity. In other words, it gives the total product concept a name that consumers can recognise and ask for. In international marketing a universal name has to have meaning and be acceptable.

The foreign interpretation of brand names has also to be taken into consideration. Sometimes a word in English, for example, translates badly into a foreign language, with a vulgar or socially unacceptable meaning in particular markets. The popular French drink PSCHITT would have difficulty in English speaking markets as would the German toilet paper brand Bum.

Trade marks are important in international marketing, especially where literacy is low. In many countries outside the EC, for example, Carlsberg lager is called Crown Bear and Guinness in South East Asia is called Red Tongue Dog or Whole Dog. Dunlop, although using its 'D' logo, also uses its 'Old Man' trade mark in many countries where the tyres are referred to as 'Old Man' tyres.

Logos and trade marks are also an endorsement of a product's quality. The ICI, Pfizer, Wilkinson Sword and Caltex logos confirm to consumers that the products originate from firms with a high reputation.

Brand name research

A brand name is a major investment. Not only will it be strongly associated with the product for which it was originated, as a property it will serve as a vehicle for future line-extension opportunities. It is therefore imperative that brand names be rigorously tested and researched in all major markets. It is important that the brand name should be suitable in a marketing sense in each and every major market – not just at home.

A new brand name must be tested at a minimum to ensure:

- it has an association with the product or, probably better, a suggestion of product benefits (Kleenex);

- the name is easily pronounceable;

- it is easily remembered (rhythm and alliteration help);

- it is quite distinguishable from other established names and has no association with the name of a product in another category which might create negative associations (eg a food product with a name similar to that of a well known brand of weedkiller); and

- it has no objectionable connotations – either spontaneous or created by the competition to rubbish the product.

It is essential to research and test brand names for both positive and negative qualities of the name. Some essential tests which must be carried out are association tests (what images are evoked); learning tests (how easily the name is pronounced); memory tests (can the name be recalled easily); and preference tests (compare a range of names for preference).

There are market research organisations which have developed quite elaborate brand-name-testing procedures and it is strongly advised that they be used when taking products into new markets.

Brand name protection

Registration of brand names and their attending properties such as logos and trade marks is absolutely vital. Without legal protection against unauthorised use by other companies the brand name is worthless. Many companies would simply go out of business if their brand names could not be protected.

In the international environment, brand names have to be registered *as soon as they are conceived*. It is surprising how quick competitors are in pre-empting the legitimate owner's registration of their new brand's name in foreign countries. Whether the aim is to block entry or to sell back to the manufacturer its name, pre-emption of registration is a problem recognised by all experienced internationalists.

Few countries do not provide a system for trade mark registration protection for both domestic and foreign companies. Laws vary from country to country but there are basically two systems. The first company to register a trademark secures protection for the name (although this may lapse if usage does not occur); or the first company to initiate the brand name registration alone is insufficient, it also demands that some sales actually be made within the country.

It is well worth selling token stocks of products each year to provide proof of sales. One British food company sold two dozen products a year through a single retailer for three years in Western Germany merely to hold onto a valuable brand name whilst it made preparations to enter the German market.

A number of conventions have been agreed between various countries to ensure that registration in one member country gives protection in all. There are difficulties in that the name has to qualify for registration under each country's own regulations. There is no automatic right of registration if the name is prohibited in a particular country.

The *Arrangement of Madrid* provides registration protection in 22 countries where a name is registered by a company domiciled in a member country. The name is passed on to a central bureau for subsequent registration in member countries.

The costs of registering brand names across a number of countries can be high. There are the legal fees of lawyers acting for the company for each registration procedure. There are usually registration fees charged by each country and search fees involved in finding if the same or similar name has already been registered. There is the cost of establishing usage and the legal costs encountered in contesting claims from companies who have the legal right to allege infringement.

Trade mark piracy, imitation and claimed compatibility

Whilst name registration provides legal protection, there is no obligation on the part of national authorities to police infringements. It is the responsibility of companies to search continuously for possible infringements and take appropriate legal action in the courts. There are three ways in which competitors can attempt to usurp the legitimate use of a name.

Trade mark piracy

Here companies register names in countries where 'the first to register assumes the legal rights to a name' with the single intention of selling the name back to the legitimate owner. This activity is deemed legal in many countries although the means through which confidential information about intended brand names is obtained may not be.

Trade mark imitation

Unscrupulous companies may well take the opportunity to 'cash-in' on the value of well known brands either by using the same or similar name or part of a name to market cheaper or inferior products with similar packaging and labelling. This is deliberate passing off and companies have to be alert to find and take legal action against offending companies. In some parts of the world this activity is quite common.

The problems may not be confined to the single country in which the offence is committed as pirated brands are often exported – even back to the country where the legally protected product is made.

Claimed compatibility

A number of companies have recognised that through marketing products compatible with highly promoted branded products they can exploit the brand name to their own advantage. The personal computer and power tools are particular targets. There is seemingly little that the legal holders of brand names can do about this except, maybe, through libel and copyright rulings. The question of product liability may yet have to be resolved where there are damages claimed against a company which sold the original but was used in conjunction with a claimed compatible accessory.

Brand names used as generic terms

Once a brand name becomes the common parlance for a particular type of product the courts may refuse to afford any legal protection for the name. It is important therefore for brand-name users to avoid anything which might be seen as allowing the name to become the generic term of a particular product. Presentation should always note the name as a brand name by the 'R' symbol, spelled as a proper noun and by differentiating between the name and the generic, eg Gordons Gin.

Some companies anticipating vulnerability such as Xerox have mounted advertising campaigns throughout the world to prevent improper use of their trade marks.

Packaging

Packaging is the front-line presentation for most portable products.

Packaging which is unattractive will adversely affect product sales. A US study, for example, showed that a third of consumers who were presold by advertising switched to different products when presented with more attractive alternatives.

Consumers have been taught to expect attractive packaging. This is also true even in lesser developed countries following years of high-quality imported packaging from advanced Western countries.

Packaging has a number of important tasks in building a total product concept. In international marketing this task is more complex and again the decision to adapt or standardise for international market becomes important.

In presenting a product, packaging has six key tasks:

- attracting consumers at point of sale (where it is merchandised);
- carrying the sales information to point of sale;
- projecting the product image;
- providing usage and function information;
- providing relevant information required by law; and
- protecting the product.

Attracting consumers at point of sale

Creating visual impact and purchase appeal is a prime task for packaging, particularly in self-service outlets. First, the packaging should tell the consumer what the product is and second, it should attract attention. Label design should also take into consideration the offerings of competitors with the intention of producing a more attractive and more desirable package.

Carrying the sales information to point of sale

The package has to tell its 'sales story' quickly as consumers will only glance at it. In most territories mass media advertising permits companies the advantage of pre-selling the product, thus the package merely needs to remind consumers of the sales message at point of sale. Yet it should still reinforce the consumers' desire to buy through projecting appeal at point of purchase.

In less sophisticated markets packages will have to carry more of a sales story, despite the clutter which this involves. This is because the package still remains its own salesman where media takes longer to pre-sell or where purchasing decisions are more important to the consumer with limited disposable income.

Packaging is also often required to carry messages for merchandising promotions such as 'price-offs', competitions and 'mail-ins' to point of sale. These need to stand out in order to attract consumers but they should not devalue the overall attractiveness and communicability of the packaging.

Projecting the product image

The image of a product is an important psychological benefit. A food product presents appetite appeal, a consumer durable projects quality and a male toiletry product may present masculinity. There are dangers in letting a package become old fashioned and overtaken by competitors with a more modern presentation.

Image projection involves considerable aptitude on the part of designers. Consumer testing of package concepts is important in ensuring that the right image is projected. Common international products' packages are themselves part of the product image, eg Coca Cola.

Providing usage and function information

Most products require some information about usage and function, particularly for technical consumer products and food products. In using the limited space available for such information it is important that the consumer receives the necessary information to be able to use the product successfully.

Such usage information should take into account variations in usage requirement in individual territories. In the USA for example, some European packet soups tend to be used for dips rather than eaten as hot soup. A secondary usage or ideas for extended usage are often carried on packages, and providing that they are relevant to consumer needs, they provide an opportunity to stimulate increased usage and hence sales.

Where instructions on usage are too lengthy or technical in nature the use of a pack insert may be necessary. It is, after all, essential that the consumer be able to use the product successfully if he or she is to become a regular user.

Providing relevant information required by law

International marketing executives know all too well that they face a minefield of laws and regulations which seem to be constantly changing the world over (a factor in deciding upon packaging inventory levels). In different countries and regions packaging regulations tend to follow similar paths based upon those of such august bodies as the US FDL or the EC basically because, between the two, most of the important aspects of the law have been exhausted. But unfortunately these aspects are treated differently in each market. The law usually demands the following:

- weight, size or capacity of the products;
- safety reminders;
- annotations that certain ingredients are present (such as in food the presence of anti-oxidising agents and colourants);
- ingredients and formula;
- country of origin (often); and
- price.

One of the major frustrations to marketers is that although laws and regulations tend to be basic there is little standardisation between countries. There are also a number of important local regulations such as multi-lingual requirements in Belgium, Canada, and South Africa. Furthermore, countries may demand that legally required information be printed a certain size or that (as in the case of Spain) food registration numbers have to be displayed.

Protecting the product

Protection of the product was undoubtedly the original primary purpose of the package. Today this purpose should not be overlooked or sacrificed in an effort to meet artistic criteria. The image of a leading cereal suffered a jolt in Germany, for example, after initial supplies packaged locally were found to contain weevils. Such problems are costly and can even cause the failure of a product through consumers losing confidence in the product.

The package will have to suffer different conditions in different markets. The problems which distance from the manufacturing base imposes can cause considerable stress on both the package and the product through handling, weather and temperature. There is little point in producing a product and embellishing it with expensive packaging if it arrives in a retailer's stockroom in an unsaleable condition.

Adapt or standardise packaging

We come back to the argument of whether we should standardise our packaging or not. There are considerable economic benefits from standardising, such as in running long batches through the production line, as well as savings in advertising, production costs, bulk buying of materials and so on. Yet is a true standardised package really feasible?

If we look at a piece of packaging which meets the six tasks assigned it, we will find that these are embodied in four overlapping features – protection features, information features, display features and legal features (see Figure 9.1). These features inter-relate and it is this inter-relationship which makes a universal standard package for a product difficult to achieve. Ultimately, because of the differences in consumer, legal and distribution factors in different markets there may be a need to change one or more of the four features of a package.

Many companies attempt to achieve some standardisation in the presentation of their packs mainly through keeping to basic design elements and maintaining key display features – yet run special packs which meet legal and language criteria for each market. Wilkinson Sword, for example, sells largely standardised shaving products around the world but adapts its packaging to meet country or regional criteria.

Reliability and service support

Reliability is a critical assessment which customers make when comparing competitive products. Thus in bringing a new product into being those aspects which will influence customer regard for reliability will need to be assessed and incorporated into the product. Service support will need to be assessed and built into the marketing structure. A new computer will need trained service engineers to support installation and provide customer back-up. A new consumer product will need merchandiser support and so on.

Product reliability, customer care and service support are important elements for marketing in competitor-intensive international markets. Every product will in some way or another require these elements if it is to achieve a significant market share.

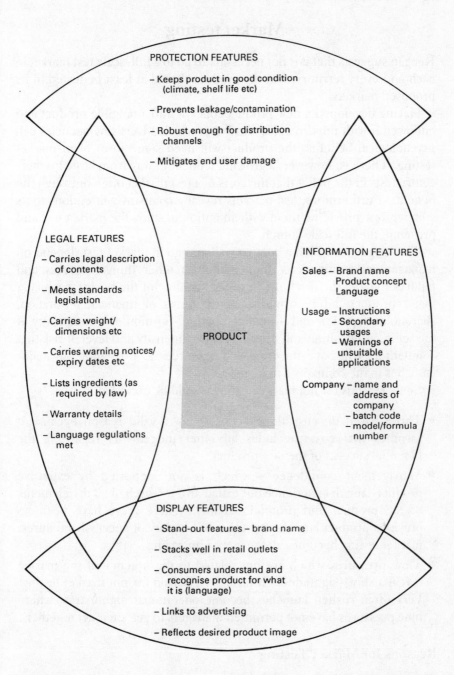

PROTECTION FEATURES

- Keeps product in good condition (climate, shelf life etc)
- Prevents leakage/contamination
- Robust enough for distribution channels
- Mitigates end user damage

LEGAL FEATURES

- Carries legal description of contents
- Meets standards legislation
- Carries weight/dimensions etc
- Carries warning notices/expiry dates etc
- Lists ingredients (as required by law)
- Warranty details
- Language regulations met

PRODUCT

INFORMATION FEATURES

Sales – Brand name
        Product concept
        Language

Usage – Instructions
      – Secondary usages
      – Warnings of unsuitable applications

Company – name and address of company
        – batch code
        – model/formula number

DISPLAY FEATURES

- Stand-out features – brand name
- Stacks well in retail outlets
- Consumers understand and recognise product for what it is (language)
- Links to advertising
- Reflects desired product image

Figure 9.1 The six key tasks of a package are embodied in four overlapping features of a pack

Market testing

Keegan suggests that it is not necessary to go to a full-scale test market in each and every territory. But the product should at least be tested in its proposed markets.

Having developed a new product concept into a tangible product and endowed it with those magical attributes which advertising agencies call psychological benefits, the product will need some form of in-market testing. There is, however, a growing tendency away from large market-centre tests in the belief that the costs of a test market often outweigh the benefits. Furthermore, test markets reveal a company's intentions to its competitors, providing them with an option to study the market test and pre-empt the full scale launch.

The lengths to which a company should go in market test depend on management assumptions about, amongst other things, success and failures to date; the level of risk to the standing of the business which a major product failure would cause in terms of financial reputation, shareholder opinion and overall competitive position; the complexity of the selling proposition and the competitive intensity and level of risk that competitors will have the time and resources to pre-empt the major launches in the company's markets.

Some reasons for not market testing should be excluded.

- Those based on cost alone – this is not a valid reason because it assumes that cost precludes all other judgements regarding the potential success of the new product.
- Management confidence – which is not supported by extensive product-launch experience nor exhaustive research of all the elements of the product and promotional mix. Where there have been no previous product launches or there is a history of successive failures, market testing becomes all the more important.
- Time pressures which are not related to the urgency of the market reveal a short-sightedness if given as a reason for not market testing. Very often rushed launches become operational nightmares, where time pressures have not permitted managers to get 'their act together'.

Reasons for Market Testing

The main reasons for market testing are more to do with assessing a company's ability to make its marketing mix work than for any other reason. They are concerned with testing and improving a company's assumptions about its success criteria in terms of:

- customer responses *vis-à-vis* competitor products in terms of awareness, trial, applications, attitudes and repeat-purchase intentions;
- trade reaction to the product and its marketing support;
- measures of the effectiveness of elements of marketing activities;
- improving the company's knowledge of potential sales;
- measuring the effectiveness of logistics and seeking out problems – especially those which reveal weaknesses in the product or its packaging;
- providing benchmarks against which to set objectives for each area of marketing activity involved in the full-scale launches;
- discovering weaknesses and problems which were not foreseen; and
- providing data upon which sales presentations to major customers can be based.

Difficulties with market tests

In planning market tests it is as well to understand their shortcomings and difficulties when used in predicting the likely success of a product in an international environment. Managers should be aware of the limitations and think carefully about solving these difficulties.

Finding a set of markets or market centres which are representative is difficult. Proliferation of market tests becomes an administrative headache when a number of markets are involved. There are also considerable difficulties involved in transposing elements of the marketing mix from one market to another.

Competitor reactions will remain an unpredictable element affecting subsequent launch activity and may be heightened as a result of the market tests.

Market tests may well be effective in giving some measure to the company's ability to bring a product to market but they do not provide any information about the future. Extraneous and uncontrollable factors such as strikes, the weather and so on may also affect results.

Kotler suggests that market testing's main value lies in a second area of managerial control. It is a way of testing for negatives in the product, promotion price, logistics and sales presentation to the channels of distribution. The general view is that test markets are a less expensive method of finding hidden problems connected with the new product than finding them after full-scale commercialisation.

On balance, some form of testing a company's ability to launch a new product and provide an opportunity for it to be competitively tested in a live market situation is advised. This is particularly the case for fast-moving consumer products and consumer durables which require high amounts of promotional activity in intensely competitive markets. Not only will the shortcomings in activity and negatives in consumer and trade reaction be spotted before full commercialisation, the company will also benefit from the valuable experience and increased understanding of the markets in which it intends to launch its product.

Choosing test markets

Test marketing has become something of a specialist area particularly in Europe and the USA. Large international companies like Unilever have considerable experience and work with their subsidiaries to run tests in different markets. Such companies have the capability to run a series of test markets simultaneously. There are also consultant companies who specialise in research activities. A C Nielson has an excellent reputation for its services in a great number of markets. Companies such as Research International in the UK can also help set up test markets.

The major decision for the international company is how and when to test all its markets.

Test initially in the lead country

Particularly if this market is to be the principal market upon which the decision to commercialise the new product will be based. Use this test as a pilot for other market tests. Then extend test markets to priority markets.

Test in metropolitan areas around the world

Do this simultaneously. This is based on the view that there will be greater similarity between metropolitan centres across countries than within them. The main constraint for this approach will be cost and practicality.

National launches in key representative markets

This is done within respective clusters of similar markets. Each national launch is in effect a test market for a region or market cluster. This alternative will require a certain amount of pre-launch experience which may in fact come from small-scale market tests.

The length of the test market

The last critical decision is in determining the length of a test market wherever it is planned to run. There are basically three factors which influence the length of time a test market should run and these are:

- the length of the repurchase cycle;
- the competitive situation; and
- the level of accumulated experience.

The repurchase cycle

This is the period of time comprising the initial purchase of a product, the length of time the purchaser takes to use the product, plus the intervening period between finishing the product and buying it again.

As information about satisfaction, brand switching and loyalty to the new product are essential data that will be collected during the test-market, the duration of the test should be long enough to allow for at least two or three repurchase cycles to occur.

The competitive situation

The effect of this is to encourage companies to keep their test markets short. Obviously, companies want test markets to last long enough to produce an adequate level of information but not so long as to give competitors sufficient time to steal a march on the company.

Level of accumulated experience

This describes the knowledge acquired by successive product launches into new territories. Marketing organisations which keep documentary records of each successive launch and the subsequent progress of their products have a valuable database of experience. By recording experiences companies can:

- avoid repeating mistakes;
- build on marketing techniques which appear to be the most effective for the product;

- provide a basis for comparing launch-phase effectiveness between territories;

- map competitors and study their reactions;

- provide comparability data which may help to reduce the need for extensive tests in similar markets (as long as comparability can be established); and

- allow management to make 'ballpark assumptions' about total volume potential.

Target information to be collected

The information requirements from a test market should be targeted in advance. Collection of data should be assigned before the test starts. Once the test market is over it will no longer be possible to track many of its activities.

It is necessary to evaluate results in both quantitative and qualitative terms. However, before the test-market results are evaluated it might be a pertinent question to ask if the test-market itself was executed adequately enough to provide a reasonably representative set of results. This really can only be done by internal management discussion – but post mortems should be carried out before the results of a test-market are presented, otherwise there is a tendency for executives to read executional shortcomings of the test market into the results. For example, 'the slow consumer trial figures indicate our lateness in bringing a major multiple into the test'.

Quantitative data such as product shipments by volume from the warehouse to the market gives an impression of overall market stock requirements for a product launch. A crude sales figure can be arrived at simply by deducting stock unsold at retail level from the original shipment figures, taking account of stock losses etc.

Store Audits are essential in that they show the speed of stock movement by outlet type and show comparative movements by competitor products. This information might provide a rough estimate of brand share expectations as well as a basis for estimating the potential growth in total market size when stimulated by the introduction of a new product. However, store audits do not tell us anything about the buyers habits and attitudes. In particular we would not know what proportions were new 'trial' buyers or repeat buyers.

Consumer studies, panels and 'dustbin audits' provide real quantitative and qualitative data about buyers' behaviour. They permit measurements of brand switching, repeat buying and the types of consumer showing the most interest in the new product as well as measuring consumer response to advertising.

Trade-buyer studies should be carried out to find buyer attitudes and reactions to the new product. Such information can prepare the sales team for trade-buyer presentations and for solving potential areas of complaint. Obviously, the more usable information the company acquires the better its chances that the right decisions will be made in planning the launch of a new product.

In essence, test results provide some reliable pointers in the assessment of a product's sales and profit potential. They will indicate the viability of the product concept. The information from the test should establish a ratio between the number of consumers who make a trial purchase and those who make a number of repeat purchases. Finally, there will also be some useful feedback regarding trade returns of unsaleable goods and consumer complaints.

Test market results should be treated with two thoughts in mind. Is the product viable as positioned and marketed? And, how much rethinking is necessary to provide the necessary success criteria for a full-scale launch (and will a further test be necessary)?

There are many cases where managers become so overconfidently committed to a launch they press ahead on the basis of very spurious evidence that they might succeed. To illustrate the point we quote from the memoirs of an ex-chairman of Beechams.

My idea was that with Brylcreem, Silvikrin Shampoo and Macleans Tooth Paste we should have three products [in the US market] and I could see us achieving a total turnover in excess of $50 million and soon the US business would be larger than that in the UK. It could have been done, I am sure, but we made too many mistakes and I failed to realise that the American reaction to success of a competitor is much more ruthless than the British.

So we chose to launch Silvikrin Shampoo. It was our most successful shampoo in England but, with hindsight, was not the brand we should have attempted to put on the US market. First of all, the name was peculiar and some people thought it was for grey or silver hair. Then, the product was an efficient cleaner but probably not the best for dry hair (there are three different Silvikrin products now for dry, normal and greasy hair). Yet in average conditions in the US, dry hair and dandruff are very prevalent. Finally, we should have tested at least one of our other brands before we took a decision. In the event, our test did not really justify a launch. We were able to manufacture evidence from it that we would achieve 3 per cent of the market and break even and were cock-a-hoop over [the success of] Brylcreem and greatly over-confident. So away we went on with what turned out to be a catastrophe . . .

10

Pricing Strategies for
International Markets

There can be few areas of business which affect a company's international standing more than those involving its pricing decisions. Yet in a globally competitive environment the cascades of conflicting dynamics make control of pricing decisions elusive to many companies. In this chapter we will, therefore, discuss the role of pricing in global business strategies and highlight conditions and constraints that create inconsistencies between prices and corporate product-marketing objectives.

Pricing is a key component of the marketing mix. It is an intrinsic element which in concert with product, promotion and logistics forms the marketing strategy. Yet all too often pricing is set independently and is inconsistent with other elements of marketing strategy. International markets are often seen as 'somewhere else' where the rules at home do not apply. Too often export pricing is cost-orientated.

Exports are often assigned the role of providing additional profit contribution to a given capacity level by 'skimming' markets at higher prices than at home. Such strategies have considerable weaknesses in application and contribute little in the way of driving up sales volume and pushing down costs. They merely divert existing capacity to short-term and often illusory opportunities which create neither a firm market standing nor improve competitiveness.

Effects of the Single Market on international pricing strategies

Traditional pricing strategies are based on what companies believe will provide the optimum trade-off between the share of customer purchases they are aiming for and the costs of recruiting those customers in a competitive environment. Most companies have different prices in different markets, reflecting their individual marketing strategies which take into account their relative competitive advantages in relation to competition; customer buying habits; the state of the market and the level of promotion, service and so on. The profitability of international operations is for a number of companies based on their ability to achieve high prices in some markets whilst contending with lower prices elsewhere.

The SEA has the ability not only to influence a firm's prices in its Community markets but to affect the prices it charges in its global markets as well.

The individual nature of markets, VAT and selective price controls in a number of countries in the EC has meant that prices for individual products vary considerably across the Community.

The various regulations and directives which are likely to appear over the next few years will reduce a number of the pricing options companies can call upon in different markets. Not only will pricing transparency narrow the price bands for products across the Community, it may affect a company's global pricing strategy.

Under Directive 79/581, amendments to ensure that prices are to be

Table 10.1 National price differences compared with intra-EC differences – the case of home electronics in Germany

	W Germany*	Community**
Compact-disc players	10.6	14.9
Radio recorders	7.3	16.2
Turntables	9.6	10.8
Video recorders	5.7	13.2
Cam recorders	6.8	11.3
Video cassettes	5.7	13.3
Washing machines	3.3	13.4
Colour TV	6.4	13.5

  * Source: Institut für Angewandte Verbraucherforschung (IFAV). The coefficient of variation has been calculated on the basis of average prices in major German towns.
** Source: Bureau Européen des Unions des consommateurs (BEUC) and Eurostat (last two products). The number of Member States taken into account varies according to the product.
Source: High Stakes for Europe 1988, 35.
By kind permission of the Office for Official Publications of the European Communities.

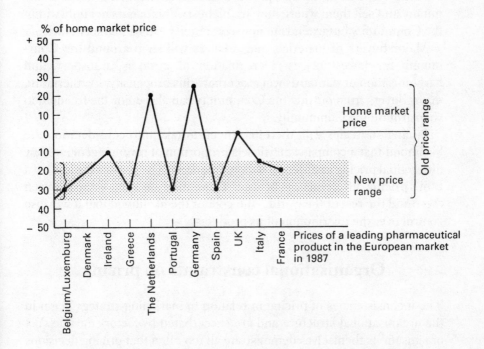

Figure 10.1 The effect of price levelling in the Single Internal Market

Levelling of prices for a major pharmaceutical product

The tendency will be for prices to level downwards. There is a 55 per cent range of prices shown in the graph. Upward movements are restrained by price control in the lower-priced markets. The stragegy adopted by the company illustrated is to accelerate market share and seek cost savings along its value chain (see Chapter 3). The short-run increase in marketing investment will smooth (downwards) profits. The resulting increase in sales plus efficiency savings will, at least in theory, replace the revenue lost as a result of price levelling. The erosion of prices should not therefore create a massive impact on the company's revenue performance in any period, although margins in the major markets will be greatly reduced.

indicated on foodstuffs is likely to be introduced. This will be extended to non-food products permitting governments, customers and consumers to see where prices in the Community are lowest.

Already consumers are allowed to buy limited amounts of product for personal importation. In continental Europe this will have no small influence on where consumers choose to buy their products. Differential VAT has already motivated consumers to shop around the Community.

Parallel traders may locate products at their lowest prices in the Community and sell them where they are highest. This occurs not only within the Community but extends to non-community export markets as well.

Major buyers of materials and retailers will shop around the Community for lowest prices. Deregulation of customs, transport, and harmonisation of standards will exacerbate this propensity. Furthermore, major buyers from outside the Community can also enjoy the freedom to shop around the Community.

Pricing strategies will, therefore, need to take into consideration the likelihood that a company may lose a proportion of revenue generated by differential pricing in different *national* markets. The greater the level of a firm's pricing differentiation between Community markets – and between these and the rest of the world – the greater the likelihood that it will lose control over the distribution of its products.

Organisational constraints on pricing

The inconsistencies of pricing in relation to marketing strategy begin in the organisational structure and are exacerbated by factors outside. Yet organisations themselves demonstrate all too often that pricing decisions are often made on poor assumptions. In export markets decisions are often made which ignore both customers and competitior and yet would not be made at home.

Costs

Cost-competitiveness depends on the efficiency a company achieves in maintaining its volume output against the resources it employs in relation to that of its competitors. Highly efficient firms with a large market share are likely to have lower costs than inefficient ones. Costs are, therefore, a poor basis upon which to base price, save that they determine the lower level against which prices can be set economically in the long term. Those firms more competitive in cost can also use their position to be either more price-competitive or allocate a higher percentage of their selling price to R & D, production investment, management and promotion. Thus companies trying to recoup costs through uncompetitive pricing doubly complicate their poor competitive situation.

Availability of investment funds

The limited availability of investment funds is a serious problem. Yet to use this constraint in pricing decisions is to compound the problem. Prices cannot be set beyond those which the market will bear. Simply to accelerate some theoretical pay back computation through excessive pricing is a dangerous decision because there is every likelihood that insufficient share will be achieved to generate the required level of revenue.

Employing a low price to enter a market as a means of reducing high entry costs of promotion may well present an attractive trade-off, especially if market investment funds are scarce. Yet the assumption that demand is influenced by price alone rarely holds true. Whereas an entry at low price alone may upset the market psychologically, such a strategy is vulnerable to attack by the market leaders through a combination of intensified promotion and short-term discounts and deals.

Disruption of pricing stability in a market is unlikely to please either competitors or distribution channels. New entrants, therefore, may find their unsupported low-price entry thwarted by a combination of competitor activity and trade hostility. An example of this occurred when a Danish pharmaceutical company attempted to launch two generic drugs against entrenched branded products in Holland – with a price advantage of up to 60 per cent. Their miscalculation was based on the premise that doctors would prescribe their lower-price drugs in preference to the higher-priced brands. Competitors reacted by promoting heavily to doctors (who did not pay for the drugs themselves) and the drug distribution channels discouraged stocking. As a result perfectly good and competitive drugs failed to achieve market share.

Where a lack of investment funds is a constraint companies should look to those other options which provide a market entry opportunity, namely: licensing, franchising, joint ventures and other co-operative deals. These may overcome the investment shortcomings whilst still providing the basis for competitive pricing and a strong marketing attack.

Short-term profit requirements

The constraint of short-term profit requirements is again a poor basis for pricing decisions. Scope always exists for exacting a better value for products by increasing the efficiency of prices (ie by better discount controls and by constantly trying to test the uper limit of prices). There is a point, however, beyond which prices can be increased and such increases become counterproductive in terms of reduced demand.

The less in touch prices are with the realities of the market place the more vulnerable a business is to customer dissatisfaction, which in turn will be exploited by competitors.

Problems of controlling prices in a global arena

A company which fails to take a position in the larger global market is vulnerable to competition. Yet global expansion itself brings with it a number of problems which result from the difficulties of controlling prices across a number of markets.

Any business which fails to avoid substantial variations in the prices customers pay for the same or similar products around the world may well find that: there are pressures for prices to be reduced by government and distribution channels comparing prices in different markets (more so in Europe after 1992).

A grey market can also develop around exporters and importers who locate the company's products in their cheapest markets and sell them in their more expensive ones. For example the parallel trade of pharmaceuticals between Belgium and the rest of the world is based on the low price of such products found there as a result of Belgian price control.

Competition can attack targeted companies through creaming off their most profitable markets before assaulting their main markets.

Factors which militate against control of prices in international marketing are:

- government measures such as price control, limiting upward movements in price, the absence or availability of retail price maintenance, margin controls which limit trade margins and consequently retail prices;
- local taxes which distort retail price comparisons between companies (for example Table 10.2 shows the different levels of VAT charged across the EC; and
- the different structures of distribution channels and the traditional margin structures which exist in different countries.

Table 10.2 Rates of VAT in the Community Member States
(situation as of January 1986)*

	lower	standard	higher
Belgium	6 & 17	19	25 & 33
Denmark	–	22	–
W Germany	7	14	–
Spain	6	12	33
France	5.5 & 7	18.6	33.3
Ireland	0 & 10	23	–
Italy	2 & 9	18	38
Luxembourg	3 & 6	12	–
The Netherlands	5	19	–
Portugal	8	16	30
UK	0	15	–

*Greece has not yet introduced VAT

By kind permission of the Office for Official Publications of The European Communities.

These factors are further exacerbated by exchange rates and relative levels of inflation between countries.

No company can hope to achieve uniform customer prices and there are too many variables to allow companies to achieve uniformity in export and trade prices. The hope, therefore, is keep the variations in price within such narrow parameters as to maintain global competitiveness in the long term whilst remaining nationally responsive in each market.

The pricing turbulence created between bona fide and grey marketers of a company's products can and often is beneficial in stimulating trade. The existence of parallel trade is a phenomenon of market forces creating equilibrium for prices where disequilibrium exists. In fact in the economic sense the market itself is finding the optimum price for a company's products. In so doing the informal trade will often inhibit the growth of lesser-known products for which there is little universal demand. In the UK, for example, the parallel importation of branded pharmaceuticals from Belgium has in this writer's opinion greatly reduced the scope for the substitution of generic equivalents.

The downsides to permitting the informal trade control of the market, however, include the loss of control of distribution and the quality of product reaching the customer, dissatisfaction and low morale amongst bona fide distributors and the loss of revenue from higher-priced markets. Many companies complain about parallel trade and divert funds to reduce it, yet few, very few, ever attempt to look closely enough at what its existence and its effect on competition is telling them about their pricing strategies!

Pricing strategies

Despite the conflicts, constraints and influence on pricing decisions in the international arena, pricing remains a key tool of marketing. Its application, therefore, must be consistent with the business objectives as an intrinsic part of the marketing mix for any product–market relationship.

In many textbooks today students are offered the choice between 'market-skimming' pricing and 'penetration' pricing. Skimming supposes that production can be beneficially diverted to markets where high prices can be found for limited volume. The assumption is that if it is done in a number of markets simultaneously the capacity utilised will generate higher returns than equivalent in the domestic market. The idea holds good providing that sufficient market share is created to motivate trade channels to support the product; parallel importers and exporters do not spoil the strategy by buying in the domestic market and selling in the export market at a discount; and that competition ignores the profitable niche carved out of the market – often a distinct possibility as long as it remains small.

The advantages, then, of skimming are in using capacity more efficiently in terms of revenue contribution. Yet there are considerable disadvantages. Skimming positions are difficult to hold and the greater the proportion of output tied up across a number of markets the more vulnerable a company's business becomes. Fragile market shares in a number of markets are difficult to sustain for competitive reasons alone. The chief danger that skimming brings with it is that cost-competitiveness is not improved from a larger share of the wider market. Hence, whilst skimming is attractive in improving contributions from an existing cost base the additional revenue generated from peripheral marketing activities does little to drive up share and tackle the cost base of the business. Furthermore, the high-priced export business is vulnerable and could well impact against business performance if lost.

Penetration pricing strategies involve pricing within the range of prevailing market prices for competitors' products. This puts products at a price advantage or at least parity with existing products on the market, thus enabling the company to compete for larger share of the market. The advantages are found in providing a larger share against which to target and fund marketing activity and providing increased volumes against which to attack costs.

Whilst such strategies benefit from greater market share and a reduction in interference from the parallel marketing channels, competition still presents a major threat. More often than not the more aggressive the pricing strategy the more hostile will be the competitor's countermoves. Thus the judgement of the viability of a market entry will be based more on the success factors built into the entire marketing programme than on price alone.

Pricing for market share strategies

Pricing for market share is a grander concept than either skimming or penetration strategies. It is based on two underlying principles: the greater the share a company holds in the market the lower its costs should become; and the greater cost-competitiveness a business acquires the greater the share of sales value can be pumped back into R & D, marketing investment, production resources and management. Furthermore, the company with lowest costs can drop its prices in defence to much lower levels than its competitors and for longer.

Yet pricing for market share does not mean that a company holds doggedly to a low-price strategy. For as it reaches its targeted share levels it can begin to increase price to match those of its competitors – or even surpass them. Both Sony, with its assault on the US television market and Seiko in Europe, have established high shares with a combination of low prices and high marketing investment and, having created a position of strength, have steadily increased prices against competition.

Pricing for market share, therefore, calls for a trade-off in short-term margins for a future lowering of costs and increases in revenue, whilst at the same time providing a sustainable level of marketing activity against which to win customers and outfight competitors. For those who may think that such a strategy is too risky and ambitious – beware. You may well become the victim of such a strategy from foreign competition in their home market.

In making commercial sense of the pricing for market-share strategy there needs to be a financial basis upon which it can be sensibly funded. A strong home or regional market base is needed upon which to sustain profitability whilst the pricing for market-share strategies are being deployed in foreign markets. By 1992 Europe will provide such a home market.

Pricing in the marketing mix

There are a number of ways in which pricing can be used in relation to the other elements of the marketing mix.

Product–price relationships

In the product–price relationship pricing can be used to differentiate one product from its competitors. For example, a product might be priced lower than equivalent competitors thus providing a pricing edge. To achieve such a strategy, however, it is necessary for the product's costs to be at least as – if not more – competitive than its competitors, otherwise the latter can retreat behind their lower cost base and disrupt the product–pricing strategy. Such a strategy is therefore vulnerable and needs a sustained level of promotional activity to maintain it. Low pricing alone, as we have discussed previously, is rarely effective.

The concept of *functionality* may however be applied. This concept is based on the assumption that customers are prepared to pay for a solution to their problems or needs rather than merely comparing prices for equivalent products. Functionality is the breaking down and analysing of customer needs and dissatisfactions in relation to what is on offer and then providing a product at which the customer is happy to pay.

The next concept is *quality*. Prices for items which are of higher quality than competitors' can be higher than poor-quality equivalents. Quality has to be both perceived and tangible because if customer quality expectations are not met then the product will suffer as a result. Setting and maintaining quality standards may be initially expensive. Yet a maintained dedication to quality may have a high economic value.

Pricing and promotion

There is no doubt that highly promoted products can command higher prices than poorly promoted competitors. The way in which highly promoted fcmg products have managed to survive against low-priced own-labels in retail multiples is proof of this. Yet the scope for pricing flexibility depends on more than just the weight of promotion: it also depends on the dominance products have achieved in the market place. Higher prices for heavily promoted products are generally won – not *imposed*.

Hertz, for example, has consistently charged higher prices than Avis or Budget and has retained position of price leader but this has come from many years of building its position out front.

Pricing and distribution

Prices for products in greater distribution than their competitors can generally be higher. Thus organisation employed to ensure a competitive distribution level may be an investment against price. Yet for many fmcg products competitive distribution can only be achieved through its promotional spend and market share. In many parts of the world sophisticated buying organisations will not touch new products without a promotional commitment on behalf of the suppliers.

Pricing and service

Service can add tremendous value to products. A history of service and reliability can be a major factor in the prices customers are prepared to pay. A feature of business often forgotten by suppliers is that satisfied customers will often be the ones most ready to purchase their new models and new products. Customer loyalty is the most valuable asset a company can have. The concept of *reliability* therefore is based on the value customers or potential customers place on the continued satisfaction they will receive through freedom from breakdowns, availability of spare parts and hassle-free service. Reliability of products and services provides an important benefit for which customers will pay. Thus a company with an edge on service and reliability will be doubly rewarded through prices and customer loyalty.

Reactive pricing competitive strategies

Many marketing textbooks explain the options for price strategies and the relationship between pricing and the marketing mix in a way which assumes that managers are in control of the market. Much is made of proactive strategies and options. Such an approach, whilst demonstrating the versatility of the marketing mix, tends to emphasise attack rather than defence. Yet if there is anything more apparent for managers in the late 1980s and 1990s it is that defensive pricing strategies are likely to be needed.

In this section we will aim to discuss the basic reactive pricing strategies which can be used in defence of market position.

One of the most common reactions to a major competitor pricing threat is to do nothing and wait and see what happens. Despite the rushing around and endless debates, managers make the fatal mistake of doing nothing. The most common error of assumption is that they wish to do nothing which will cause a downward price spiral in the market. Firms will tend to follow each other's prices. An oligopoly holds good until a firm disrupts the pricing structure by moving prices downwards. Other firms may then move their prices downwards in line with the maverick competitor. Such movements will occur until weaker companies can no longer support costs. However the impact of a pricing attack by a key contender in the market is more likely to upset the 'pricing psychology' of the market before any clear change in market price occurs.

To do nothing therefore has two dangers. The psychology of the market without firm leadership will revert to pricing anarchy; and the attacking company will absorb market share initially at least from the demise of the weaker contenders in the market thus reinforcing its competitive position.

It also has to be remembered that very often it may take time before the loss of a competitive pricing position begins to affect revenue. Managers may persist in holding their pricing position as long as they can, often simply to complete their current budget obligations!

The role of price leader

The role of price leader should be to attempt to restore the psychological position of the market with utmost speed before anarchy prevails. The price leader should target a lower point on the pricing scale behind which to defend the market price. (This may not have to be much lower than its current market price.)

The market leader starts off in the fray with a number of strengths. These relate to its customer loyalty and reputation, trade support and its experience in the market.

Len Hardy, ex-chairman of Lever Brothers, emphasises the role of a company which holds a leadership position with its brands.

A leader must enforce market discipline, must be ruthless in dealing with *any* competitive challenge. If you make a price move and a competitor undercuts it, then he should be shown that this action has been noticed and will be punished. If he is not punished he will repeat the move – and soon your leadership will be eroded.

Any strategy which is based on blindly holding onto present revenue targets through trying to hold up prices or cutting operational costs will in the short term waste strengths and miss opportunities.

The defensive strategy, therefore, should be based on three basic criteria:

- restoring confidence;
- utilising company strengths; and
- determining the true nature of the competitor threat and respond.

Restore confidence

Be seen to be making a firm response, for example by increasing promotional activity and by such activities as 'hit and run' price promotions.

Utilise company strengths

Reinforce service levels, increase sales force activities, hold and expand distribution etc.

Determine the true nature of the competitor threat

Use research and information-gathering by marketing and sales person-nel to find out whether *price* is the only competitive offering or whether it is reinforcing product, service or promotional superiority. Responses to the price assault alone are easier to deal with than a combination of other competitive advantages. From a strong market base a company can sustain countermeasures through price discounting, increased promo-tional activity and improving service levels.

Price followers

Compared to the price leader price followers are doubly disadvantaged by the entry of a low-priced competitor. They have little positive influence over the market's pricing psychology and they are most likely to become victims of both the new entrant's activities and those of the leader's response.

They are, in effect, between hammer and anvil. Their immediate reaction, therefore, may determine their longer-term viability as contenders in the market. Any move they make to encourage reactive price reductions will exacerbate the overall pricing psychology of the market, leading ultimately to the collapse of prices to around the new entrant's level.

The follower has three choices:

- act in concert with the leader;
- act in concert with the aggressor; or
- find a defendable niche.

Acting in concert with the leader

This implies following the leader's strategies of increasing promotion and using price promotions. The effect of the whole market responding in apparent concert will make the competitor's life difficult and lengthen the time the competitor will have to sustain activity to secure a footing in the market. (Such strategies cannot, however, be done in collusion with other companies without breaking national and EC anti-trust regulations.)

Acting in concert with the aggressor

This means focusing response on the leader. Where a leader has a large market share, is inflexible and complacent, following the aggressor may lead to the leader's market share being divided up between those following the aggressor. Once a leader has squandered its strengths and lost market share it will lose both cost advantages and customer loyalty.

Finding a defendable niche

This allows a follower to escape from the situation of not being able to sustain a prolonged price war. Whilst the leader and larger competitors may yield market share to an aggressor, too often the smaller players are displaced. The distribution channels alone will often delist or disregard smaller companies in favour of a new aggressive entrant. The strategy of finding a defendable niche therefore may be imperative for survival.

Discouraging price competition

Discouraging competition by pre-emptive defence to pricing competition is a typical Japanese strategy. For example, Casio introduced a thin calculator and, rather than hold onto a price premium until competitors attacked the market, they reduced price and introduced a new model. This strategy provided neither a product nor a price target for competition.

The need to be continually aware of competition threats and constantly seek out weaknesses in the marketing mix are axiomatic. Yet all too often companies fail to identify their weaknesses and are consequently overtaken by events.

Pre-emptive strategies involve discouraging competition by attention to the following areas:

- cost-competitiveness;
- product competitiveness;
- promotional strengths;
- distribution dominance; and
- service levels.

In other words to focus on their competitive advantages. (See Chapter 3.)

Premium price positions

It is a fact of life that companies which have striven for tenure of premium price position tend to hold on to them and are less vulnerable to price competition. Premium price positions are created at the end of the market where price comparisons are not primary points of difference for products which customers are seeking. Examples are Concorde, Mercedes, Joy Perfume and Rolex. All operate in markets in which price competition prevails but have aimed products, promotion and high-quality service at those segments of the market where price is not so important in customer choice.

Unfair competition regulations

Few countries do not have regulations which prevent, limit or prohibit any activities adopted by companies to set prices unfairly. Unfair pricing can be considered from two points of view. Firstly, setting prices below a realistic economic level thus damaging local industry in the importing country (*dumping*). Secondly, continuing, through agreements or concerted practices, to effect higher prices through the prevention, restriction or distortion of competition (trusts).

Anti-dumping Regulations

The prevention of dumping is controlled under the General Agreement on Tariffs and Trade (GATT). Consumers in importing countries chiefly benefit from cheaply priced foreign products, yet governments may well attempt to restrict the entry of such products where they are seen as being unfair competition to local industries. Governments may impose a 'dumping duty'.

Determining a definition for dumping is, however, difficult. Dumping implies that products are exported at prices set somewhat below the economic cost of production. However, from the point of view of legal argument, such a definition is inadequate. This is because it is difficult to calculate an exporter's costs.

Article VI of GATT deals with anti-dumping legislation. The definition of dumping focuses on the concept of 'normal value'.

If the price of the product exported from one country to another is less than the comparable price, in the ordinary course of trade, for the like product when destined for consumption in the exporting country; or, in the absence of such domestic price is less than either the highest comparable price for the like product for export to any third country in the ordinary course of trade, or the cost of production of the product in the country of origin plus reasonable addition for setting cost and profit.

However, GATT is still a poor response to dumping. Whilst it provides a legal framework for complaint, drawn-out procedures and the rights of exporters to be heard make it difficult to deter short-term dumpers. Many companies frequently breach anti-dumping controls on the basis of seizing short-term opportunities to break into markets. However, some countries deal with such breaches by invoking temporary anti-dumping duty rates (eg UK).

Restrictive practices – anti-trust legislation

Whilst dumping regulations protect companies, anti-trust legislation protects consumers from manipulation of competition to effect high prices in a market. EC articles, 85, 86 can be evoked where trading practices affect trade between member states but their jurisdiction is limited to the EC.

Article 85

This order attacks activities which are deemed to prevent, restrict or distort competition. Thus price fixing, market sharing, restrictions on output and discriminatory terms of supply contravene the terms of Article 85.

However, exemptions are allowed where the Commission can be convinced that agreements and practices are in the best interest of the community, ie practices which improve production, distribution, promote technical and economic production. The Commission may also grant exemptions in other cases under the Article.

Article 86

The purpose of Article 86 is to prohibit improper advantage being taken by companies occupying a dominant position within the EC. This Article prohibits discriminatory, or inequitable selling or purchase prices or terms in respect of equivalent supplies.

Transfer pricing

Transfer prices are those charged between profit centres of a single company. These include charges for products from the centre to subsidiaries or vice versa and between subsidiaries themselves.

The essential aim of transfer prices is to ensure that there is no loss of value incurred when products are transferred between profit centres. Thus production costs, administrative costs, shipping and insurance costs are passed on from one to another. However, the complexities of intra-company trading across national frontiers invoke a host of considerations.

Because different countries have different duty rates and levels of corporation tax, varying policies on dividend remittances and varying inflation and interest rates, corporate accountants need to seek an optimum transfer-pricing strategy which on the one hand maximises the efficiency of the internal value-added system and yet on the other continues to reduce the adverse impact of duty, tax, dividend remittance and restrictions and inflation on the business as a whole.

Forgetting for a moment the watchful eye of governments, it may be prudent to transfer goods at low prices to markets demanding high duty so that (where *ad valorem* duty rates apply) the cost of importing is reduced. Where there are difficulties or penalties involved in remitting profits, high-transfer prices may be charged thus reducing revenue earned in the country by taking it at the point of manufacture. The options then are legion, depending upon the circumstances in each market and the overall policy of each individual company.

Governments, however, do not sit by and watch profits and funds being manipulated by transfer prices. Governments are motivated to act against companies in their countries which continue to reduce collective tax revenue or export profits as a means of avoiding remittance controls. Government controls – or the threat of them – limit the extent to which transfer prices can be manipulated.

11

International Advertising Policies

Advertising plays a vital role in business development, and appropriations represent a sizeable proportion of marketing funds yet it is a fact appreciated by all marketing managers that the level of investment in an effective advertising programme can be little different from that spent upon an ineffective one. There is, however, no comparison between the results achieved. Thus the question of how advertising should be used internationally has commanded considerable debate for the best part of three decades.

The elements of cost and risk demand of managers to look into ways in which funds can be economically deployed to achieve the objectives they set for product and market development. Through international advertising management a company seeks to control geographically-dispersed marketing activities to find the best ways of spending advertising monies as economically as possible. Yet despite the experience, money, time and attention of large international advertisers more attempts to internationalise advertising fail than succeed.

In building a global foundation for the international business we need to revisit the principal issues which influence advertising decisions and then examine the options open to managers.

Advertising in the international marketing mix

In examining the role which advertising plays in the international marketing mix we have to look at it both in terms of global objectives and in its role at local market level. Advertising, it must be remembered, is a method of communicating messages. In a diverse world, the methods of communication and even the messages themselves must vary considerably depending upon the structure of the organisation, its products, and the characteristics of individual markets in which it operates. Therefore, managers should thoroughly examine product–market relationships to establish exactly what advertising missions are to achieve.

We should therefore look at the following issues:

The role advertising will play

Demand-pull

Advertising used to pre-sell mass-market fast-moving consumer products (fmcg) will play a major role in influencing consumer demand. In this respect advertising will have to create considerable *demand-pull* from consumers. Thus both expenditure and risks will be high and this will demand considerable management input in ensuring that funds spent result in the achievement of sufficient market share to ensure that revenue objectives are achieved.

Where advertising is used to create demand-pull marketing, activities will have to be concentrated around the maintenance of adequate distribution to ensure that the pull is worked to maximum effect.

Direct response – Demand-push

Where advertising is used to create enquiries and leads for direct selling activities it takes on much more of push emphasis. Here advertising will demand of management fine targeting of audiences and considerable innovation in developing advertising techniques to stimulate response. Marketing activities will have to be concentrated on following up leads and servicing response.

Sales Support

In a sales-supporting role advertising is used to:

- add credibility to the selling proposition by making a public commitment to it through media advertising;
- remind buyers and users of the product and provide supporting information to reinforce selling activities; and
- add quality to the product image through the way it is presented – a feature of pharmaceutical advertising.

Managers using advertising in these roles will need to plan advertising activities around the selling programme, eg launching campaigns for products to coincide with a major sales programme or supporting demand for products during periods when they are not featured in sales activities.

Reinforcing company image-building

An increasing role of advertising is in reinforcing company image. This can be an important role where a high reliance on the company is important in differentiating the products it sells. Airline advertising is an example. Seats on competitive routes present a choice for consumers based upon their perceptions of the airline rather than anything more tangible. Other examples are found in the marketing of hotels, stores, courier services and car-hire organisations offering services difficult for the consumer to distinguish between.

It has to be emphasised that services have to live up to the image packaging created through advertising. Management, therefore, has to concentrate on achieving the service level promoted as well as spending considerable time and investment in packaging every aspect of the company – from its letter-headings to livery, staff uniforms to showrooms etc to project its image to the user or consumer. Furthermore, motivation and training staff to meet customer-care expectations must be rigorously enforced.

Also, companies involved in high technology, such as electronics firms, defence systems, chemical and pharmaceutical discovery and the like, need to reinforce their credibility to make their innovations acceptable. For example, should a small unknown pharmaceutical company discover a new drug it will find it a lot harder to establish credibility for the drug than if a major name were to do so. Management needs to market its company image through its product successes and innovations. Both product and corporate advertising need to be linked, as company image will be created through product success.

Furthermore, in both types of company mentioned above managers need to realise that they are appealing to an international audience and therefore advertising should reflect this.

Standardisation of creative policies

Having looked at the different roles which advertising might play it is incumbent upon us to discuss the relative merits of transnational standardisation of advertising. Much is made of this argument particularly where high costs and risks are involved.

When advertising is used specifically in the push role or in support of selling activity, the nature of the product and the complexity of selling programmes may exclude these roles from the standardisation argument. Yet in advertising used in pre-selling internationally distributed fmcg and in promoting a company image arguments for and against standardisation become important.

Opinion is divided on the philosophy of standardising advertising. In the 1950s advertising professionals were urging clients to delegate the preparation of campaigns to local agencies. A decade later this view was challenged. Eric Elinder, for example, as head of a Swedish agency wrote 'Why should three artists in three different countries sit drawing the same electric iron and three copywriters write about what is largely the same copy for the iron?' Elinder was emphasising the concentration of top talent at the centre to produce an international campaign. Twenty-five years later the argument still prevails.

For the product sold in a number of countries and, more importantly, for products which are global or destined to be so, the alternative options which can be evaluated are to:

- produce specific advertising for specific markets;

- standardise world-wide with minimal changes to copy and presentation; and

- adapt campaigns in terms of copy and presentation to meet individual market needs.

Produce local advertising specifically for each market

Many companies advertise their products in different ways in different markets.

- Product usage, presentation and consumer perceptions are different in each market (for example coffee).

- Companies simply do not have the organisation and structures which would make an international approach to advertising a feasible option.

- Company philosophy may be such that in pursuing high local accountability all advertising decisions should be made by local management.

- There may be no common approach by individual governments in legislation covering specific types of products, eg pharmaceuticals, alcohol and tobacco, thus necessitating a market-by-market approach to meet local legal conditions.
- Availability or non-availability of mainstream media may restrict the adaptation of otherwise-international campaigns in certain markets.

However, the following may not be considered as responsible approaches.

- Internecine relationships between local management and central staff which compromise the successful internationalising of the advertising mission.
- A lack of control over international operations stemming from a poor awareness by management of the benefits of the internationalisation of advertising.
- Inability of management to co-ordinate the international marketing function of a business.
- The dominance of individual local managers who are unhelpful and too inflexible to evaluate the benefits of any advertising strategy option other than those which they recommend. (Such managers tend to be successful in their local markets. Consequently they are not pushed by central management to look at organisational points of view for fear of demotivating or losing them.)

Advantages of the decentralisation option in international advertising however are that campaigns are market-specific and finely tuned to local conditions. In highly accountable management systems, local managers have complete control over all aspects of the marketing mix.

Organisational economies may also be drawn from having a few managers at central office co-ordinating the function. Decentralisation allows a great number of advertising approaches to be created offering opportunities for cross-pollinisation of ideas.

The disadvantages of the purely local approach are quite numerous.

- The global attack, particularly in regard to international competition, may be reduced due to a lack of cohesiveness and the varying effectiveness, quality and standards of advertising executions around the company's markets.

- Large numbers of central managers may be required to approve each local execution where high local accountability is not a company's management practice.

- There is no international identity for a product, thus losing transnational opportunities from migrant and tourist consumers. (This point, however, is frequently over-emphasised as a benefit for international standardisation of advertising.)

- There may be a loss in economies in such areas as production of advertising materials, creative work and the need to employ large marketing departments in each market.

- A lack of cohesive policy and co-ordination of the advertising mission may reflect inadequacies in a company's overall approach to its international markets.

- Companies may be exposed to criticism regarding ethics, codes of practice and legal problems either within each market or, more likely, in its domestic market. (For example, the criticism levelled at certain baby-food manufacturers for their activities in lesser developed countries, the backlash of which invoked controls on the promotion of certain types of baby food in Europe.)

- There are also probabilities that confusion may be created in the consumer's mind where different advertising executions in adjacent countries lead to consumers seeing or hearing different campaigns for the same product (eg German and Italian advertising impacting on Switzerland and Austria, and French and Dutch advertising impacting on Belgium).

Standardise world-wide with minimal changes to copy and presentation

Here the international advertiser seeks to present a standardised campaign throughout the company's markets. Adaptations are minimal. Obviously interpretations need to reflect racial and cultural issues as well as meeting legal and voluntary codes of practice in each territory.

The advantages of this approach are:

- using internationally proven campaigns which are likely to increase the success potential of each local campaign (ie successful campaigns are transferred from one country to the next);

- the competitive position against other international products formed on a global basis;

- there is a universal quality standard in creative presentation, message and copy;

- there are a number of opportunities to save costs, particularly in producing commercials, press advertisements and point-of-sale material;

- central co-ordination of the global advertising attack becomes feasible; and

- less local origination of advertising obviates the need for expensive marketing people, thus personnel resources can be focused on the selling mission.

There are also disadvantages to the standardised approach.

- Products may be at an earlier or later stage in their life-cycle in different markets. This makes it difficult to find a creative approach capable of meeting varying advertising objectives in each different market. These are particularly emphasised where a product is being introduced in some markets and where at the same time it is mature, fighting to retain share in others. This does not, however, preclude managers from standardising at each stage of the brand's development, eg a common launch programme, and an evolving sequence of campaigns as the product matures as was achieved by Boots' launch of Nurofen (Nerofen) in the UK and northern Europe between 1984 and 1987.

- The danger that advertising fails to work effectively in some markets may lead to under-exploitation of demand. It is often difficult to transfer the exact meaning and atmosphere of advertising from one country to another.

- Inflexibility and a lack of fine tuning of campaigns may lead to weaknesses in defending a product against competition particularly where the product's competitors are not universal.

- Local managers may become dispirited by what they see as central headquarters' domination of marketing leaving them with a feeling that they cannot control their marketing attack.

- Changes in direction may be difficult to perform as they will involve steering brand-positioning the same way in all markets together. Even changes to campaigns may be extremely difficult to make given that such changes will have to be acceptable to every market.

- Cost savings for promotional material may be wiped out by the need for local language adaptation in media and language changes.

- Media availability is very different from market to market, hence advertising skewed towards say, television, transposes badly to press in West Germany or Sweden.

A standardised approach needs a universal product meeting similar needs occupying similar segments in key markets, eg Marlboro, Levi, Coke, Strepsils. Also essential is international competitors occupying universal competitive positions and having similar market share in key markets.

The international marketing organisation has to be matched to manage the marketing programme and advertising has to be based upon the global market and not simply transferred from what does well in the domestic market. The UK, for example, is very untypical a market within Europe.

Adapted campaigns

By tailoring a general concept to each market and making adaptations to meet local conditions especially in terms of presentation and competitive positioning, the marketing attack can become considerably sharper.

The way in which this can be done most effectively is described by James Killough in an article he wrote for the *Harvard Business Review*. Although this was written back in 1978 it still holds good today. James Killough breaks down advertising into two essential elements – the buying proposal and the creative presentation.

'I call the first element the buying proposal of the seller's product or service judged by him to be most persuasive and relevant to the potential buyer.' In the context of an advertisement, the buying proposal is what one says. It is the content not the form. All the other components which do not belong to the buying proposal are concerned with the method of communication: in other words the presentation. 'This starts with the headline idea (eg Esso puts a tiger in your tank) and all the visual and verbal elements which surround that central statement.'

Buying proposals and creative presentations are distinct from each other but not independent. James Killough postulates that buying proposals generally have a good chance of acceptance across large geographic areas. However, creative presentations do not. Table 11.1 shows examples of the differences between advertising propositions and presentations as described by James Killough.

Table 11.1 Differences between advertising proposition and presentation

Product category	Buying proposal	Creative presentation
Leisure-time driving	Off-the-road technology	Jeep's 'We wrote the book on 4-wheel drive'
Toothpaste	Cosmetic benefits	Colgate's 'Ring of confidence'
Bank trust department	Conservative management	Chase Manhattan's 'Nest egg'
Laundry detergents	Heavy-duty cleaning	Procter & Gamble's 'Tide gets out the dirt kids get into'
Airline travel	In-flight service quality	British Caledonian's 'The airline other airlines hate'

If a consumer target can be identified as showing a similar set of needs and interests to those in established markets, then the chances of successfully adapting the buying proposal are favourable. Conversely, if transnational profiles are very dissimilar, the chances of successful adaptation are considerably reduced. The trend towards similarities in consumer segments, particularly in metropolitan areas, is significant even to the extent that transnationally metropolitan areas are showing more similarities than urban and rural areas within national boundaries.

The reasons for this are the similarities in city infrastructures, social pressures, international films, TV programmes and journals, plus a common flow of communications through news media. Further, the trend towards regional integration in, say, the European Common Market, parts of Africa and South East Asia, as well as in the Middle East, have led more and more to cultural interplay both within regions and without.

Primary benefits

In producing a common buying proposal, therefore, we are looking for common expectations in transnational segments, where target audiences are similar. High-technology and industrial products frequently meet similar target audience because their needs are highly specialised. The influence of Western and particularly North-American culture through films, literature and direct influence through tourism, have led to superimposed norms on other cultures. The world strategies of Stuyvesant, Levi Jeans and Coca Cola have succeeded in universally selling Westernised American Culture.

Lufthansa Airlines maintained a universal theme of punctuality for two decades and 'Barbie Doll' has a broad scope of costume changes to meet every little girl's breadth of imagination. In all these examples we are concerned with the universality of primary benefits upon which the buying proposal can be based. There are, however, dangers in assuming a commonality in consumer perceptions of primary benefits. Bovril, for instance, is perceived by the Chinese as a health drink whereas in Britain it is perceived as a nourishing food to replace lost energy. Sales of cavity-reducing fluoride toothpaste are high in countries where there is an awareness of the benefits of healthy teeth. Yet, in some areas of Britain and French areas of Canada the principal reason for purchasing dental creams is breath control, hence the primary benefit of fluoride toothpaste is limited. In cigarette marketing, a universal trend has been to market 'low tar' except in Germany where low nicotine has become the trend.

James Killough describes a further set of qualitative factors which determine the target audience's 'frame of mind' and which go beyond determining the primary benefit. Here the buying proposal has to check out with three self-explanatory reference points – traditional beliefs, contemporary behaviour and product familiarity.

When buying proposal cannot be transferred

There are two situations under which it becomes difficult to transfer a buying proposal and these are:

- when values are highly personalised; and
- when products and services truly have independent appeals.

In the former, food is an example. It seems that consumers are difficult to segment on taste and perceptions of nutritional values. Even in Europe, for example, studies of the uses and attitudes to soup show broad differences between France, Germany, The Netherlands and the UK.

In the latter, James Killough cites an example of the advertising-supported programme for commemorative coins for the Royal Canadian Mint, where two clear buying motivations became apparent. The product had an appeal to investors on the one hand, yet on the other, it appealed to the seeker of intrinsic value. It was not practical to put both motivations together and as a result different buying proposals were created to reach each important consumer group.

Creative presentation

The trend since the 1950s away from universal creative presentations has, to a great extent, mirrored two changes in consumer behaviour. Firstly, advertising has become more sophisticated, and possibly even more creative, in its expression and consequently the need to reflect consumer expectations more accurately is important. Secondly, consumers are becoming more conscious of their own identities. In the 1950s much of Europe and the Far East were desolate. After 30 years of rebuilding, the populations have become culturally more nationalistic: General Motors, for example, used an advertisement in Germany depicting a blond with big diamond earrings and a backless dress entering an Opal Diplomat following a successful creative presentation in the USA. Research showed the image to be too frivolous so GM changed the model to a late middle aged woman in a coat to give the solid and dignified image demanded by the German market.

Legal barriers

It is a fact of life that what is permitted in one country may not be allowed in another. In Germany, for example, there are strict rules on truth advertising which rule out even mild attempts at puffery. The law there is backed up by heavy penalties. There are also rules covering advertising to specific audiences, such as children, and this applies to Canada and the USA. There are less obvious rules that may prevent its message in certain media, for example sanitary protection has only recently been permitted on television, or rules which prevent advertisers specifying the time an advertisement will appear on radio or TV.

Cultural barriers

There are not only a number of cultural taboos such as those associated with religion, sex and the role of women but also a number associated with habits and lifestyle. Nestlé, for example, found great difficulty in the early years of marketing instant coffee in the UK because the product and advertising were insufficiently addressing UK consumer needs. Alcoholic drinks manufacturers have found difficulty penetrating the British market where people go out for a drink rather than consume at home.

Communication barriers

There are problems always in communicating ideas transnationally even from one English speaking country to another or one French speaking country to another. The problems stem not only from translating words but in the whole business of translating the idea intact. An advertising image often fails in its transportation either because the idea cannot be transferred or because the idea itself is meaningless in another culture, such as connections about English cricket in some cultures or baseball in others.

Another factor, of course, is literacy. Whereas most advertisers have now got over the idea that foreign nationals are just as literate as themselves, we do have to face the fact that in many developing countries general literacy is low, which obviously limits the amount of explanation in advertising.

Aspects of presentation concerning humour, puns and animation have to be carefully considered. They are used on the assumption of a general reaction to an exaggeration of some kind. 'In the case of animation, in fact, there has to be an ability to distinguish fantasy from reality. Some cultures are too literal-minded to routinely make these distinctions. Even in his hey-day the friendly Esso Tiger was regarded with some scepticism by the Swedes . . .'

Occupied positions

Ford in Europe used 'safety engineering' successfully in many countries in the 1970s but were unable to do so in Sweden because this position was occupied by Volvo. Here, then, is another problem in producing an international creative presentation. Research and observation must be used to ensure that positioning is centred in a gap not already filled by another product's advertising.

National identity

There is, too, the question of the nationality of the product being advertised. Should companies, for example, emphasise the pedigree of their products or create a locally-made image, that of being non-foreign. Some countries tend to carry images of higher quality and prestige than do others. Studies in the USA and also in Central America indicate that products from developed countries are more highly acceptable than those from the lesser developed countries.

Research also shows that among specific products, countries of origin are all important. The creative presentation, therefore, has to overcome the problems of identifying the product's source of origin if this is perceived to be beneficial in the market, or avoiding the issue where it is not. For example, Marathon Oil made a point of stressing its US association in Italy where the American high technology image is beneficial, but in Germany Marathon avoids the issue of its American parentage because of the German concern over the US control in the German energy industry. IBM attempts to create an image of Britishness and Germanness in its European markets.

Problems of transferring finished advertising

There are pitfalls in this area which can completely spoil what might otherwise be an effective piece of advertising. Variations in print quality, transfers of film on to video, language dubbing and so on can adversely affect the actual execution of a campaign. Attempts using international-ised models so often come unstuck. One British food company made television commercials using Chinese models in Singapore. These were not so well received in Hong Kong because there the models were seen as too dark in complexion. In Malaysia the films were not used because they were considered by the censors as not being culturally representative.

Unfortunately, many bad executions of otherwise good campaigns appear on the market to the detriment of products being advertised often before executives realise what is happening and precious appropriations are used up.

Market orientation and economics

In attempting to bring some direction back to the argument for common or adapted advertising policies, two key considerations need to be re-emphasised. Firstly, we are concerned with the product being marketed and secondly, with its place in the market. We have seen examples of how buying proposals can become transnational, and also the limitations imposed upon creative treatments. It is important to look at international advertising policies, not from the position of a company-wide policy to standardise or not to standardise, but to *express the policy as a product policy*. A company emphasis is too blunt.

The nature and size of the product is the most important factor in deciding whether or not it is practical to employ a common, transnational advertising programme or whether the programme needs to be adapted on an individual or regional basis. Coca Cola is one of the best examples of international standardised advertising but it has to be remembered that Coke is low priced and appeals to a basic biological need – thirst – and that its potential market embraces a large number of consumers wherever it is introduced in the world. (Yet their major rivals, Pepsi, have gradually moved away from highly centralised advertising.)

Thus for companies operating with a number of brands in a number of markets there is a danger that mangement philosophy towards advertising will be applied too generally to all of the company's products and markets. However, if each product is taken on its own merits, those which might benefit from an international advertising approach should be treated as such, and those for which such an approach is inappropriate must be subject to a local advertising approach.

The option for international advertising should then be evaluated on a product-by-market basis excluding any market for which the option would be unsuitable. Such an approach would have clear advantages through exploiting the strengths of the international option whilst excluding it where it does not make sense. Products suitable for a local approach should be treated that way with local management entirely accountable for advertising activity.

The decision regarding each product market relationship should, however, be thoroughly and rigorously evaluated. When Nurofen was launched in Europe, it seemed highly suitable for a standardised campaign adapted to meet local regulatory and media constraints. In the UK, Ireland, Belgium and Finland (the first batch of countries to receive the product) the advertising campaign was fairly uniform. The Netherlands, however, were seen to have some differences and an alternative campaign was used. The former countries were performing substantially better than the Netherlands twelve months after launch and in the face of a competitive threat the campaign was switched to conform with the other early launches in Europe. This action made a major change for the better in the fortunes of Nurofen (Nerofen) in the Netherlands.

It is likely that companies with established product portfolios will have a number of options working at the same time in their international operations. We have already pointed out in this book that the founding of global competitiveness will be based upon each company creating a significant share of its business through an international product strategy. Part of this strategy, however, will involve ensuring that local activities are not compromised by too great a desire to control advertising too rigidly from the centre.

12

Media Policies for International Products

One of the problems associated with internationalising advertising is that advertising media structures are so varied in the markets around the world. Few countries have similar media structures thus making it exceedingly difficult to set international media policies for individual brands. This chapter discusses the key issues affecting media decisions in the context of international advertising programmes.

Media structures

By taking a single market and mapping its media structure it is possible to build up a picture of media availability from which media planning options can be determined. However, this process becomes very complex when the options in each country differ so greatly. Not only will managers find that there are considerable differences in predominant types of mainstream media and media availability between countries, there are also areas in the world where media overlap, significantly affecting the 'media map' of closely adjacent countries.

If we take continental Europe, for example, there are a number of areas where no mainstream method of communication really dominates as an effective advertising medium. At the same time there is such a considerable amount of overlapping media, that noise levels and audience viewing options make reach and frequency targets extremely difficult to achieve. Add to these the complexities, differences in cultural attitudes to information sources, and the divergent nature of distribution channel structures, and it is a wonder that any advertising-based marketing strategy can ever be successful. For UK and US companies used to selling fast-moving consumer products with high-spend television campaigns, there comes a rude awakening when the complexities of media structures within many countries make such an approach extremely difficult.

The relative availability of media for individual product advertising is a major factor which needs to be addressed when inernationalising advertising. The diversity of options has to be fully understood if advertising is ever to reach its target audiences with sufficient weight and frequency to make a commercial impact on sales. It is a fact of life that continental European companies have a far more straightforward set of options for advertising in Britain than the British companies have on the European continent. In the UK, two television channels carry frequent advertising breaks. There are national press and magazines available, radio advertising and a well-organised poster medium. Furthermore, where television and magazine advertising in places like West Germany tends to overlap into adjacent countries (which may or may not be an advantage), there is virtually no overlapping media affecting Britain (other than to Eire).

It is critical, therefore, that international problems associated with media options are understood by managers charged with allocating funds for media expenditure. Many British managers need to break from the relative ease of making fairly uncomplicated proposals for media expenditure from clearly defined options to trying to put together complex media plans aimed at audiences which, however easy to identify, are difficult to reach. It is extremely difficult to persuade otherwise-good UK product managers that they need to be far more rigorous in approving media plans when operating in markets outside the UK.

There is a need to look at media structures from different points of view, namely:

- nature of media structures in each country;
- significance of media overlapping between countries;
- legal restrictions on media use; and
- availability of media information at territory, regional and international levels.

The Nature of Media Structures

In an ideal market mainstream media, television, radio, newspapers, magazines and posters will be well organised, offering advertisers the options of media choice based on economy, effectiveness and suitability for the products advertised. The greater the degree to which any single territory meets this ideal the stronger the media structure might be considered to be. Countries may then be classified into three groups.

Strong media structures

Countries which have strong media structures favouring the advertiser are those which:

- have well-organised mainstream media, ie television, radio, press, cinema and posters;
- permit audience targets to be defined both demographically and geographically and reached using the minimum spread of different media;
- enable reach and frequency objectives to be achieved rapidly;
- present few competitive viewing, listening or reading options for the target audience;
- provide mainstream media as an information source which is believable and well regarded by the target audience;
- regulate to provide quality and standards of advertising but few enough restrictions not to hinder the bona fide advertiser; and
- provide adequate media information to enable buyers to spend advertising funds effectively.

The strong media structure presents the ideal for each advertiser permitting defined audiences to be easily and efficiently targeted using a limited number of media-mix options. The UK exemplifies a relatively strong media structure which allows advertisers to choose their media mix based on the aims of the creative strategy and the media through which the target audience can be reached effectively. The disadvantage of media structures providing a limited number of 'best options' however is that competitors will be using similar lines of attack. This means that competitive spend levels will often be a deciding factor in winning market share.

Diverse media structures

These are structures where there is very wide and complex range of media available, which does not allow an advertiser to select from a small number of media options to reach its target audience regardless of how easy it is to define. Also, there are considerable competitive viewing, listening and reading options which make it difficult to create an impact on audiences economically eg large number of television channels in Japan, the USA, and Italy, and the wide range of press options in other parts of Europe.

There is typically a wide variety of mainstream media available yet none predominates with sufficient weight to enable advertisers to create campaigns which have a high and rapid impact on the market. For example, in Germany and Holland, the limitations of television advertising force advertisers to select from a very wide range of magazines to create campaigns.

The diversity of media options often means that advertisers have to spend both highly and continuously just to hit reach and frequency targets. Reaching competitive spend levels becomes increasingly difficult when the availability of many competitive media waters down the impact of advertisers' spend. New products are thus severely disadvantaged against entrenched competitors who have established their positions over a number of years.

Inadequate media structures

Here we find that, regardless of any combination of media selected, campaigns fail to reach audiences effectively. This situation occurs frequently in developing countries.

Inadequate media structures occur where:

- there are too few media available through which to reach audiences;
- audiences do not have the financial means to acquire television sets, radios or even newspapers;
- there are low literacy levels making it difficult to communicate with audiences through the press;
- media information is inadequate;
- media are poorly organised;
- advertising standards are low and poorly regulated, making available media unreliable as a source of information to sceptical audiences; and
- governments control media, reducing efficiency and making them instruments of propaganda.

Here, advertisers find it difficult both to plan campaigns and allocate funds economically.

Planners face the problems of too few options combined with over-saturation of advertising in those media which do exist. Media plans may need to be reinforced with other activities including producing poster plates, point-of-sale material and running their own mobile cinemas. Unilever and BAT do this in East Africa. Advertising in territories with inadequate media structures will limit changes to product presentation and reduce options for making changes to advertisements for very long periods. Products with established positions are very difficult to displace and new entrants will often take a very long time to establish themselves. Planning, therefore will need to take a time element based on years rather than weeks or months for awareness levels for new product introductions to be achieved.

Furthermore, media planning must often be based on experience and feel rather than on media information. The choice of agency will need to take account of experience and historical success in handling media problems in territories where inadequate media structures exist. Whereas this approach may not appeal to sophisticated marketing managers, more attempts to introduce analytical targeting methods to media plans fail than succeed in developing countries.

Advertising standards and legal controls

Where advertising standards and legal controls do not exist audiences have a low propensity to accept advertising as a reliable source of information for selecting products. Therefore in most sophisti-cated environments the advertising industry has formed voluntary bodies through which standards can be set to ensure that consumers can place some reliance on information they receive through the media.

Furthermore, advertisers are conscious of the hindrances that legal controls can put in their way in both the use and selection of media. They have therefore sharpened voluntary codes of practice to head off legal controls. Voluntary and legal controls have an advantage to advertisers in reinforcing advertising credibility. Unfortunately both voluntary and legal controls are so different in each country that it makes creative and media strategies difficult to internationalise.

Media options can be limited in many ways.

- Restrictions may be placed on the use of certain media for specific products, eg the limitations placed on the use of television for tobacco and alcohol-based products in some countries.

- Restrictions are sometimes used concerning the times certain products may be advertised to avoid the child audience.

- Restrictions can cover the amount of time that can be allowed for advertising, particularly on television and radio in different countries (eg Holland and Germany with high limits on television airtime devoted to advertising).

- There may be maximum limits on the proportion of monies in relation to turnover that advertisers can spend on advertising (eg pharmaceutical advertising in the UK).

- Regulations can affect the advertising of imported products.

- Restrictions may be placed on the creative presentation of advertising, either as a general rule or specific to individual media.

The impact of controls on media selection and usage will obviously have a constraining influence on the options open to media planners for any single campaign in any single country. This will often limit the full exploitation of international advertising themes and present obstacles for managers trying to introduce advertising media policies for global application. What should be avoided, however, is the watering-down of advertising campaigns in each territory in an attempt to mount campaigns which are universally acceptable. Furthermore, attempts to impose inflexible media usage policies (eg television advertising as the major medium) where it is either unworkable or impractical demonstrates immaturity and inexperience on behalf of marketing policy makers.

Media options have to be evaluated on the basis of what is possible and practical in both an economic and executional terms. The suitability of the chosen options in relation to the advertising objectives must be considered, as must finding supporting promotional activities to complement the media mission and make up deficiencies where all practical efforts still lead to shortfalls in its effectiveness (in terms of coverage, frequency, impact and timing).

In less developed markets information is difficult to obtain outside the EC. In Kenya, for example, Research Bureau Limited has managed to carry out only two fully comprehensive media surveys in six years – due in the main to a lack of client interest. Media planning is expensive and,

where media information does not exist, the chances of optimising cost
and effectiveness in campaigns is difficult.

The chief sources of information are:

- advertising agencies themselves;
- media owners and their representatives based in foreign countries;
- research bureaux;
- company research data;
- marketing and advertising societies; and
- government licensing centres for radio and television receivers.

These six sources are self-explanatory. Their relative value to the
advertiser and media planner is dependent upon the reliability of
information given out by each source. In many of the less developed
countries where direct access to published media information is not
available, media surveys can be done by privately sponsored research and
often by consortia of companies.

Media information

Availability of media information is the obvious key to planning. In North
America, Europe and many other parts of the world research companies
provide a substantial amount of data which agencies will store on
computer. For example, many international agencies such as Saatchi and
Saatchi produce media digests each year to help their international
clients.

Examples of major research companies concerned with media data in
Europe include:

Austria	Nielson Werbeforschung
Belgium	CIM Readership Survey, Advertising Audit Service, People Meter
Denmark	Danish Circulation Control
France	IREP, SECODIP, Taril Media and Dailies, OJD, CESP, SOFRES
Italy	Auditel, ISAR
The Netherlands	Intomart, SSC Amsterdam

Spain	Repress, Nielsen, EGM, Metra-Seis TV Ratings
UK	Advertising Association, BARB, MEAL/ JICTAR/JICRAR/JICCAR/JICNAR, ABC/AGB, British Rade and Data
W Germany	Schmidt and Pohlmann Annual report, GWA IVW
Scandinavia	Media Scandinavia
Satellite	Pan European TV Audiences Research (PETAR)

Table 12.1 Distribution of advertising expenditure by media

(percentage of total)

	Total 1986 Adv Exp in US$	News-papers	Maga-zines	TV	Radio	Cinema	Outdoor/ Transport
Austria	495.7	34.4	17.1	28.4	12.2	0.7	7.0
Belgium	450.4	33.5	32.6	15.8	2.1	1.6	14.4
Denmark	651.6	72.5	23.5	0.0	0.0	1.1	2.9
Finland	991.2	75.1	10.6	11.6	0.8	0.1	1.8
France	4,425.9	20.9	38.1	18.5	8.5	1.5	12.5
Greece	156.4	14.7	25.6	52.9	6.8	n/a	n/a
Ireland	143.1	31.9	10.2	39.4	11.3	0.7	6.6
Italy	3,028.2	22.6	19.5	48.7	3.7	0.3	5.2
The Netherlands	1,452.2	55.5	20.5	8.4	2.1	0.3	13.2
Norway	628.8	81.7	15.1	0.0	0.0	1.1	2.2
Portugal	95.9	26.3	0.0[1]	54.3	13.2	n/a	6.3
Spain	2,249.2	33.6	16.8	31.6	13.0	0.7	4.4
Sweden	952.5	73.7	22.1	0.0	0.0	0.5	3.7
Switzerland	1,351.9	60.9	19.3	7.2	1.4	0.9	10.3
Turkey	178.2	33.3	0.0[1]	58.6	2.5	n/a	5.7
UK	7,506.7	41.7	19.6	32.7	1.8	0.4	3.8
W Germany	6,689.0	44.9	36.3	10.3	4.0	1.0	3.5
Europe	31,447.0	41.4	25.3	22.2	4.3	0.7	6.0
Japan	18,107.6	28.8	6.9	35.3	5.2	n/a	23.9[2]
USA	102,675.0	26.3	7.8	22.5	7.0	35.4[3]	1.0

Note: These figures have not been adjusted to account for different methods of compilation and are therefore not fully comparable.
  (1) Magazine expenditure is included with Newspapers.
  (2) Direct mail expenditure is included with Outdoor and Transport.
  (3) Cinema data is unavailable, this percentage is miscellaneous expenditure and includes direct mail and farm and business publications.
By kind permission of Saatchi and Saatchi Advertising Worldwide.

Broadcasting media in Europe

For European countries both within and outside the EC broadcast media is very restricted with the exception of Italy. Of the 14 principal European countries, four offer no national television advertising facility and three greatly restrict the amount of time available.

Table 12.1 showing the availability of television advertising in Europe's 14 principal countries clearly shows the lack of general availability of television as an advertising media when compared to the UK, Japan or the USA.

The paucity of television advertising shows the proportion of individual country national advertising expenditures towards newspapers and magazines. For example, in Italy and the UK television's share of advertising is 49 per cent and 33 per cent respectively. Yet in Western Germany and Holland, it represents approximately 10 per cent of advertising. Table 12.2 shows how advertising is shared between the media in Europe compared to Japan and the USA.

Table 12.2 Number of commercial stations – radio

Austria	2	Portugal	21
Belgium	800+	Spain	500+
Denmark	–	Sweden	–
Finland	18	Switzerland	35
France	1,000+	Turkey	10
Greece	29	UK	47
Ireland	2	W Germany	14
Italy	400+		
The Netherlands	3	USA	8,807
Norway	–	Japan	71

By kind permission of Saatchi and Saatchi Advertising Worldwide.

Radio is an important medium in some countries in Europe. France, for example, has over 1,000 commercial stations, Belgium 800, Spain 500 and Italy 400.

Pan-European satellite television

One of the most exciting media breakthroughs this decade has been the growth of satellite and cable television in Europe.

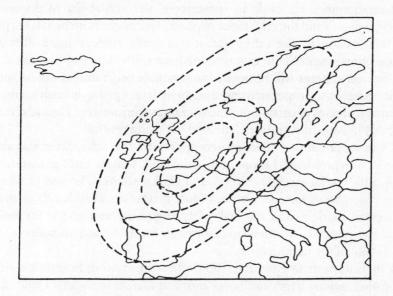

Figure 12.1 Intelsat 5 – the big media footprint on Europe satellite broadcasting

As we have already discussed, the UK is well served by three commercial television networks. The European advertiser, however, is presented with great difficulties. Much of European commercial television, where it exists at all, suffers from restricted airtime, blocked spots and myriad complicated regulations.

Covering Europe today are nearly 20 satellite stations offering choice to 21 million viewers in 8 million homes (spending an average 16 per cent of their viewing time except in Germany where it is as high as 30 per cent according to PETAR in 1987).

Sky and Super channel have the highest penetration, 92 per cent and 74 per cent respectively, of satellite television viewing homes. Both use ECS3, one of the two low-powered telecommunication satellites that covers Europe (the other being Intelsat 1).

In the next few years a number of high-power direct broadcast satellites (DBS) will offer scope for many more satellite stations giving viewers huge programme choice.

Amongst the problems that satellite stations will have are whether to gain their revenue through subscription or advertising. Whereas, previously, satellite broadcasts were connected to ground-receiving stations to channel programmes via cable to subscribers, the availability of domestic satellite dishes and the reluctance of people (particularly in the UK) to pay for connection to the cable system has made cable a more difficult proposition to sell. Yet to gain revenue from DBS stations will mean that encryption systems will be needed to scramble programmes unless subscribers have the proper viewing equipment. It may prove difficult to create meaningful sales of costly equipment amongst consumers. Thus advertising may become the preferred method of raising revenue.

Even so, satellite-channel owners appreciate that advertising may also have its own problems. Europe, unlike the USA, is made up of 20 countries with different languages, cultures and legal systems. The way in which many companies have set up individual marketing subsidiaries in their European markets and the lack of homogeneity amongst many fmcg products may make it difficult to co-ordinate funds and activities to take full advantage of the new medium.

Pan-European satellite television offers an exciting future as a new medium reaching larger audiences and clear market segments. Table 12.3 shows the availability of television advertising time in 14 European countries whereas Table 12.4 lists the major satellite stations and shows the types of programmes shown and the ownership.

Ownership comes from many national and independent television companies, together with media owners, telecommunication companies, film distributors and major financial institutions.

The development of cable and satellite capabilities has the potential to make television a truly international medium. In response, European countries have begun to create international regulations for television services.

- Ensuring programmes meet basic standards in terms of taste and decency.
- Harmonising basic rules to enable countries to remove restrictions on the reception of foreign television programmes.
- Harmonising laws on advertising and protection of children.
- Protecting copyright.
- Developing programming within Community states.
- Developing common standards for new kinds of equipment as these are developed. This includes such aspects as high-definition television.

Table 12.3 Availability of TV advertising in 14 European countries

Country	No of commercial channels	Advertising general availability	Language
Austria	1 national	20 mins per day none on Sundays	German
Belgium	none	none	French Flemish
Denmark	none	none	Danish
Finland	3 national	yes	Finnish
France	3 national	18 minutes per day	French
Greece	2 national	yes	Greek
Ireland	2 national	yes	English
Italy	3 state 350 independent	yes	Italian
The Netherlands	1 national	5 blocks between programmes	Dutch
Norway	none	none	Norwegian
Portugal	1 national 1 regional service	yes	Portuguese
Sweden	none	none	Swedish
UK	2 national 14 Regional (ITV)	yes	English
W Germany	1 national 9 regional	yes	German

Media overlapping from one country to another

Draw a media map across any of the major regions of the world and there will be evidence of considerable media overlap between countries.

Where national boundaries meet there is more often than not an overlap of media between countries. Countries receive each other's broadcast media, newspapers and magazines. For example, Hong Kong TV penetrates well into mainland China; Voice of Kenya radio and some television reaches Uganda, Tanzania and Somalia; Malays and Singaporeans listen to each other's radio and watch each other's television. There is considerable media overlap along the Canadian and US border. However, European media overlaps are probably the most complex in advanced countries.

Much is made of overlapping media particularly in classroom situations. Yet the impact of imported overlapping media has only a marginal beneficial effect on audiences. My own view from experience is

Table 12.4 Satellite and cable broadcasting companies in Europe

Station	Programme Type	Ownership	Advertising	Language
Arts Channel	Cultural-classical music drama, opera	WH Smith, TVS, John Griffiths, Commercial Union Assurance	yes	English
Cable News Network	US news and current affairs. Live broadcast via UK from USA	Turner Broadcasting International	yes	English
Childrens Channel	Childrens entertainment	British Telecom, Central TV, Thames TV, Thorn EMI	yes	English
Eins Plus	General entertaiment	ARD Germany, SRG, Switzerland	—	English Dutch German French
Film Net/ATN	Film channel	Esselk, VNU/ATN, United Dutch Film Co.	no	Dutch
Life Style Channel	Womens interests, fashion, cooking, travel, general interest	WH Smith, Yorkshire TV, TVS, DC Thompson	yes	English
MTV	Youth culture, pop videos, music, news, competitions	British Telecom, Mirror Group Newspapers, Viacom	yes	English
Musikbox	Youth culture	Kabel Media Programmescellschaft	yes	German
Premiere	Film channel	British Cable Services, British Telecom, Columbia Pictures, Home Box Office Showtime/ Movie Channel 20th Century	no	English

RAI UND	News, current affairs, sport	Radio Television Italiana	yes	Italian
RTL Plus	General entertainment—Luxembourg Channel 7	Audiofina Schlumberger Paribas, Moet-Hennessy	yes	German
SAT 1	News, current affairs, films, general entertainment	Consortium	yes	German
3 Sat	Public service channel, ZDF, ORF, SRG programmes	Zweikes Deutche Fernsehen, ORF, SRG, ZDF	yes	German
Screen Sport	European sports channel	WH Smith, ESPN, ABC, Ladbroke Group and others	yes (incl sponsorship)	English
Sky Channel	General entertainment, pop videos, sports, soap operas	News International, DC Thompson, Ladbroke Group, Ferranti, Equity & Law	yes (incl sponsorship)	English
Superchannel	Programmes from BBC and ITV, Australia, EC and USA, News from ITN	The Music Channel Ltd, Virgin Group, ITV contractors (excl TV AM and Thames)	yes	English
TV5	General service, Francophone service from BRTF, TF1, A1, FR3 SFR	TFI, Antennae 2, FR3, RBTF, SFR	no	French
Teleclub	Film channel	Rediffusion, AG	—	German
Worldnet	US news and current affairs	Reuters	—	English

that any gains accruing from overlaps are a bonus and should not be calculated into a media programme's coverage and frequency targets. The reason for this is that where advertising occurs in adjoining countries, substitution of viewing, listening and reading by nationals receiving each other's media undermines the increased frequency potential.

Evidence from Ireland, Austria and Switzerland indicates that where advertising is coming in from adjacent countries it is largely ignored unless the product is also advertised locally, thus undermining the increased coverage potential.

There is a need to harmonise creative presentation where overlaps occur to prevent confusion in the minds of potential customers.

International centralisation–decentralisation issues

Again, as with many aspects of international marketing, the question of whether to centralise or decentralise media planning is an issue for discussion. Given the local nature of mainstream media in most markets and the need to integrate selling programmes at the local level, any approach which mitigates against the achievement of an integrated promotional programme at the local level has to be weighed against arguments in favour of centralised planning.

Many attempts at running media programmes from the centre have failed. Poor co-ordination of advertising and selling programmes have resulted in lost opportunities to maximise both distribution and merchandising activities to coincide with the impact of advertising campaigns. Also, inertia created through centralised planning reduces the flexibility of changing advertising programmes in response to competitor activity, production or supply problems etc.

Media are often planned on central management's preferred ways of doing things rather than what is best for the market place. Due to distance, best media deals are lost to local advertisers, thus losing for the local company prime space and time as well as economies from bulk-buying rates and special purchase packages.

Lastly, there is no accountability for sales and revenue results between those responsible for planning and those placing the advertising.

The advantages for centring responsibility for planning and purchasing media to local management are that:

- all promotional activity can be properly and effectively integrated into an overall promotional plan;

- flexibility can be more easily achieved by providing local management with responses to competitor activities, moving or reducing advertising during stock shortages or increasing advertising to take advantage of short-run opportunities;

- local management selects media appropriate to the achievement of its advertising objectives;

- through personal communication and good knowledge, local advertising agency planners and buyers can obtain good deals from media owners and can often negotiate excellent rates and packages for their clients on the basis of their total local billings; and

- local accountability is high with local management not only responsible for spending funds but also accountable for results achieved.

The disadvantages of local responsibility for media planning and buying are:

- the quality of advertising planning is dependent upon the available expertise in local management and advertising agencies;

- unless high standards of discipline exist at the operational end of an international business, promotional activity may be prone to delays and postponements of activities, thus reducing the overall development of individual products;

- media budgets may become victims of cost-saving exercises where local operations are hard pressed to meet revenue targets – thus advertising campaigns are cancelled to the detriment of the longer-term competitive position; and

- economies from exploiting regional advertising opportunities are very often missed.

The ideal situation for media planning on an international scale is to find a method which:

- allows for a totally co-ordinated and integrated programme to be run locally, flexible enough to respond to short-term changes and developments in the local market;

- ensures that the media time and space purchased is the most appropriate for its market and is bought competitively;

- ensures responsibility for spend is reflected by accountability for the achievement of objectives and overall financial results;

- executes events effectively within the time frames planned; and

- exploits regional overlaps and regional advertising opportunities, where significant.

To achieve the ideal and find the right balance in international media management, general management must identify those areas where central policy and direction can influence local decision-making yet at the same time leave local management to shape and execute activities.

- Set overall product policies recommending media of choice in specific territories.

- Agree spend levels for each product in each territory with local management as part of the planned marketing programme.

- Agree activity programmes with local management together with a reporting system to ensure adequate execution of programmes.

- Control the effect of media overlaps through harmonising creative presentations.

Having established a co-ordinated approach to planning between the centre and local operations, local management then becomes free to run media programmes with enough local autonomy to ensure that sharp and responsive decisions can be made.

International client–agency relations

The relationship between an advertising agency and its client can be viewed as being somewhat more than merely a simple interaction between the advisor and the advised, since both parties are complex organisations in their own right. Through the joining of both organisations in a common project, there is a definite synergy created by the interaction. The sociometric overlay will of course reveal personality harmonies and discords. Functional overlays will cut across authority boundaries and the decision-making processes will confirm the intricate forces which essentially cement the contractual arrangement between the two parties.

In international marketing, agency and client relationships are far more complex than in a simple one-to-one relationship in the domestic environment. In international advertising, organisation usually calls for a number of client-and-agency relationships at both head office and in marketing territories. Thus complexity of the organisation depends greatly on the client's requirements and business philosophy, as well as on the ability of agencies to adjust to their client's needs.

Every client has a certain amount of choice and flexibility in setting up an advertising organisation – as do agencies in being flexible enough to adjust their organisation to meet client needs.

Client–agency alignments

As with every aspect of international management there is a basic choice between local autonomy and centralised control over the way advertising agencies are appointed and assigned campaigns. Structures can thus be loosely formed by local marketing operations appointing local agencies or more tightly controlled through the central appointment of an interational agency whose network of branches and associates provides the vehicle for central control for advertising activities.

Whatever the basis used, it should reflect the structures of the marketing organisation. Inevitably there will be in most companies areas where local control is preferable and others where central control is forced on management.

Local autonomy means that territorial management (be it subsidiary, distributor or the travelling export executive) have the authority to set up and control an advertising organisation and programmes independently of other territories and central office control. There are several advantages to this system.

- Management has control over its advertising structure enabling it to be highly accountable for its performance.

- Flexibility and control of advertising at market level permit management to respond rapidly to market changes.

- Local control (at least in theory) means that local management's and agency staff's combined local knowledge of the market, customers and competitors provides the basis for highly tuned campaigns.

- Local control facilitates the co-ordination of advertising, promotional and selling activities to be played on to the market in concert.

- The appointment of local agencies will be based on merit and not be merely a matter of whether they are branches or associates of an international agency.

There are, however, a number of disadvantages which may outweigh many of the operational benefits.

- Loss of control of advertising policy from the centre.

- Duplication of advertising development activities: 'the wheel may be reinvented many times'.

- A variable output of advertising in terms of standards, quality and effectiveness.

- The possibility that selection of local advertising agencies may be based on reasons other than merit (ie long-standing relationships, nepotism or favours) may lead to a lower quality of advertising than the organisation might otherwise achieve.

- The difficulties in generating the cross-fertilisation of ideas and transferring skills and standards within the global structure denies the organisation deployment of one of its key strengths.

The main reasons for local autonomy are that local organisations are marketing products which are sold only in their territories, central control has little advantage except in terms of financial control. Also, markets can have a special status in the international organisation. For example, the USA because of its size is often managed separately to other markets or a highly European-based company has a number of developing country markets for which European advertising policies do not apply.

Centralised control often favoured by organisations such as the British Tourist Authority and many industrial product suppliers such as John Deere in Europe has a number of advantages. Through controlling the global advertising agency network from central or regional centres companies have hands-on control of advertising policies at the centre. Central development of advertising provides both an opportunity to test and develop international programmes as well as reducing the duplication of effort from a number of local agencies. Quality and standards should, at least in theory, be universal.

The disadvantages are axiomatic. The distance from each centre of local activity makes it difficult to harmonise advertising with local operations; remoteness may also undermine the organisation's ability to provide finely tuned competitive advertising. Worst of all, local management's accountability for sales is not supported by ability to control and direct advertising.

Co-ordinated decentralisation through international agency alignment

The principal difference between this approach and the two preceding, according to Keegan, is that it generates more effective advertising at a lower cost. In a world which is becoming increasingly more competitive and where international standards of marketing communication are rising rapidly, 'Major international businesses are looking for a middle ground between local laissez-faire and central direction'.

In its launch of the instant camera in Europe, Kodak aligned with J Walter Thompson, and ran several similar campaigns in Europe to meet individual market nuances. But the overall campaign was centrally co-ordinated. As Kodak and JWT found, it was necessary to apply a level of local operational supervision. Where companies can align themselves to agencies either on a regional or international basis, centralised co-ordination becomes a reality. The advantage is in producing effective advertising with centralised guidance but benefiting from local agency and client inputs without really losing the economies which arise from co-ordinated budgeting and common production. Where there is a common product and a common brand image this type of approach is very practical.

The main advantages are:

- central co-ordination of advertising policy can occur between central management and the agency's central office;

- international standards can (to a certain extent) be imposed through the agency's disciplines in all the client's markets;

- the client has a certain amount of muscle with the agency because of the world-wide value of the account;

- global experience records of brand successes and failures can be maintained at the centre;

- international workshops of agency creative groups working on the same product in different markets are feasible; and
- the international standards to which client and agency work internationally will have a beneficial effect on transferring skills and affording a cross-fertilisation of ideas to company marketing management around its areas of operation.

There are, however, a number of potential disadvantages that should be looked at and pre-empted if this superior option in international client–agency relationships is adopted:

- a tendency for over-management of a brand from the two central co-ordinating functions – to the detriment of local management;
- an unnecessary over-standardisation of creative production throughout the agency network, which may stifle local contributions to advertising ideas;
- although the global billing may put a client high on the agency's head office list of accounts, it is frequently the case that at the local level the account is uneconomic and receives very modest attention by local agency management; and
- the more countries in which a brand is handled by an agency network, the more probable that there will be conflicts with competing accounts, to the detriment of both client and agency.

By and large international agency networks work best where the arrangement is based upon key company international products and *not* on total company advertising spent on a variety of brands around the world. Multinational brands usually benefit from co-ordination through an international client–agency alignment. Obviously, where there is a centrally co-ordinated export organisation, such an alignment also has a major benefit – providing that operational decisions are devolved to such an extent as to ensure that advertising can be effectively tied into local promotional and selling activities.

How agencies meet the needs of international clients

Not unnaturally, clients needing an international service will look towards agencies offering such a service. Some clients may themselves be in the process of expansion and require the services of an agency both to aid in their expansion by providing contacts and by generally assisting mission-ary executives to survey and plan market entry.

Multinational agencies certainly have the edge in these circumstances. There are occasions where a smallish client begins to look abroad and seeks its agency's assistance. Where the agency itself has yet to set up in the client's target territories (it may lack foreign experience) it may actively look for ways of servicing its clients through setting up confederation agreements with foreign agencies or looking for compatible associates. The client, of course, may get the worst of both worlds when its own lack of experience is coupled to the inexperience of its agency!

James Benson at Ogilvy and Mather in London once quoted 'flexibility in matching clients' needs' as a key to servicing and gaining business from multinational clients.

The following agency structures are the most commonly found.

Multinational agencies

Agencies which are really multinational enterprises in their own right, such as Saatchi and Saatchi, Ogilvy and Mather, and J W Thompson, are international established companies operating wholly- or partly-owned sudsidiary branches in major world centres. To the multinational agency can be added the joint ventures or partnerships.

Confederations of agencies

A confederation of agencies describes a situation where two or more agencies work together to service common clients. In many cases the ties between agencies are often very close, with strong co-ordinating managements which allow for a cross-fertilisation of ideas. There emerges a strong and effective client service. This gives the confederation the ability to mount and operate multinational advertising campaigns. In other cases, organisation and co-ordination are less effective and demand a high level of co-ordination by the client's own management.

Associate agencies

Some agencies use associates located in foreign centres to place business with local media on a share-commission basis. Such arrangements are very suitable to smaller agencies with relatively low-spending clients or where the level of business potential in a market is not large enough to justify investment in a branch. Most agencies using local associates as agents work on a reciprocal basis.

Centrally based one-office structure

Another method of operating internationally is by running a central agency which deals directly with media internationally.

This is not as difficult as it seems. In major centres such as New York and London there are central media representatives. These act as brokers for groups of publications, or act for a major media conglomerate which owns journals, newspapers, radio, television and cinema advertiser concessionaires.

This method (as used, for example, by John Deere in Europe) has a number of advantages in terms of control, and obviously offers economies over previously discussed structural methods of international management. Distance may be a problem in that the centre may be remote from its markets, and executives are not in daily touch with them.

13

Management of Logistics, Physical Distribution and Customer Service

The costs of physical distribution both to and within markets can absorb considerable amounts of revenue. Whilst such costs may have paused lately, their rise has been astronomical in recent years. The effects of the
Single Market, as we saw in Chapter 1, will probably lead to a general reduction in road and rail transport costs.

Regardless of relative costs, customers are demanding higher and higher levels of service. A survey in the United States amongst grocery buyers, for example, rated physical distribution in four out of ten key service factors they believed to be essential criteria for dealing with suppliers, as can be seen from Table 13.1 below:

Table 13.1 Rank ordering of service levels – grocery buyers USA

1. Product availability
2. Promotional activity
3. Representation
4. Order status
5. Physical distribution
6. Delivery time
7. Pricing
8. Merchandising
9. Product positioning
10. Advertising

The absence of good customer service is a major factor in undermining a company's competitive position. The consequences of poor customer service manifest themselves in:

- lost sales, missed opportunities and a lack of future support for promotional activity by affected outlets;

- providing competitors with a window of opportunity;

- creating potential de-listings by major customers;

- causing conflicts between distributors and their principals; and

- undermining company sales force morale.

The need to meet customer service criteria is paramount. Yet at the same time the aim of each manufacturer, according to Len Hardy, 'is to get his finished product, that is his brands, packed in appropriate cases or trays, from the end of his production line to the point of sale, efficiently and at as low a cost per unit as possible . . .'

The problem facing companies is how to provide a competitive level of service which supports the marketing attack whilst keeping costs to a minimum.

This problem can be approached through analysing marketing needs and cost-benefit analysis for selecting alternative physical distribution options. To this end managers need to:

- understand the distribution channel structures of subject markets;

- look for opportunities to increase volume and minimise costs;

- examine the constraints imposed on importers in subject markets; and

- evaluate opportunities for transferring production to subject markets.

Understanding distribution channel structures

It will come as no surprise to the reader that like every other single aspect of international business, distribution channel structures tend to vary between markets. They also vary between product categories. An understanding of differing distribution systems in each market is important for it will help managers to match their company's distribution system to the demands of the market.

The main factors which influence the nature of distribution systems in different markets are the types of the distribution channels themselves, and the changes from traditional (independent) systems to multiple-dominated systems.

Types of distribution channel system

Highly developed countries in the main have short distribution channel systems; in lesser developed countries longer channel systems predominate.

Channel length can be determined by the number of intermediary stages between production and the procurement of the product by the consumer. The shortest channel provides for a direct sale to the consumer from the source of production. A long channel will involve the product passing through a series of intermediaries: say, distributors, wholesalers, sub-wholesalers, retailers, bazaar traders and pedlars and so on, to the final consumer.

Where long channels exist there is often a tendency for them to be circuitous in nature. In long channels of distribution the total value of transactions can exceed the total value of sales. Empirical study has shown in Turkey, for example, that food merchandise passes through multiple channel intermediaries. 'Particularly circuitous is the wholesaling structure. This is evident when one notes that the volume of transactions value among food wholesalers far exceeds total retail food sales.' (Erdener Kaynak)

In a long-channel system goods tend to spend time in the system and there are considerable numbers of intermediate transactions taking place. In many parts of Asia investigations lead us to believe that, in the provisions market, as few as six retail outlets could be served by a single sub-wholesaler who in turn is supplied second or third hand by different levels of wholesaler on a daily replenishment basis.

A long channel is thus much less controllable for suppliers than a short channel – and the length of the stock pipeline of goods in the system is greater. This latter point is important in that during the market recessions in the early and late 1970s and early 1980s the effect of unpredicted shortenings of pipeline stocks in the face of trade liquidity problems cut many suppliers' sales by the equivalent of three months' stock cover in Asia and Africa.

Servicing long channel systems frequently calls for more sales force intervention in pushing goods through the system as well as sufficient marketing activity to pull goods through. In many parts of Africa both distributors and multinational companies employ expensive van sales forces to intervene in the system by uplifting stocks from stockists and wholesalers and redistributing them to smaller shops and market-place stalls.

Long channel systems exist where retail oligopolies do not dominate the distribution system. In traditional long channel systems, there is a high retail density (approaching market saturation) occupied by independent retailers. Such systems are prevalent in developing countries but not entirely confined to such. For example, merchandise wholesalers proliferate in both France and Italy, in much the same way as they did in Britain before 1960. In France, for example, there are upwards of 1500 local wholesalers for vehicle spare parts, of which nearly 80 per cent are small independent concerns. In Japan, families dominate distribution chains for many products.

Short-channel systems are generally more controllable in terms of product distribution despite the strength of buying oligopolies. Pipeline stocks tend to be considerably shorter. This has the advantage of keeping stocks in a better condition than in long channels and it allows promotional stocks to reach the consumer more quickly. It does mean, however, that the supplier has to provide a highly efficient distribution service.

In Britain and France, for example, major multiples demand a weekly delivery service and, with so many companies providing such a service, delivery vehicles have to queue for long periods. This leads to a need for large vehicle fleets or contracting out distribution to one of the major service organisations.

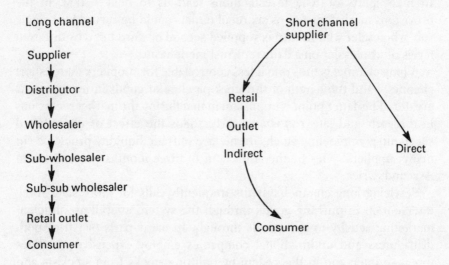

Figure 13.1 Long and short distribution channels

In most markets, long-channel and short-channel systems co-exist. There is a gradual attrition of the smaller independent sectors in Europe. The increased dominance and escalating costs of prime shopping-space rental have done a lot to push the independent out of the market in Europe. This trend is increasing in South East Asia and Japan.

Survival tactics for the independent sector are found in the establishment of buying organisations, symbol groups and franchises. There is also a developing symbiotic relationship between multiples and the independent sector. Out-of-town superstores offer concessionaries to supporting retail units within their developments. Developers of shopping malls realise the need to offer a wider range of shopping opportunities (which the independent sector can offer more easily than multiples) if they are to compete for consumer traffic and to attract 'blue chip' multiples.

Minimising costs, maximising volume

There are two main ways of minimising costs per unit shipped. First, reduce inefficiencies and uneconomic activities. Second, maximise volume shipped to each drop point. The value analysis of different options for both reducing inefficiencies and maximising loads leads to a basketful of reasons for differentiating physical distribution options both across different markets and outlet types within markets.

The costs of the different methods of distribution employed have to be weighed against their impact on the market. The relationship between volume and cost must be brought into the equation. Yet the greater the dominance a company achieves with its brands the more opportunities it has to focus on volume shipments. A dominating brand allows for large single shipments to multiples and allows the smaller independent sector to be serviced by large drops to wholesalers (dominant brands having the demand to pull product through to retail level).

This flexibility with its scope for cost-efficiency opportunities provides yet another argument against skimming strategies!

Figure 13.2 helps to explain the relationship between the scale efficiencies in production and distribution and differentiated distribution systems. Cost minimisation increases with the level of market share for three reasons:

- the higher the volume the lower the unit costs of production and (where properly managed) the lower the unit costs of shipment;

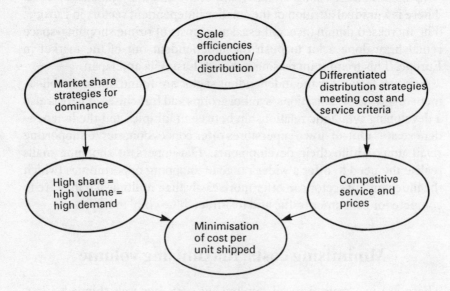

Figure 13.2 Matching scale advantages to market share strategies to achieve a competitive service while minimising costs

- with greater market share there is less need for direct service to uneconomic independent retailers (there will be greater demand-pull on wholesalers); and

- market dominance (or potential dominance) allows companies a number of different supply options including forms of local production etc which would, in critical-mass terms alone, be denied to marginal suppliers.

Furthermore, the synergy between market penetration strategies and competitive levels of cost-efficient service not only reinforces the market position but potentially releases additional revenue for reinvestment in marketing expenditure, service and R & D.

Constraints

As with all good theories there are a number of constraints thrown in the way of practical application. Yet there are very few markets in the free world, with the possible exception of some of the more badly managed

LDCs where there are no dominant brands exploiting their cost-efficiency positions.

Constraints by and large only affect companies whose management lacks a problem-solving capability or is over-constrained by inflexibility itself. The secret, therefore, in developing competitive physical distribution systems is to find ways of overcoming constraints which allow marketing objectives to be achieved profitably.

In the international context the role assigned to physical distribution strategies is often to overcome constraints which would otherwise deny a marketing opportunity to a company. It will be selection of the best option in many cases which will smooth the way for market-share strategies.

Some such constraints can be anticipated.

Barriers to trade

These constrain imported products by duty, prohibitions, quotas and other hidden barriers, either denying companies the opportunity to enter a market or distorting costs.

Availability and accessibility

In relation to types of retail outlet, there may be a constraint where companies are used to marketing their products through specific outlet types – for example, there is no equivalent to Boots in the EC outside Britain; wines and spirits are sold through state-controlled outlets in Sweden and Canada; few pharmacies in Germany have self-selection layouts etc.

Through legal controls, certain types of outlet may be inaccessible to certain types of product. Sales of over-the-counter medicines are more strongly regulated in Europe (although less so in North America) for example.

Legal constraints

Outside Western Europe and North America many countries have evolved laws to keep corporate ownership and distribution in the hands of their nationals. These are particularly prevalent in developing countries but exist in Japan and Switzerland.

Competition

Dominant competitors may exclude imported products from many types of outlet, particularly tied wholesalers and multiples.

Transport

Costs and practicalities of transport have a limiting effect on the movement of certain goods to markets any great distance from the source of production.

It is the job of management to overcome constraints which impinge on the company's ability to both enter a new market and exploit its potential competitively. What managers need to do is to analyse their markets properly and identify those success requirements needed for a competitive position to be established. Again, they need to set success-criteria objectives, and then find the best options for meeting them. All too often greater attention is paid to the promotional aspects of marketing than to the practicalities of physical distribution. Yet without a physical distribution strategy which matches both customer needs and marketing strategy requirements a company is unnecessarily constraining itself.

Options for devolving production

In Chapter 3 we looked at the different options for modes of marketing entry and organisation for international business. These need to be revisited by the reader in seeking options for overcoming physical distribution constraints as well as rationalising production options. In this section we aim to draw attention to the potential for devolving production at any of its various stages.

Reasons for devolving production

The principal reasons usually given for devolving production are to:

- overcome barriers to trade;
- reduce transport costs of either low-value items, or products for which the cost of transport would be prohibitive;
- increase competitiveness of customer service;
- spin-off production of 'specials' to their relevant markets to facilitate an economic rationalisation of production at home;
- increase production capacity generally, using the opportunity to bring production closer to major markets;
- spread production around the world to reduce exchange-rate risks;

- devolve production to low-cost markets in order to achieve cost and price competitiveness; and

- move production to centres of excellence.

The downsides to production devolution are of course numerous. The most commonly quoted (and from experience the most frequently voiced) is the loss of production at home. Loss of home production, however, is probably the weakest of all arguments set against transferring production abroad. For, in the reasons given above, not one really impinges on volume economies. Where markets are competitively inaccessible other than through some form of local production, domestic volume economies can in fact be improved by finding points in the stages of production where market accessibility becomes competitively feasible (eg production intermediates are shipped at pre-packaging or pre-assembly stage) and at which optimum value added in the production stage has been reached (eg production of intermediates or bulk product).

The closer the two points can be brought together the greater will be the cost benefit in terms of maximising both the use of production capacity and achieving market accessibility competitiveness.

By judicious cost-benefit analysis, production efficiency may be raised by spinning-off production at a point beyond which 'export specials' begin to impinge on marginal cost efficiency.

This point can be quite easily identified. It is the point in the production stage where marginal production costs begin to rise more rapidly for specials than for mainstream production. It follows, therefore, that if any loss of contribution were noticed as a result of devolving production after such careful analysis then production costing is awry. (Usually because too great a proportion of fixed costs is allocated to those products which should be correctly treated as marginal contribution.)

There are more telling downsides to transferring production.

Loss of control over quality
Of all the downsides, this is probably the one most likely seriously to injure a brand's competitive position, particularly where products enjoy a high-quality, imported image.

Risks involved in transferring technological know-how
This could provide opportunities for competitors.

Reimportation

A risk where production is transferred abroad to meet lower price criteria than at home. (Traders pick up goods at low local prices and ship them back for sale in the country of origin often picking up export rebates on the way!)

Loss of control over production logistics and administration

This may well occur, especially where production is subcontracted. This could lead to a reduced customer service and sales lost through stock-outs.

Losing the perceived quality image

Potentially a major marketing problem for high-priced, quality imported products when customers notice their familiar products are made locally. Branded imported spirits could enjoy much lower duty levels in Japan if they were produced locally – yet suppliers continue to import major brands for marketing reasons.

Other obvious risks involve those attending arrangements with third parties, political risks and potential losses should projects fail.

Devolution of production has, however, quite a considerable number of benefits. The rationale for proceeding has to be based on sound financial analysis and meeting customer-service needs. Management will often have to break down innate psychological barriers within its production functions to ensure that reasons for opposing transfer are based on sound financial arguments and not mere obduracy. At the same time, territory management holding on to production will have to be persuaded to ensure that their recommendations are based commercially on competitive advantage and meet success criteria objectives which they have identified.

Local production options

Once the need for transferring production has been identified, management has to decide which of the production options to pursue. The decision will obviously be affected by the level of volume; the stage at which production should be transferred; and the level of commitment to investment they are prepared to make.

Generally speaking there are four basic options, each calling for higher levels of production commitment and investment: contract packing, contract manufacture or assembly, joint ventures (franchises), and subsidiary production facilities.

Contract packing

Contract packing involves subcontracting the lowest value-added stage of the production process. The cost benefit is calculated on the basis of:

- savings accruing from marginal costs of production incurred in packing 'specials'; *plus*
- savings accruing from shipping bulk materials; *plus*
- duty savings where appropriate; *less*
- the price paid to the subcontractor; *plus*
- any contribution from increased sales should duty and shipment cost savings be effectively reinvested through achieving competitive price levels or increasing marketing expenditure.

It may also be necessary to take account of costs of stock held at both intermediate stages and by the subcontractor prior to it being transferred to the designated marketing organisation – if these are appreciably higher than exporting finished goods.

By subcontracting packing the company only has to concern itself with quality and standards. There is barely any financial risk, and investment commitment would usually involve little more than purchasing necessary filling or packing machinery (which could be supplied on loan). Subcontracting packaging allows for rationalisation of domestic-based packing whilst allowing the benefits of value added to the main processes to contribute to overhead recovery at home.

Contract packing facilities are not difficult to locate for most types of product and therefore there is little need to transfer production technological know-how to third parties (local distributors or government services can be employed in locating candidate packers).

Contract manufacture or assembly

Through contract manufacture or assembly marketing opportunities are made feasible by avoiding barriers to trade, overcoming transport problems or making products otherwise cost-efficient for their markets.

The cost benefits are probably more difficult to define except where the transfer of production of specials permits production rationalisation. Again, decisions relating to the point in manufacture at which production is transferred to subcontractors is important. (Both contributions to overhead recovery and minimising the technological risks are factors to be considered.)

Costs and risks involved in transferring production or assembly rise appreciably with the number of stages of production the subcontractor undertakes. Not only will the subcontractor's costs increase but the costs of capital equipment investment also rise. Furthermore, the more involved the subcontractor is in company product and production technology, the harder it is to protect them. Even so, the subcontractor undertakes most of the risks involved with providing facilities and taking on labour. In sub-contracting production, however, companies also delegate their control of standards. Quality control risks therefore increase and it will be necessary for the company to provide both rigorous controls and provide production support.

Joint ventures (franchises)

These have all the advantages of transferring production to subcontractors except that the company shares all the risks involved in financing the joint venture. The principal risk (probably greater than those which apply to subcontracting production) stems from those associated with the possible break-up of the joint venture.

Whilst the joint ventures so far discussed in this book concern themselves with marketing and joint arrangements to finance R & D, production may be involved where:

- it is used as a trade-off in financing the joint venture (ie production volume helps provide the critical mass for the joint venture);

- production forms part of the marketing logistics rationale for a joint venture;

- (as in R & D joint venture) production technology is part of the outcome of the combined approach. If one partner develops the production technology it is often logical for it to continue to produce for both parties for their respective markets. This ensures benefits from acquired experience. It negates the need to duplicate production facilities especially where the combined volume requirements of both parties provides high economies of scale.

Where the joint venture is run as a franchise the franchisee usually stumps up the investment capital in order to obtain the production and marketing end of the deal. In such cases the risks borne by the franchisor are marketing risks.

Subsidiary production company

The total devolution of production for a company's brands is a major investment decision. Reasons for such decisions, other than those which apply to previous options, are:

- to increase production capacity where logistical, financial and marketing advantages accrue as a result;
- the need to devolve production but a reluctance to trust subcontractors to maintain quality or share in knowledge, product and production technology;
- the costs and difficulties of subcontracting highly technological processes outweigh any advantages gained from subcontracting;
- the award of grants, aid and tax concessions from a host government provide major financial incentives; and
- a company may simply seek to stamp the mark of its commitment onto a territory which it sees as providing a potential opportunity (for which a reasonable financial rationale is found).

The advantages of control and ownership are supplemented with products assuming a national identity (like IBM in Germany); the local company being seen by its customers and employees as more than a marketing organisation; and having a highly flexible production facility close to its market. Furthermore, through the owning of a production company, local management have a foundation upon which to develop local R & D facilities. Whereas the corporate risks of investment, buildings, plant, facilities and employees rise considerably, these are often mitigated where good local management can reinforce corporate commitment to the market (shown by production investment) through leadership and corporate culture.

To reinforce the advantages so far listed, local production can be used in multiple sourcing as part of the global business play to reduce exchange rate risks, reduce production costs and provide centres of specialisation and excellence for production and processes.

With the devolution of production comes an increasing need for central co-ordination, planning and supervision. The chemical disaster at Bhopal alone points to the risks which companies take once they embark on the trail to transfer production abroad. Despite the risks, the transfer of production to national markets provides a formidable competitive advantage in matching resident competitors and providing superiority over those not resident. The advantages, however, are only secured where:

- the rationale for production is based on meeting marketing success requirements;
- investments are based in strategically targeted markets;
- adequate investment is made to meet market needs and match competitor advantages;
- cost-benefit analysis is carried out and involves trade-offs between production rationalisation in existing facilities and meeting market needs competitively; and
- transferred production operations are well managed, quality control is supervised and the company can provide an adequate production and technical support.

Customer service and customer care

We began this chapter by discussing physical distribution from the customer point of view and the customer will feature in this final section.

Many managers forget that customer satisfaction begins after the sales transaction has occurred. Whilst product and sales managers pore over the latest brand-barometer information many forget that these statistics reflect the buying behaviour of customers. All the statistics indicate customer-loyalty movements between a company's brands and those of its competitors. Yet it is a fact of business life that loyal customers are the most likely to provide the longer-term security for a product's franchise. Poor service in meeting customer demands (as we have already shown) or areas which follow purchase transactions are major disincentives to customer loyalty.

Customer service and customer care are vital tools of marketing. Yet so often the sales and marketing echelons have little control over them.

Given the high costs of marketing, R & D and production investment, together with their risks, corporate management must involve itself in ensuring that standards of service and customer care are matched to the success requirements of the market. They must ensure that they are competitive and supportive of the marketing attack and not a constraint to it.

Managers are so often deaf to service deficiencies abroad which they would not tolerate at home. Foreign customers will provide the foundation for global competitiveness. Yet in each national market maintaining a competitive service and customer-card edge will reinforce the global position.

14

Foreign Exchange

EC capital movements and financial services

The running of a pan European business involves the movement of funds in terms of paying for goods and services, investment and loans. The creation of the Single Market means that both corporate and private individuals need to be able to move funds around the Community unhindered. In Chapter 1, page 39, the question of capital movement and financial services showed the potential savings to the Community that the harmonisation of capital movements and the derestrictions on financial services would bring if all the measures are adopted.

In this chapter we are concerned with the issues as they affect risks and transactions. The Single European Act influences capital markets, financial services and the liberalisation of capital movements.

'During the transitional period and to the extent necessary to ensure the proper functioning of the common market, Member States shall progressively abolish between themselves all restrictions on the movement of capital belonging to persons resident in Member States and any discrimination based on the nationality or on the place of residence of the parties or on the place where such capital is invested.

For this purpose, the Council shall issue directives, acting by a qualified majority. It shall endeavour to attain the highest possible degree of liberalisation. Unanimity shall be required for measures which constitute a step back as regards the liberalisation of capital movement.' (Articles 67 and 70 of the Treaty of Rome)

A new Chapter 1 is added to Part Three of Title II of the EEC Treaty to reinforce the co-operation between members states in managing the

monetary capacity of the Community, as the extract from the Single
European Act shows:

'Sub-Section II – Monetary Capacity
Article 20

1. A new Chapter 1 shall be inserted in Part Three, Title II of the EEC
   Treaty reading as follows:
   Chapter 1
   Co-operation in economic and monetary policy (economic and
   monetary union)

Article 102a

1. In order to ensure the convergence of economic and monetary
   policies which is necessary for the further development of the
   Community, Member States shall co-operate in accordance with
   the objectives of Article 104. In so doing, they shall take account of
   the experience acquired in co-operation within the framework of
   the European Monetary System (EMS) and in developing the
   ECU, and shall respect existing powers in this field.
2. In so far as further development in the field of economic and
   monetary policy necessitates institutional changes, the provisions of
   Article 236 shall be applicable. The Monetary Committee and the
   Committee of Governors of the Central Banks shall also be
   consulted regarding institutional changes in the monetary area.
   Chapters 1, 2 and 3 shall become Chapters 2, 3 and 4 respectively.

European financial area

The achievement of a European financial area is the goal of the
Commission. The proposals put forward are:

- For a directive to extend liberalisation of all capital movements. These,
  however, are subject to safeguards which allow for temporary controls
  to be reimposed in certain specified circumstances.

- An amendment to the 1972 directive regulating international capital
  flows. The proposal will almost certainly require member states fiscal
  authorities to put certain controls into effect immediately, without

enacting measures. It also contains a clause which is a statement of intent to liberalise capital flows with countries external to the EEC.

- There is a proposal for a regulation establishing a single facility for providing medium financial support for individual Member States balance of payments.

These measures are still very much under consideration and may well be modified substantially before enactment.

The banking sector

Articles 59–62 of the EEC Treaty provide for the progressive abolition of restrictions on the provision of financial services. This, despite its costs to the Community (7 per cent of Community GDP) has been slower in progress than the lifting of barriers on goods.

The European Commission recognises that unless banking activities across the Community are co-ordinated, then the means to facilitate capital movements will not exist. The first task has been to allow banks from individual member states to establish themselves in each others territories. Britain has long permitted this which means that more than 60 per cent of banks operating in the UK are, in fact, foreign owned.

The Directive on freedom of establishment and services issued in 1977 sought to ensure that there were no restrictions that would prevent banks and other financial institutions from establishing themselves or providing services in other member states.

The First Banking Co-ordination Directive sought to secure a common system of authorisation. It outlined the basic principles that would be adopted towards achieving co-operation between member states and it was implemented in the UK though the 1979 Banking Act.

The most significant of the main proposals (according to an Ernst & Whinney report) include those in the Second Banking Co-ordination Directive, at the core of which is the single banking licence. This will permit a bank to undertake a wide range of activities throughout the Community, provided they are permitted in the bank's home country, subject to home country control – services will be exportable across frontiers more freely, branches will not need 'endowment capital', and individuals and firms will be free to open accounts throughout the EC. Harmonisation of regulations is also proposed over large exposures and, the kinds of people and institutions fit to be major shareholders.

Related proposals include those to liberalise capital movement and cross-frontier data transfer.

Particular considerations apply to the subsidiaries of banks and non-EC countries. Those already established are considered to be EC institutions and thus will benefit from the right to establish new branches and from the freedom to provide services throughout the Community. However, a prospective new entrant, by establishment or acquisition, will be permitted in an EC country only if reciprocal rights exist in its country of origin for the banks of all EC countries.

Liberalisation of capital movements

Roger Gray, writing in *Management Accounting* in May 1988, summarises the present initiative and proposals of the European Commission in response to the recognition of the need to liberalise capital movement. He points to the need for companies to prepare for the consequences of the latest communication of the Council of Ministers outlining its recommendations for the liberalisation of capital movements.

'It calls on Member States to abolish all restrictions on capital movements taking place within the Community and requires transfers to be made on the same exchange rate conditions as those in place for current transactions. The different categories of capital movement covered by the proposal include all operations necessary for the purpose of such movement; the conclusion and performance of the transaction and related transfers and access to all the financial techniques available on the market.

The categories covered are extensive: direct investments; operations in capital market securities; money market transactions; financial loans and credits; sureties and the performance of insurance contracts. Direct investments are perhaps the most interesting category and must be interpreted in its widest sense. It covers investments of all kinds made by natural persons or commercial, industrial or financial undertakings; those which serve to establish, or maintain, lasting and direct links between the persons providing capital and the consumer; the establishment and extension of branches or new undertakings belonging solely to the person providing the capital; the acquisition in full of existing undertakings; participation in new or existing undertakings made with a view to establishing or maintaining economic links;

long term loans made with a view to establishing or maintaining lasting economic links.

It will be some time before the proposal is adopted and implemented but, yet again, it provides an excellent example of the sort of measures that are being produced in the lead up to 1992 which will have such wide ranging consequences for companies. Planning for these cannot begin too soon.'

The benefits for companies

In Chapter 1, page 41, Table 1.1 shows the relative costs of financial services and the huge disparities between countries. The table demonstrates the range of financial services costs relative to the average of the four lowest national prices. Price Waterhouse, the organisation carrying out the research, found that bank loans to customers in the UK, France and West Germany, for example, carry more than three times the spread over money market rates than they do in Belgium. Yet, by 1992, companies will have a wide range of services and instruments to select from. The increasing proliferation of services and new entrants in the financial services sector will create greater competition and hence provide cheaper services.

Even outside the banking sector, insurance brokerage and factoring services will become more competitive. Treasury and financial managers will need to become more procurement-orientated if the benefits of the financial services are to be secured in terms of cost reduction.

The effects of risks and transactions in currencies across the Community will, however, have to be borne. Despite the growing pressure for the creation of a European Central Bank and evolution of the ECU, at least as a commercial currency, progress is very slow.

Giscard d'Estaing has advocated the creation of a joint central bank and wider use of the ECU. He has emphasised, however, that the ECU will never replace the Dollar or Yen as a reserve currency – 'We do not want the ECU to become the world's reserve currency, but Europe must be able to make its voice heard with one not eleven currencies'.

Managers need to be concerned with the risks and transactions of operating in a multi-currency environment. To prepare for international business some knowledge of the problems of foreign exchange is necessary, for the European Community and the markets in the wider world will involve foreign exchange transactions and the risks they bring to the business.

Risks and transactions

Once a company begins to operate across national boundaries, it encounters the risks and complexities of foreign exchange. Operating in the Community brings with it the need to understand foreign exchange. In this chapter we will examine the general issues of foreign-exchange risks and transactions. For not only do they apply generally to the European Community – the more a company expands into the global arena the more important many of the issues become.

Additional to all the complexities of running an international business are the risks associated with foreign exchange. Every transnational business transaction will involve at least two currencies – that of the seller and that of the buyer.

The three principal risks the international company faces are losses incurred through fluctuating currency rates; failure of the buyer to secure foreign exchange with which to pay for goods received; and defaults on payment by the importer.

The aim of this chapter is to raise the main issues surrounding transactions involving two or more currencies.

Exchange rates

An exchange rate is quite simply the number of units of one currency required to buy one unit of another. The essential, if not obvious, fact about exchange rates is that they fluctuate constantly.

Exchange rates are normally expressed in spot rates or forward rates. The spot rate is the rate which would apply for an immediate transaction. Forward rates are those quoted for future delivery.

A third category is the cross rate. This is an exchange rate calculated between two currencies when only the rate of each is known against, say, dollars or pounds. For example, in finding the rate between French francs and Italian lira, given that the rates of the franc and lira between sterling are known:

Ff   9.31 per £1 sterling

Lira 425 per £1 sterling

therefore

$$\text{Lira } 425 = \frac{\text{Lira } 45.7 \text{ per Ff}}{\text{Ff } 9.31}$$

Rates are quoted in either *direct* terms or *indirect* terms. A direct quote is the number of units of the domestic currency for one unit of a foreign currency. An indirect quote is the number of foreign units of currency for one domestic unit.

Two rates of exchange are always quoted: the *bid* rate, that is the rate at which a bank is prepared to buy, and the *offer* rate, the rate at which the bank is prepared to sell.

Many companies monitor cross rates because any significant change between countries, particularly those which are major trading partners like France and Italy, could signal major changes in prices for goods.

The forward market

By allowing forward purchases of foreign currency, buyers and sellers can reduce their risk of loss through foreign-exchange fluctuations. For example, a British company selling products to Germany using a rate of exchange of DM2.9 to the pound and offering 90-day credit would lose if the rate moved to DM3.05 on the date payment was due.

If, however, the company was able to purchase marks at 90 days at DM3.03 then the rate of exchange would be fixed for the transaction. The risks would then pass to the bank.

The difference between spot and forward rates is known as the 'spread in the forward market'. The size of the spread reflects the level of confidence within the money market to the level of fluctuation expected between any two currencies. The spread may reflect a percentage premium if it is anticipated that there will be an upward movement in the exchange rate between the currency being bought and that being sold, or a discount percentage when a downward movement is expected.

Convertibility

The 'convertibility' of a currency expresses the relative amount of ease by which a currency can be exchanged for another. The Swiss franc, the dollar, the deutschmark and the pound are truly convertible because they can be exchanged for any currency. Yet the Nigerian naira is far less convertible in that, even though exchange rates for buying are obtainable, people wishing to exchange hard currency for naira are far more difficult to find. The naira, then, has relatively poor convertibility.

Convertibility may be full or partial. Full convertibility implies that both residents and non-residents can convert any amount of a currency. Partial convertibility implies that there are restrictions on the ability of residents to convert their currency but that non-residents can convert any amount. Such a currency is said to have external convertibility.

The trend in Europe is for convertibility. Since 1958 the Nordic countries, Benelux, Austria, France, Italy, Ireland, the UK and Western Germany agreed external convertibility between their countries. Greece joined the agreement in 1959.

'Hard' currencies are those which are usually fully convertible; based on relatively strong economic performance of the issuing country; and relatively stable.

The prime currencies used in foreign transactions around the world are the US dollar, the deutschmark, Japanese yen, pound sterling, Swiss franc and the Canadian dollar.

'Soft' currencies, on the other hand, are those which are not easily convertible, because they are hampered by government controls on exchange and/or are not backed by the sort of economy which would inspire confidence in the money market.

Black markets for soft currencies often exist to enable residents to acquire hard currency. These represent a free market for a currency which is outside the control of the government and usually illegal. In Nigeria at one time it was possible to get up to five times the official rate of exchange for sterling and dollars. In Tanzania the black market for the shilling has exceeded by ten times the official rate of exchange.

European Currency Units – ECUs

The creation of the European Monetary System in 1979 was designed to facilitate trade amongst member states by minimising exchange-rate fluctuations. The ECU is the central exchange rate for the participating members of the EMS currency. Whilst pounds sterling are used in the computation, Britain is not a member of the EMS.

The EMS system works on bilateral currency rates between countries. There is, therefore, a parity rate between the Dutch guilder and French franc, and the deutschmark and Italian lira, and so on. Exchange rate fluctuations are minimised by controlling the deviations in bilateral currency rates and the central exchange rate. All participating members are permitted a 2.25 per cent fluctuation (except Italy which has 6 per cent). If currencies deviate beyond the permitted levels, central banks of the participating members are obliged to intervene to protect the integrity of the central rate.

Whilst there is no ECU printed currency in circulation, financial transactions can be carried out in ECUs. The approximate value of the ECU is about $1.2. (It has fluctuated between 1987 and 1988 by six or seven cents.)

Foreign exchange restrictions

Foreign governments of many countries, including most developing countries as well as the Eastern Bloc (as well as certain other countries for whom the rising cost of managing foreign debt and importing vital materials such as oil has limited their foreign currency reserves) have found a number of effective ways to reduce the outflows of foreign exchange.

Licensing

In order to regulate and allocate foreign exchange on a priority basis, governments, usually through their central banks, will use a system of licences. The aim of the licensing system is to act as 'test of essentiality'. Thus importers involved in acquiring raw materials, pharmaceuticals, fuel etc gain priority over those attempting to seek foreign exchange for non-essential items.

Multiple exchange rates

Governments will often establish more than one exchange rate. For example there may be an advantageous rate to a company wishing to set up a factory in a country against a punitive rate given to residents wishing to travel abroad.

Import deposits

Many governments have found that the use of import deposits, ie an amount calculated as a percentage of the FOB or CIF value of goods for which an importer wishes to use foreign exchange. Import deposits allow the central bank to test for essentiality.

Import deposits do not bear interest and as a result can drain cash away from importers, thus further reducing their propensity to accrue high stock levels of imported products. From personal experience this writer has experienced the frustrations of complying with the Nigerian central bank's procedures where deposits have been held for many months pending a foreign-exchange allocation.

Controls on amounts of foreign exchange allocated

Controls on amounts of foreign exchange allocated are more commonly applied to residents, and these may limit the amount allocated for foreign travel. Prior to the lifting of foreign-exchange restrictions in the UK, residents were allowed a maximum allowance for pleasure travel and businessmen were restricted to a daily allowance. This still applies to many LDCs today. There may also be limitations on the amounts expatriates can remit home or the amount of capital emigrants can take with them.

Compensatory trade

There are many governments who, through necessity or desire, have experimented quite successfully with trade arrangements which force either the importer or exporter to link foreign exchange allocations to compensatory inflows.

Barter is the oldest and commonest form of compensatory trade. Nigeria, for example, in its budgets for 1982 and 1983 actively encouraged barter trade for non-oil items. Indonesia bartered oil for foreign goods.

Pepsico bartered Pepsi syrup for Russian Vodka and Occidental took Russian ammonia as payment for fertiliser plants and pipelines.

'Countertrade' is another form of compensatory trade. The Indian government has used import licences for raw materials to motivate companies to undertake export of a certain proportion of their production. Spain in the past has made agreements with those acquiring companies in Spain to find a market for Spanish-made products.

Levi Strauss agreed with the Hungarian government to build them a factory to produce jeans and received payment in the form of output from the factory. Levi Strauss also undertook to supply part of their European market from the Hungarian factory whilst selling the balance in Africa.

Banks as facilitators for foreign exchange

It is banks which manage the aspects of foreign exchange in the sense that they are collectors, lenders, buyers and sellers of foreign exchange. Whilst the activities of banks and the workings of the foreign-exchange market are interesting topics, it would not be possible to cover them within the remits of this text. However, the areas of study which are relevant, are those concerned with the instruments of foreign exchange and the management of risk.

Instruments of foreign exchange

In order to facilitate the conversion and movement of currencies, banks have over the last three centuries created instruments of foreign exchange. These are common the world over – each, however, offers varying degrees of risk for the exporter.

Commercial bills of exchange

This instrument is an instruction to an importer to make payment to an exporter immediately or at a specified time in the future. Commercial bills of exchange may be '*sight drafts*', meaning that payment must be made immediately the importer is presented with the bill of exchange, or *time drafts*, allowing the importer to pay at a specified time in the future (eg 90 days, 120 days etc).

Selling bills of exchange

Selling bills of exchange to a financial institution is known as 'discounting'. Once a bill is 'accepted' the exporter can, if so desired, endorse the bill and sell it on the money market. The bill cannot be sold at its face value and is therefore acquired by the buyer at a discount. The rate of discount will be calculated by the buying institution on the level of risk that is involved and the time which will lapse between discounting and maturity. Obviously, the buying institution will need to consider the likelihood of the bill being honoured and the prevailing conditions in the money market.

Commercial bills of exchange offer no security that they will be honoured by the importer who may for one reason or another not accept the bill.

Bank drafts

The principal disadvantage that a bill of exchange has is being a demand on the importer. Bank drafts are a preferable instrument of foreign exchange because they are bills of exchange which instruct a bank, rather than the importer, to pay.

Letters of credit

By using a letter of credit the importer knows that the bank has extended the credit to the importer and undertakes to pay the exporter. Thus the letter of credit obliges the importer's bank to accept a bill of exchange. However, the bank will insist that the bill of exchange be accompanied with documents satisfying the bank that goods relating to the bill of exchange have been properly imported and cleared by the importer.

The principal advantage of a letter of credit is that it relies on the credit of a bank and not the standing of an importer. There is still no guarantee that the bank can obtain sufficient foreign exchange to remit where such problems are likely. It is safer, therefore, to ensure that a line of credit is opened through a corresponding bank in the exporter's own country. This leads to a confirming bank adding its guarantee of payment. Such an instrument is called a 'confirmed letter of credit'.

The greatest security for an exporter is an instrument called a 'confirmed irrevocable letter of credit'. The added security stems from the confirmed line of credit being irrevocable. It cannot be altered without the agreements of all the parties involved.

Obviously a letter of credit which is in the exporter's own currency is free from any possible losses due to fluctuations in exchange rates.

Electronic Transfer

Often called 'telegraphic transfer', electronic transfer involves the rapid transfer of monies by telex or computer.

Documentary acceptance drafts – D/A

For importers who present little risk of not paying the D/A permits the release of goods to an importer once the obligation to pay is accepted by the importer.

Documentary on payment drafts – D/P

A D/P is used to ensure that goods are paid for before they are released.

Open account

A highly creditworthy importer or subsidiary company may be granted unsecured credit through open-account dealings in the same way as the exporter may deal with a home market customer.

Open account should not be used for countries where foreign exchange is often difficult to obtain. For some reason central banks seem to place a lower priority on allocations of foreign exchange to open accounts than to bank instruments, probably because the central banks are aware that confirmed letters of credit are the risk of the banking system whilst open accounts are the risks of the exporter.

Finding confirmed lines of credit

In dealings with countries where foreign exchange difficulties exist it may often be difficult to find banks prepared to confirm letters of credit. If export guarantees can be found then banks may be prepared to accept the risks. From experience, deals can be offered to banks. These may include offering equal amounts of low-risk business to cover the amount of the confirmed line of credit required, or depositing funds in markets where the bank most needs them.

It should be remembered, however, that it is the importer for whom the confirmed line of credit is required and efforts should be made for the importer and exporter together to find and provide acceptable deals to confirming banks.

Management of exchange loss risks

The risks of incurring losses through exchange-rate fluctuations are high for both exporter and importer.

Where exporters sell in their own currency the importer takes the exchange loss risk. Where importers buy in their own currency the exporter takes the risk. A business which involves frequent transactions of roughly the same value might permit a general smoothing of risk over a fairly long period and this may suit buyer and seller to continue on such a basis.

Where sales are infrequent, such as for tightly priced tenders, or are seasonal, the foreign-exchange loss may be too critical for either exporter or importer to bear. Here, either party has the option of passing such a risk to the bank – if one can be found to accept the risk. Either buyer or seller is in a position to buy the other's currency forward.

Banks will secure a forward exchange rate for the transaction at either a premium or discount according to the prevailing money-market conditions. By so doing, the exchange rate for the transaction is fixed and the bank then takes the risk.

Where no forward rate is available or where a high premium exists, two parties may agree to a 'currency swap'. This usually involves the parent company and one of its overseas subsidiaries. Here both parties swap currencies with an agreement to swap them back at a fixed time in the future.

A development of the currency swap is the 'credit swap'. Take a situation where a subsidiary needs credit in a country where there is no forward market and where local credit is restricted. Here, the parent, not wishing to convert hard currency or tie up capital in a particular company, may decide to make available a sum of hard currency to the subsidiary's bank on the understanding that it will be returned at a given time in the future. Using the hard currency as collateral, the local bank is then able to lend local currency to the subsidiary at its local interest rates. The local subsidiary pays back the local bank and the hard currency is returned to the parent.

Those aspects of foreign exchange which are of principal concern in running an international business are the risks involved in effecting transactions.

The effects of fluctuating exchange rates and the creditability of foreign customers are accommodated by the way banks facilitate exchange processes and reduce risks for clients in the money markets. Through the spot and forward markets and the instruments of foreign exchange, banks can collect, lend, buy and sell foreign exchange. The risks are much reduced (at a price) for those companies availing themselves of their banks' facilities plus governmental risk agencies, such as Britain's ECGD.

15

Organisation for International Business

Organisational structure is probably the hardest issue facing management in running a complex international business today. The fact is there is no perfect model upon which to base an organisation's structure. Because every business has different strategic and operating requirements it is even more difficult to prescribe the ideal approach.

In tackling the question we need to ask ourselves what the key criteria are and then to look at the ways in which a typical organisation might meet them.

Criteria for the international organisation

In forming criteria for the international organisational structure we need to find ways in which the business can be globally competitive on the one hand whilst being nationally responsive on the other. This means we need a management and organisational structure which permits the control and direction of strategy, resources and operations at the centre but which at the same time allows for a flexible response to pressures within local markets, allows for product adaptation and for the motivation of local employees.

It is imperative to consider the structure as more than a set of organisational charts and remember that most companies rely upon sets of informal relationships for the real management of their day-to-day activities. An international organisation should be seen as a management system which is concerned with the deployment of all the resources through which management can direct, control and support the business's international operations.

Furthermore, any system of management should be concerned not only with the rigorous setting of marketing, production and financial targets but should embrace:

- the strategic management of people;
- the development of an international climate and corporate culture;
- the strategic management of innovation in terms of products, production and methods of operating and administrating the company.

An organisation which fails to reflect the way in which the market is organised will fail to permit the proper focusing of resources on the company's competitive advantages, thus putting it at a disadvantage *vis-à-vis* competition. Furthermore, any structure which focuses only on opportunities and disregards threats will ultimately find that it cannot respond effectively to competitor incursions.

An organisational system can therefore be viewed from two points. Firstly, from the point of view of those hard components reflecting structure, planning needs, control and information systems and performance measures and rewards. Secondly, with a view to those soft components which affect the management environment, including those critical driving forces such as vision and wisdom; the style of the top management cadre, the ways in which co-ordination and conflict resolution mechanisms work; and the quality of management and people available within the structure.

An international organisation with a relatively simple structure and clear goals can, in all probability, achieve a superior performance to a more complex and matrix structure. In simple structures there is a greater likelihood that effective diffusion and acceptance of common visions and values will drive the business and that co-ordinating and conflict-resolving mechanisms will create a more effective working environment.

Alternative structures

By looking at a wide number of international businesses, some common structures appear. These involve:

- functional activities involved;

- relative age of the business;
- types of products marketed and manufactured;
- geographical areas to be covered; and
- degree of commitment to the international market.

Let us look at some typical structures, beginning with those where the international commitment is still relatively immature.

Diversified business with a centralised export structure

Such a business will be young in the field of international business and will be characterised by:

- limited product ranges;
- little or no attempt to modify or adapt product ranges to local conditions;
- marketing strategies not highly differentiated between markets;
- limited geographic spread of the business;
- production centred in one country;
- few executives with international experience;
- export business small in relation to domestic sales; and
- no foreign-based structure for the business, leaving sales to be managed by distributors or agents.

As can be seen from Figure 15.1 the export division is an 'add on' to the structure of the domestic business offering a range of products drawn from the other divisions.

The advantages of the structure are that:

- a provision to sell domestic products abroad allows for additional sales opportunities to be achieved;
- the size and importance are relative to the commitment to sales objectives; and
- the reporting structure to the chief executive allows for the export division to form a nucleus from which an international strategy can evolve.

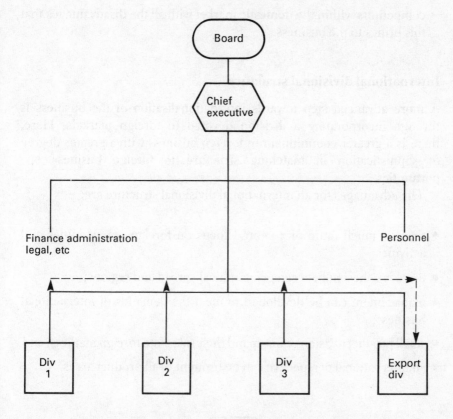

Figure 15.1 Diversified business with a centralised export structure

The disadvantages however might be seen as:

- the position of the export division in the structure may make it difficult to influence product policy;

- unless the export division is formed with the intention of growing the importance of foreign markets the structure will only permit a limited contribution by the export division to corporate strategy;

- the organisation's exports will be vulnerable to foreign competitors because there is no depth in the international organisational structure; and

- the company itself is highly vulnerable to foreign attack in that its only strategic option with its present structure would be to fight off competitors within the domestic market with all the disadvantages that this brings to the business.

International divisional structure

A more advanced step towards internationalisation of the business is through incorporating a division devoted to foreign markets. Here, there is a greater commitment to foreign business with a greater degree of sophistication in matching structure to foreign business opportunities.

The advantages for an international divisional structure are:

- there is much more of a central focus on foreign opportunities and activities;

- there is cohesion between geographical spread and regions;

- management can be developed to meet the demands of international business;

- small product divisions can expand their sales into foreign markets; and

- an international perspective can be brought to all product areas.

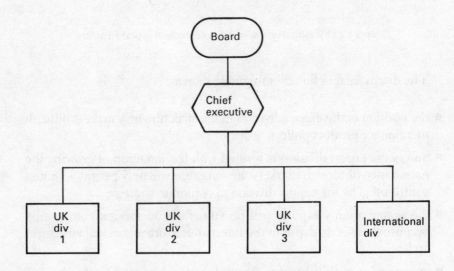

Figure 15.2 International divisional structure

The disadvantages are:

- the business is still very vulnerable to foreign competition in its domestic market although it does have in place an organisational capability to meet competition in foreign markets; and

- without top management commitment to the success and evolution of the company's international business, it will rely on the forcefulness of the international division's management.

A company with an international divisional structure is not displaying a global perspective to opportunities and competitor threats, albeit the commitment is much greater than that shown by the largely domestic business with a centralised export division.

The next set of structures we will discuss are those where the need for a global outlook has been recognised and different options adopted.

Mother-daughter structure

The mother-daughter structure is the archetypal structure found amongst many older European companies. The structure offers little in the way of control through a head-office network. Subsidiaries are set up to run country operations and there is little or no means of co-ordinating a global strategy for products within the structure. The organisation divides its operations between domestic and overseas.

The advantages are:

- local autonomy for national subsidiaries, giving them a capability for responses to local market opportunities and threats;

- a high level of local-management accountability for the successes of local subsidiary company activities; and

- relatively low costs in running global activities at headquarters.

The disadvantages:

- no strategy-formulating structure to co-ordinate product and geo-graphical emphasis;

- limited opportunities to create consistency in the use and tools of marketing; and

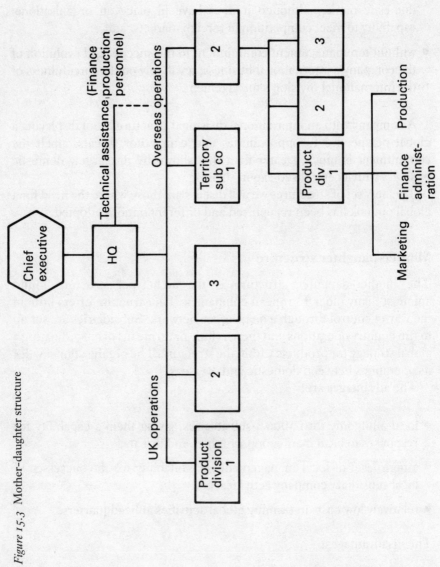

Figure 15.3 Mother–daughter structure

- a high probability that the continuance of a relatively 'old-fashioned' structure reflects a management lacking in vision and perception of the needs for international competitiveness.

The mother-daughter structure acknowledges the opportunities for international business without really addressing the threats. Each national company operates relatively independently and is insulated from the problems facing the organisation either in its domestic operations or in other countries. Such a structure is highly vulnerable to global competitive threats.

Global functional structure

The global functional structure is often adopted where there is little product differentiation between local markets and considerable economies found in scale and integration of production processes being carried out on a global scale. There is normally demand for a high degree of central co-ordination. Considerable levels of inter-regional trading prevail.

The global functional structure has a number of advantages, namely:

- a total commitment to global business at top management level;
- high levels of exploitation of economies of scale;
- central control of product quality standards; and
- the ability for the company to carry out its business play on a global scale, thus using foreign production facilities and local marketing organisation to compete effectively against foreign competitors in their own markets.

The disadvantages are, however:

- a high propensity for decision-making to be centrally controlled, thus reducing flexibility at local levels;
- a need to have a large number of central staff to oversee foreign operations;
- the spread of functional management at the centre may, without a powerful board direction lead to conflicting manufacturing and marketing strategies being adopted;
- the success of the business in each market is dependent upon good

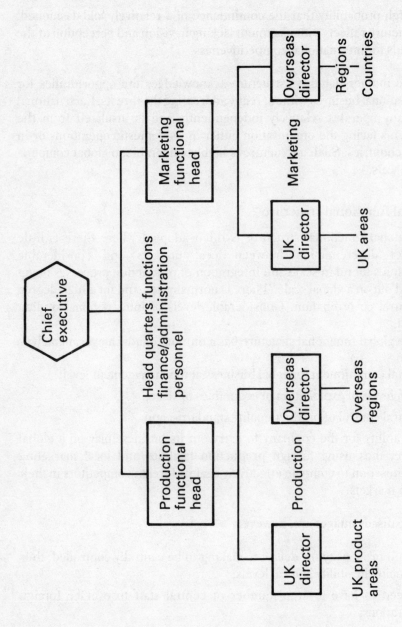

Figure 15.4 Global functional structure

communications and co-operation between marketing and production functions there – where this breaks down considerable inefficiencies will undermine the organisation's ability to meet competition and satisfy customer needs; and

● the organisation is based upon production efficiency thus hampering local responses to changes or differences in consumer tastes and preferences within local markets. This may put local operations at a distinct competitor disadvantage.

Product divisional structure

Here, individual product divisions operate autonomously. Research and development needs to be focused on global products limited the need for product adaptation or modification. Marketing and production activities will tend towards standardisation in each local market. There is little in the way of integration of activities, marketing channels and promotional tools between divisions.

The advantages of a product divisional structure are seen as:

● a single line of communication for product information and technology throughout each division;

● local marketing and production facilities are totally dedicated to the products offered by the division, leading to excellence in the selling and production of products in each local market – giving a strong marketing edge to local activities; and

● each division can develop its international business separately. Those with a more international range of products can expand into global markets unhindered by other divisions with less international products.

The disadvantages are:

● the autonomy of each division may result in poor communication and co-ordination of activities between divisions, thus losing opportunities for synergy and co-operation in foreign markets;

● each division will be responsible for setting up and developing its international operations and can thus only enter markets for which it can find cash and resources – thus smaller divisions may be discouraged from becoming international (a corporate approach on the other hand might provide a larger pool of cash and resources to enable divisions to enter bigger markets more effectively);

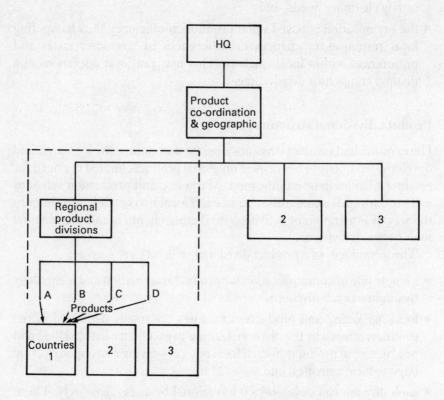

Figure 15.5 Product divisional structure

- each division will be responsible for its international strategy leaving divisions to opt in or out of a global orientation; and
- unless there is a corporate drive towards globalisation for all divisions, the business will end up with a very fragmented commitment to a global marketing presence.

Local umbrella company structure

Looking at Figure 15.6 it would appear that an umbrella structure is top-heavy. In fact it is the evolution of a product-divisional-structure-type organisation. The structure is typically headquarters-orientated but, through putting all the divisions into a local holding company there is a unified structure at local level within the host country.

The advantages of the local umbrella structure are:

- a channel of communication concerning all activities in each principal local market can be focused through the local holding company through to corporate headquarters, thus allowing a high degree of accountability for the performance of product divisions within each market;
- divisional activity can be co-ordinated at market level;
- a unified corporate entity through which the whole organisation can interface with the local market;

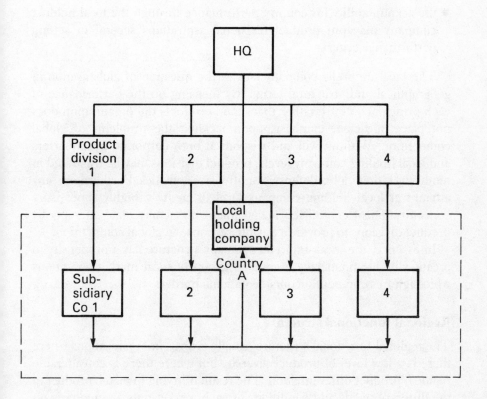

Figure 15.6 Local umbrella company structure

- a vehicle through which centralised administration, supporting services, eg personnel management training, computer services etc can be carried; and
- a centre through which the financial management of all the divisions can be focused, namely, consolidation of divisional funds, accounts, centralised borrowing, treasury management and a means through which tax can be optimised.

The main disadvantages of this structure are:

- an apparent lack of independence amongst divisional operations at local level;
- a matrix of managerial input stemming from headquarters and divisional activities has the propensity to cause conflict; and
- the accountability for country performance through the local holding company may put product divisional aspirations second in setting performance criteria.

The local umbrella company tackles the question of globalisation in geographical and structural terms. By focusing on the performance of each principal country rather than upon products the organisation does not place sufficient emphasis upon tackling the problems of global competition. Without will and wisdom at both corporate headquarters and local holding company levels, product divisions may be frustrated in mounting either global defensive or offensive activities. Furthermore, any attempt at local-holding-company level to create a highly supervisory concentration of centralised management may emasculate attempts by product divisions to provide a flexible response to global competition.

In essence, the local umbrella company structure has a propensity to create a highly financially orientated group of local market operations which ignores competition outside national borders.

Regional functional structure

The regional functional structure usually evolves in organisations where there is a low level of product diversity but where there is considerable regional product differentiation. The result of trying to match product to the different needs and conditions of each market puts an emphasis on creating regional manufacturing facilities and decentralising marketing functions.

The advantages are:

- a structure which allows for autonomy and independence in manufacture and marketing at local level – thus permitting a response to changes in local market conditions;
- economies of scale attainable through regional products help to ensure that products are competitive in cost and price in each of the regional markets; and
- high levels of accountability for regional and country activities through a relatively unencumbered structure.

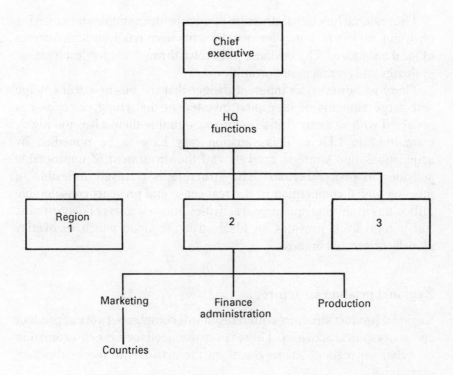

Figure 15.7 Regional functional structure

Disadvantages of such a structure are:

- there is little opportunity to transfer products between regions, thus limiting the organisation's ability to source from its lowest-cost production areas;

- the question of tackling competition globally is answered by creating local strengths through local product differentiation in areas where there is sufficient demand to enable it to make and market its products competitively – if large gaps occur in the organisation's global presence these will offer opportunity windows to competition;

- the direction in which growth will evolve for this type of organisation will stem from the regions which do best and which can attract funds to expand production capacity rather than from a policy of occupying strategic areas of geography.

The regional functional structure often provides a simple and satisfying environment in which management benefits from relatively high degrees of local autonomy. The business will evolve through the way each region evaluates and embraces opportunities.

There is, however, an inherent danger that the business will emerge with large amounts of its capital invested in the wrong place, as has occurred with so many British companies finding themselves too highly committed to LDCs. This situation may have to be remedied by acquisitions into strategic markets and the divestment of unprofitable activities in poorer regions. The structure is relatively inflexible in meeting global competition in the real sense and presents considerable difficulties in shifting operational activities into new areas of opportunity. Yet potentially it provides an ideal structure upon which to overlay globally orientated brands.

Regional product structures

Regional product structures often result in a complex network of product and geographical activities. There is a major need for tight co-ordination on behalf of regional management on the activities of local subsidiary companies.

The advantages of the regional product structure are:

- there is no home-market dominance, thus global activities are integrated in a truly international sense;

- the tight co-ordination of activities of product and geographic activities at headquarters provides the organisation with the ability to compete on a truly global basis;

- the business is product-led from the centre, providing opportunities for a clear focus on innovation, excellence in production and central co-ordination of marketing activities; and

- there is ample opportunity for developing a consistency in the use of various marketing tools and overcoming the relative strengths and weaknesses between product divisions operating in the same areas of geography.

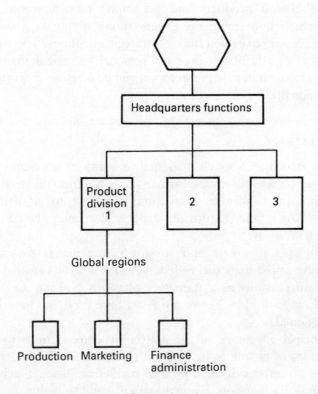

Figure 15.8 Regional product structure

The principal disadvantages are:

- the structure is complex, requiring high levels of managerial input across both product and geographical areas of the business, and thus carries with it considerable potential for conflict;

- setting performance criteria between products and regions will present difficulties unless senior management can find a formula for account-ability; and

- local response to competition and sudden market changes may be severely hampered by the complexity of product management and regional co-ordination activities.

The regional product structure, whilst providing a truly global organisation, is highly complex in nature. The need for tight co-ordination between products and geography may, however, create situations which undermine the organisation's ability to provide the sensitivity necessary to exploit fully its strategic intentions. The structure has a number of advantages over the regional functional structure in developing global strategy – the question will be whether it provides the teeth operationally.

Matrix structure

The matrix structure is much maligned as being an unnatural way of organising people and resources. Born in the 1960s from the needs of the aerospace industry to advance science and technology to put man on the moon, it has largely failed to provide a tenable base upon which to run an international business.

More attempts to create and sustain a true matrix management structure have failed than succeeded. Yet matrix structures have been used quite successfully as a transitory phase in evolving an ultimate structure. Companies like Xerox and Astra have tried, but have left the matrix abandoned.

The principal advantage of the matrix structure is to provide and harness groups of people to focus upon resolving conflicting strategies and seeking advantages through product marketing, product technology and geographical expansion. If only harmony could be maintained and a common sense of direction achieved, this multiple advocacy approach could be harnessed to produce exceptional success.

Yet the conflicts and lack of accountability which matrix management produce lead to:

- stagnation of strategic thinking;
- a lattice-work of conflicting channels of communication which cause confusion and frustrating working environments; and

- unpredictable outcomes in the market place, where headquarters and subsidiary companies have equal power.

The matrix structure has very little to say for itself in a business setting and its proneness to conflict and the creation of organisational impotence makes it a poor structure for coping with the threats of global competition. The matrix structure is difficult to direct and, except where energies are focused on a limited range of problems, is too unwieldy to provide the basis for the structure of global organisation.

Degree of autonomy for subsidiary companies

A major issue in the management of international activities is in deciding how much autonomy should be allowed at subsidiary levels. The issue is important because it involves the management of the global strategy of products on the one hand and the accountability of local management matching performance criteria on the other.

A low level of local autonomy may have a number of advantages for those managers at corporate headquarters:

- a high level of control on the global strategy in terms of product marketing, technology, innovation and manufacturing;
- clear lines of communication and authority;
- a corporate culture dedicated to marketing given product lines throughout the company's international operations;
- clear performance criteria can be set for headquarters management thus ensuring that managers close to the centre are highly accountable;
- the effects on company performance of poor decision-making in subsidiary companies is reduced; and
- pooling of central administrative resources at the centre to administer personnel, financial matters etc is possible.

The disadvantages, however, are considerable.

- There is a high demand for control at the centre in terms of large numbers of experienced managers, availability of considerable amounts of research and intelligence data.

- Local responses to short-term market changes at the subsidiary level may become headquarters decisions, thus creating delay and causing frustration amongst local managers.

- Firefighting problems in subsidiary companies by head-office personnel may become routine.

- Frustration amongst local managers may create morale problems and indecision.

- A 'them-and-us' situation may develop between headquarters and local subsidiaries.

- Accountability at local-management level may become difficult to enforce.

- Transfers of managers at headquarters may be discouraged because of the 'experience hole' they leave behind, thus leading to a situation where potentially mobile managers are kept too long in any one position.

- Decisions affecting local companies may be over-influenced by those centrally based managers who have a closer and more intimate reporting relationship with senior management at the centre.

Too great an orientation towards central control and low local autonomy, although having a number of strategic and apparent administrative advantages, will in all likelihood result in an inward-looking corporate culture. Why companies become overly managed at the centre seems to be where:

- there is a highly internationalised business commanding a significant level of experience at headquarters;

- key subsidiaries creating for themselves such a strategic importance to the business in terms of profit contribution that central management feels uncomfortable unless it is in control;

- the complexity of technology demands considerable central control;

- a strategic need to manage interflows of products and technologies between subsidiaries exists; and

- there is a high number of newly acquired companies in the global network needing integration and direction from the centre.

The advantages of giving local subsidiary managers a high degree of autonomy are:

- managers will take on a great amount of accountability for the success of their subsidiary companies;
- (in theory at least) the local companies will have considerable flexibility in challenging market changes and seizing opportunities;
- there is likely to be considerable scope for managers to take an entrepreneurial attitude towards their local markets, thus making the most out of the opportunities which exist; and
- given reasonable leadership within each subsidiary company, independence should give employees a local point of corporate focus leading to a healthy level of morale and a lively corporate culture.

The disadvantages of too much local autonomy, however, may be outweighed by the disadvantages.

- Subsidiaries will each evolve in their own way, thus when the company is looked at as a whole, the business may be very diversified with few strengths in strategic areas.
- The further each subsidiary company drifts away from core technology and products, the more it must muster its own resources and seize opportunities locally.
- The strength of each local subsidiary company will depend largely on the quality of its local management and their perceptions regarding opportunities and threats in their own environment.
- With little strategic and operational control at the centre, there is little scope for directing a concerted global attack on competitors, thus leaving the company vulnerable to competitor attacks on its key markets.

Balancing control and autonomy

The secret of running a global network of subsidiaries effectively is in finding the right balance between central control and local autonomy. Too great a movement towards local autonomy will lead inevitably to subsidiaries going their own way. Too much central control will lead to stifling of local initiative.

The balance of management, therefore, must be based around the central creation of a strategy which everyone must follow combined with high levels of local accountability for the success of local subsidiaries. This ideal relationship is easier said than done.

Attempts to create the right balance, as is often shown, can only in part be solved by structure. As in all organisation matters, it is people – and the wisdom and vision they bring to the business – which make it successful.

The ingredients for establishing the right sort of environment will evolve if organisations place a great deal of emphasis on:

- accountability of individual managers at all levels;
- creating effective lines of communication which build around a line-management structure;
- introducing training at all levels to create a pool of skills that can be drawn upon for the good of the business;
- reducing bureaucracy to a minimum to allow the decision-making chain to act swiftly; and
- harnessing the soft components of the structure into the strategy.

In a global, strategically orientated business, central management will keep subsidiary companies moving in the right direction if they keep local managers informed of their intentions.

Local managers should be given the opportunity to match strategic requirements to their area of geography in a way which demands a careful appraisal of success criteria rather than by central dictate. Local chief executives should be involved in the strategic processes of the business and their contribution should be made through setting and agreeing performance objectives for their areas of operation.

Strategic management should devote itself to:

- planning and directing the global attack;
- providing resources;
- communicating intentions through line management;
- creating a corporate culture;
- providing a set of staff functions to support and contribute to administering strategy as well as a quality-control function on marketing activities, production and financial management; and

- receiving and diffusing business intelligence.

Operational management should be charged with:

- executing corporate strategy;
- agreeing and being accountable for performance objectives for their areas of operation;
- finding and building resources in terms of people, facilities, and logistics sufficient to meet operational needs effectively;
- sending intelligence on markets, competitors, economics and government matters to the centre;
- seeking and exploiting local market opportunities;
- providing an effective response to changes in local market conditions;
- identifying and targeting local and international competitors operating locally; and
- administering local operations efficiently.

Paul Girolami, Chairman of Glaxo, describes how his company has evolved from a centrally controlled business into a globally competitive organisation in terms of management philosophy.

'What then is the new philosophy? The first point is that we are very conscious now that the holding company, the people here in Clarges Street, are not managing the worldwide business: we are conscious that we have to see that the company is managed. That's quite a different philosophy.

'Even six or seven years ago Clarges Street actively was direct or attempting to direct in detail what went on in the operating companies. Managers would say "Oh, I can't do this. I've got to get through to the centre." Not any more.

'We have delegated management. We haven't delegated control, we haven't delegated direction – but we have delegated management to where the market place is.' (Glaxo World)

And if the people in the operating companies are now to be judged according to how they can show 'get up and go' within the guidelines established by the Group, then the people at the centre will also be judged according to how they acquit themselves against a new standard. This Mr Girolami describes as 'high-class leadership'.

Paul Girolami sees the role of central management as a guiding force but emphasises that whilst it should keep in touch with its territories, it should not interfere but instead provide a unifying role which projects the corporate 'philosophy', the plans and the ambitions of the group.

EC impacts on organisational management – social rights and participation

Article 118 of the Treaty of Rome is amended by the Single European Act. The result will be to open a Pandora's box of employment and social legislation, the impact of which may well effect how and where companies choose to locate across the Community. The following extract forewarns of the intentions.

'... the Commission shall have the task of promoting close co-operation between Member States in the social field, particularly in matters relating to:

- employment
- labour law and working conditions
- basic and advanced vocational training
- social security
- prevention of occupational accidents and diseases
- occupational hygiene
- the right of association, and collective bargaining between employers and workers

The Commission shall endeavour to develop the dialogue between management and labour at European level which could, if the two sides consider it desirable, lead to relations based on agreement.'

The evolution of the European tendency towards social rights and worker participation in management of industry has been an objective of the socialist influence in the Community. Jacques Delors, President of the

Commission, has already made overtures to the trade union movement across the Community.

In his address to the European Trade Union Confederation Conference earlier in the year Jacques Delors declared his intention to press forward three main areas:

- changes in company law to develop worker participation in decision-making. This, of course, has its background in the proposed Fifth Company Law Directive and 'Vredeling' proposals;

- a minimum threshold of social rights for workers to be negotiated between a 'European union' and employers; and

- the right for every worker in the EC to have permanent training. This would be based on a system of credits gained throughout an individual's working life.

Worker participation

The Commission's Fifth Directive has been the subject of much debate 1and publicity, yet has achieved little progress. As an article in *Management Accounting* in July/August 1988 points out:

'When first published in 1972 the proposal was coolly received. The little excitement that it did arouse was caused by its separation of a "two-tier" board structure. The first level, a Management Board, would compromise company executives, the second, a Supervisory Board, would represent the interests of shareholders and employees. This would meet infrequently and would essentially be responsible for rubber stamping decisions already taken by management.

'In 1983 the proposal was amended to provide an optional approach for companies; the original two-tier board (on the German model) or the more conventional one-tier board as in the UK. Although such an approach sounds uncontroversial the difficulty that it causes is that within the one-tier board a distinction would need to be drawn between the functions of "executive" directors, who would manage, and "non-executive" directors, who would supervise. This is contrary to present law and practice both in the UK and indeed many other Member States.

'Employee participation in company decision making would be required through board representation of employees at the supervisory level, or by means of a works council, or through collective agreements which would give employees at least the same rights as either of the other two methods.

'The UK Government has consistently opposed the introduction of compulsory measures in the belief that they are best promoted voluntarily. They have received widespread support for this both from within the business community and from other interested parties.

'In successive changes over its long history the Directive's proposals have gradually been rendered more flexible and the indications are that this flexibility will increase. Any rules eventually laid down are likely to be general and conceptual, limited to fundamental minimum requirements, rather than requiring the adoption of specific methods. Approaches to worker participation providing possible models for adoption include the FRG system of co-determination and the factory committees of France and Belgium.'

The Vredeling Directive

An attempt by the Dutch Commissioner Vredeling to achieve a major socialist goal by adding to the Community's labour law was through a Directive proposed under his name.

Published in 1980, the proposal would require head offices of large companies and other major employers to inform and consult employees of subsidiaries or separate establishments through the local management structure. Employee representatives would be entitled to receive regular information, both on the subsidiary in which they were employed and on the group as a whole.

In addition, employees would have the right to be consulted over any decision that the parent board may take that could affect them as employees of the subsidiary.

The Directive was virtually killed off in 1985. It was seen as unworkable unless heavily modified. However, in June 1986 the European Council offered an olive branch to its 'social partners' by scheduling a re-opening of discussion in early 1989.

The impact of social legislation, which will surely be reinforced by cross-community trade union links, will provide formidable labour management problems across the community. The prospect of trade union strategies to collaborate on equalising pay, employment and social issues and the relocation of production could return industrial relations to those fractious times of the 1960s and 1970s.

Following the progress of legislation, trade union activity will need to feature strongly in planning for the Single Market. The location of plant and organisation may well need to take into consideration the propensity for the differences in industrial relations practices in each member state to create strife and problems in the longer term. The concept of wage parity could well undermine the viability of organisational decisions made in the short term.

Harmonisation of health and safety

All three treaties establishing the EC contain provisions relating to worker conditions and there have been a number of action programmes designed to achieve their effective implementation. The main objective is to ensure health and safety in the workplace and to improve protection against industrial diseases and injuries. To these ends the Commission has identified a number of programmes designed to:

- improve working conditions by promoting greater safety and respecting health requirements in the organisation of work;

- improve knowledge with a view to identifying and assessing risks and improving methods of control and prevention; and to

- improve human behaviour with a view to developing and promoting the spirit of health and safety.

These are in addition to proposals concerning specific sectors of the economy, for example the construction and the transport industries and those on specific hazardous substances.

Despite not being directly linked to the 1992 programme, the Commission has declared its wish and intention to align the 'social' aspect of the Single European Market with those Directives on technical harmonisation and thereafter to progress these in tandem. Safety standards will, therefore, relate both to machine design and construction and will be supplemented by requirements concerning their safe operation.

The whole issue of health and safety regulations will impose considerable strains on company facilities. The need to ensure that the personnel are kept up to date on developments, attend courses and work closely with legal advisors is vital. Changes may well prove to be expensive as the longer the period of planning and gradual implementation, the longer a company will have in adjusting to regulations both in terms of cost and activity. Here again, as we stated in Chapter 1, it is essential for companies to involve themselves at the political level in contributing to the formulation of rules.

16
Making It Happen

To conclude this book I offer some thoughts on how to approach the management of the Single Market. We have discussed the Single Market scenario, the evaluation of strategic options, the exploitation of inward and outward opportunities, marketing and logistics operations and global opportunities. Yet just pointing out these issues can be of mere academic interest unless they are put into a framework for implementation.

There can be no better a time for companies to re-evaluate their strategic positions and to use the Single Market as a reason to bring strategic management back on to the boardroom agenda. By giving the firm a mission for 1992 it will kindle energy and enthusiasm throughout the organisation. Not only is 1992 a reason to make plans, it is a *theme* by which productivity and cost-efficiency programmes can be made to have meaning to everyone in the business. It is an opportunity to give everyone a goal to aim for; a platform for conferences, incentive schemes and internal PR.

Even so, management and staff will be looking to their corporate management for leadership and direction. For they will be keenly interested to see if their corporate leaders have the capability to respond to the European challenge. The very level of publicity being put out by Community governments is making staff at all levels aware of the Single Market. Now is the time that management will come under scrutiny from the organisations they lead. So getting strategy right will play a major part in the evolution of corporate culture, the level of morale and the values staff place on working for their organisations.

Inspired and creative managers will be itching to make initiatives. In many companies, holding back enthusiasm for the European concept will be the problem. Management will have to find ways of harnessing enthusiasm and directing energies rather than falling into either of the two traps of squashing initiatives or letting things run out of control.

Therefore, implementing a process which will result in a viable company strategy which can be effectively executed will call heavily on senior management leadership. The chief executive must play an important role in winning boardroom support on one hand, and co-ordinating management activity on the other.

The approach we are recommending is to make the Single Market the focus of corporate strategy. To this end it must:

- be company-embracing;

- involve all functions of the business at all levels;

- introduce company-wide planning systems; and

- above all, be a co-ordinated plan designed around matching company competitive advantages to the business development programme.

For companies which have hitherto not been involved in strategic planning, a period of time will need to be invested in training managers in the art of strategic management. This is a wonderful business school in its own right. In companies where strategic planning is already adopted, changes or additions to strategy will need to be overlaid on to the existing planning system. The strategy for the Single Market should not be seen as a separate issue to the normal planning of the business – it must become a central feature of it. For as we have already seen, the very size of the European challenge will have its impact on both the domestic and the global competitive position of a company.

So, to make the Single Market strategy happen will demand considerable inputs across all the company's functions. It will call for co-ordination of planning and require (for the first time for many companies) a political strategy.

This chapter provides an outline for planning a Single Market strategy. It is a planning guide that can be used as the basis for management briefing and the rubrics of a work programme. It will obviously have to be tailored to meet individual company needs and management styles. More importantly however, is that it should not be used to write a plan which is simply filed away to gather dust for the next five years. It should be a plan which is used as a working document. One which sets projects and missions. A plan which can be monitored and revised at will. It must be an *action plan*.

The Single-Market plan

The planning methodology is based on five key components:

- a manageable database;
- a set of key objectives;
- a political and legal strategy;
- an overlay of projects and missions which form the basis of the strategic management process; and
- a management and organisational system to co-ordinate the planning and to ensure that activities are implemented.

The guide which follows outlines the principal areas which companies will need to address:

- outline for a strategic plan;
- time horizons and the construction of the database;
- marketing, R & D, production, logistics and organisational strategy outlines;
- compilation of a strategic budget;
- financial strategy outline;
- political strategy;
- internal organisation for managing the Single Market;
- a cascade for corporate briefing; and
- using 1992 as a motivational theme to enhance productivity.

Outline for a strategic plan

Before we begin the detail of a plan it is a useful starting point to see where we intend to end up.

Figure 16.1 illustrates how the four components of the strategic plan can be put into a logical framework. In effect the strategic plan is led by the company's overall objectives. The critical area will be matching resources to the product/market development element of the strategy.

The plan is then tested by the creation of a strategic budget. This translates strategy into a set of financial statements against which:

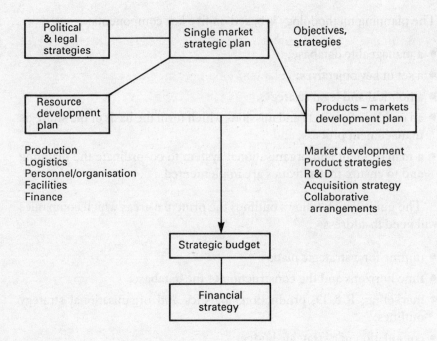

Figure 16.1 Strategic plan for the Single Market

- financial outcomes of the plan can be demonstrated;
- sensitivity analysis can be carried out to test the financial plausibility of recommended projects;
- future projects can be tested against a running database;
- a basis for the progress of the plan can be measured and gaps identified;
- foundation of a database can be organised, to be updated periodically to meet new planning horizons or changes in assumptions; and
- most importantly it provides the basis upon which the company's financial strategy can be based.

Time horizons

The problem of fitting time horizons to planning stems from trying to hold in balance realistic assumptions about the future and the long-term effects of future risks created by present-day decisions. The quality of future scenarios falls away as time horizons are extended. Where projects have relatively short-term returns, the assumptions about the future can be expected to hold fairly true. For projects involving years before payback or significant returns on investment arise, this is more difficult. For example, a pharmaceutical R & D project, if successful, may cost $30m or more and take five years before a commercial product is ready to launch. A major industrial plant development may take 20 years before its return on investment repays the investment costs.

The problem of setting time horizons in planning for the Single Market is exacerbated by the fact that it crosses a period of change. As pointed out in Chapter 2, this may upset the composition of customers, competitors and suppliers. Therefore, in setting time horizons, an assessment of likely changes is necessary. Even so, the problem of setting time horizons can be overcome in three ways:

- basing future planning horizons on the future length of time it takes to justify key investment decisions;

- building a picture of business development against the evolution of activity arrived at from the gap analysis activity – say three to five years; and

- setting a minimum forward-planning horizon based on either of the above and revising it regularly against changes in assumptions.

Whichever method is selected should be determined by what is most suitable for the company. However, it must be emphasised that forward planning must involve periodic updates which enable the firm's managers to monitor progress and input changes in circumstances, performance and assumptions. This, in effect, creates a rolling plan which provides both the basis for measuring and adjusting activity and the flexibility required to allow for changes in assumptions.

Creating the database

The database will comprise of a set of assumptions about the company's capabilities, its existing strengths, weaknesses, opportunities and threats. It will also include any statements about adjustments needed to conform to EC legal issues, health and safety regulations, product standards, and so forth. It might also include an inventory of the company's skills and resources.

There should also be a quantified database showing the company's capabilities in terms of sales, production, costs, financial resources, head count, distribution systems and so forth along the company's value chain. In other words it provides the necessary database upon which the future resource development and marketing strategies can be constructed.

The database should thus provide the foundation of the plan in terms of providing information and assumptions against which it can develop.

An initial set of objectives

To create any plan, some initial objectives need to be set. These provide the scope and direction for creating the individual consequent strategies. They will be the trigger for the development of all the component strategies – but they need to be more than a set of financial-performance goals.

The suggested method is to provide:

- a statement of corporate mission (see page 81);
- an outline of success criteria and parameters; and
- a set of performance objectives.

This then provides the overall basis for briefing management charged with producing components of the plan. For it will state the strategic intentions of the business and the focus of strategy in terms of developing or exploiting the competitive advantages of the firm. It also provides a set of challenging objectives against which managers will need to match development plans.

The management briefing sets the course for the strategic plan development and provides challenges for management to create projects and plan activity to meet objectives. In effect it says 'this is where we want to go'; 'these are the parameters of the route to find the best way of getting there'! Gap analysis will be useful here. As the plan evolves, the initial objectives may need to be modified to ensure that the best options for development of the business can be adopted and performance optimised.

Political and legal strategies

Influencing the evolution of legislation standards and so forth should be part of the Single Market strategy for every firm.

Without such a strategy, the firm's interests may well be compromised either directly by the way regulations impinge on the company's operations, or indirectly through the advantages they provide competition.

Statement of criteria

This will focus the company's political influence on those areas of EC legislation and those areas of national legislation affecting the firm's interests.

Statement of intention

This covers products, competition, labour, environmental issues and difficulties in individual markets.

Outline of organisation

Consider whether to appoint specific people to manage the legal, political and PR issues or to use outside consultants.

Creation of databases

Keep abreast of developments.

Political objectives

Set objectives in terms of those interests which concern the company as being either beneficial or adverse to the company's operations and competitive advantages.

Outline the political strategy

This is done in terms of methods and operation. Whether to involve trade associations or to act individually; consider sponsorship or executives to various national and Community committees; assess the relative values of lobbying, PR and participation in the various arenas of legal and regulatory activity.

Determine Costs

For example of PR consultancy and participation projects.

Resource development and product-markets-development plans

Here we face the proverbial chicken-and-egg situation. What is the best way of ensuring that the marketing and resource development plans match?

If resource development follows the marketing development plan then it is likely that the best utilisation of resources can only be achieved if the product development and sales-volume plans coincide with optimum production levels.

If the plan is resource-development-led then the marketing strategy will be constrained by the limited availability of resources. Conversely the marketing strategy may be compromised by unrealistic levels of business needed to cover the costs of added resources or to meet optimum capacity levels.

The solution has to be based on the market, its needs and competition. Therefore, first create a draft marketing strategy and use this as the basis for drafting the resource-development strategy. Identify critical aspects of the marketing strategy and use these as fundamental criteria for resource development.

Logic then demands that the matching of the two fundamental strategies will require a certain amount of forcing out of efficiencies. For example by forcing out projected sales it may be possible to make significant cost reductions. By forcing out production performance or relocating plant, for example, it may be possible to achieve more competitive levels of cost through better utilisation.

Planning at this stage may well require a number of reviews and 'horse trading' between marketing and the other functions. The aim is to achieve the best fit to ensure that a competitive market development strategy is not compromised by the failure of company resources to match its needs, whilst ensuring that the firm's value chain continues to provide the company's competitive advantage.

Marketing development strategy

The marketing development strategy will comprise a number of features.

- *A statement of marketing criteria*, for example to focus on products and technologies around which the company's knowledge, competence and advantages are best exploited (cost advantages or differentiation advantages) and on market segments in specific markets which best match the organisation's marketing capabilities (broad market or narrow niches).

- *A statement of intention* covering products, product development, markets, market shares, modes of entry into new markets, modes of operation in existing markets.

- *An outline of the marketing organisation*; dispositions at home and abroad; management and staff development.

- *Market-by-market product strategies*, forecasts of volume, revenue, marketing investment, market research etc.

- *Market-by-market pricing strategies* (constraints of differential pricing). A pricing strategy needs to weigh the value assumptions that customers will place on the company's products on a market-by-market basis and the effects that inconsistencies in prices across the company's markets will have in distorting demand. The likely incidence of parallel trade and procurement prevalence by multi-market customers should also be part of the decision equation.

- *A product-development programme* – in terms of new technology, new products, product improvement, standard modifications etc.

- *Distribution-channel objectives* – determining distribution channels, sales strategies, customer management, service needs etc, in each market, and spotting where significant differences in types of distribution system are likely to create different demands.

- *Acquisition objectives* in terms of access to markets, brands, products and technology: synergies; defensive or offensive strategies.

- *Collaborative objectives* as above.

- *Divestment objectives*, in terms of shedding unprofitable or poor-fitting activities; releasing funds for reinvestment into new products, market or targeted acquisitions.

- *Financial projections* showing the development of revenue, marketing investment, organisational expenses for existing products and markets overlaid by those for new ventures, products and markets. A statement of capital investment requirements, acquisitions costs etc.

R & D strategy

R & D activities present a major part of the overall marketing mission for a business. Therefore there has to be a very close relationship between the overall direction of the marketing strategy and the R & D strategy. At the same time R & D and production strategies need to be closely co-ordinated.

- *Technological criteria.* Fully exploit existing technology within the cope of the company's capabilities (allowing for adequate experience time or the bringing-in of acquisitions or collaborative arrangements).

- *A statement of intentions* to cover main areas of project development in terms of exploiting existing technologies; seeking new break-through opportunities; acquiring new technologies; product and production improvement programmes; programmes to develop common product and range standards initiated within the European Community etc.

- *Outline of R & D organisation,* facilities, project capabilities and capacity for projects to be done in-house, subcontracted etc.

- *R & D projects to be listed,* for example involvement in trade associated product standardisation programmes, new products, product adaptations for new markets, production economies, quality etc; new technology screening, licensing-in, collaboration, acquisition prop-osals, involvement in EC joint programmes.

- *Financial projections* in terms of operational revenue expenses, royalty payments, subcontract expenses, capital expenditures for equipment, facilities lump-sum payments for technology acquisitions etc.

Production strategy

Production strategy needs to address those issues involved in matching marketing objectives and meeting R & D future specifications in terms of capability, capacity, cost, quality and location. The effect of standardising some elements of production may have a dramatic effect on production planning and methods of operation for example. The production strategy will cover a wide variety of issues.

- *A production criteria statement* along the lines, say, of concentrating on production processes which meet product, market and R & D technol-ogy requirements effectively in terms of cost, capacity, capability and proximity to markets. Seeking to subcontract those processes which are relatively uneconomic or for which specialist subcontractors can provide a more competitive product.

- *A statement of intention* in terms of meeting capability, capacity cost and location criteria.

- *An outline of the production organisation* in terms of production location, facility dispositions, process systems, management and staff development.

- *Production development objectives* in terms of meeting capability, capacity and cost criteria covering such areas as new investment, rationalisation, location of plant, quality programmes, procurement strategies, adjusting to new standards etc.

- *Acquisition objectives* in terms of acquiring production technology, skills, rationalising production, vertical integration synergies etc.

- *Production and R & D projects* to develop production technology. This might cover internal projects, joint projects with suppliers, collaborative projects etc.

- *Involvement in national and EC regional-development programmes* to take advantage of incentives in terms of relocation, new factories, etc.

- *Financial projections* to provide product-cost forecasts which will need to be fed into the revenue statements provided in the marketing strategy. Capital expenditure forecasts involving new plant, machinery etc are also required.

Inbound logistics strategies

The need to develop strategies for the management of supplies involved in the production process will become increasingly important in terms of the benefits accruing to the value-creation process (through production and stock control efficiencies) and in managing the movement of materials to foreign-based production units, subcontractors etc.

The inbound logistics strategy will also be very wide ranging.

- A statement of procurement criteria reflecting the role played in production strategy by inbound logistics and procurement in meeting quality, cost and production-efficiency requirements. This avoids the situation say, where, for example, procurement criteria are based on lower cost whilst production strategy involves suppliers meeting specific service levels and minimum defect levels.

- A statement of intentions in terms of finding sources of materials, setting supplier standards, rationalising procurement, spreading procurement risks, meeting production materials, handling objectives, gaining co-operation from suppliers in service, R & D and production projects, setting up management information systems to control the movements of materials to link in with production planning systems.

- Outline of the inbound logistics organisation in terms of people, facilities, systems, location etc.

- Policies regarding procurement and supplies of components and part-made products for foreign production units.

- Supplier standards in terms of quality, volume, delivery, service levels etc.

- Rationalisation of suppliers to achieve best prices, long-term contracts, shared IT systems, quality support and service criteria.

- Projects to link suppliers to R & D and production-development programmes.

- Materials-handling systems in terms of procurement scheduling, quality-control systems, goods-inwards controls, warehousing etc.

- Make-or-buy proposals to reduce cost or to improve quality.

- Financial projections in terms of material-cost forecasts, cost benefits accruing to an effective inbound logistics strategy, capital expenditure costs in terms of facilities, IT etc. These are probably best assimilated into the production strategy's financial projections.

Physical distribution strategies

These involve the movement of goods from production units to the market place. The need to match customer service requirements can provide critical competitive advantages. The SEA allows substantial changes to both the restrictions on transporters and the speed at which goods can be moved across the Community.

Opportunities to reduce costs and improve service should thus be sought out.

Physical distribution strategies will therefore involve the whole plethora of transport issues.

- A statement of physical distribution criteria which states the role of physical distribution in meeting customer-service levels (a marketing objective) across the entire geography embraced by the company. (This avoids distribution management overriding marketing's distribution criteria.)

- A statement of intentions in terms of the methods, means and systems to be introduced to meet the company's distribution objectives.

- An outline of the physical distribution organisation, warehousing dispositions, export capability, information, paperwork, and transport network, its own vehicles, subcontracting arrangements, freight forwarding systems for export etc.

- Physical-distribution development objectives in terms of warehousing efficiency, evaluating and selecting transport, computerisation of physical-distribution control and information both internally and as a customer service etc.

- Cost containment projects through such areas as inventory control, shipment volumes, transport methods and selecting transporters etc.

- Managing customer service in terms of developing systems and practices: meeting customer delivery requirements, providing progress information, stock availability information, reducing errors between delivery notes, invoices and ensuring accuracy of export documentation etc.

- Financial projections in terms of forecasting distribution costs, organisational costs etc. Capital expenditure in terms of meeting the distribution system needs, eg facilities, depots, vehicles, computer systems etc.

Organisational strategies

Organisational strategies involve shaping, structuring and administering the company in such a way that it meets the needs of the corporate strategy. Organisation strategies should evolve rather than suffer sudden traumas of reorganisation. This means that in developing organisational strategy it is important to establish the overall strategy first and then allow the organisation to fit to it. This means establishing firm criteria as regards centralising or decentralising controls, the style of organisation, production division, geographic division etc (see Chapter 15).

Parameters involving the size of the head count, quality of management, skills and languages, training and development are all vital elements of the organisational strategy. The most important aspect of organisational strategy is to make things happen; to develop a productive corporate culture; emphasise excellence and achieve loyalty and commitment from all employees. A mission-based corporate culture, good leadership, sound organisation and a motivated workforce all make a major difference to a firm's competitive position.

In outlining the strategy, particular care and attention will need to be taken in reviewing legal issues affecting personnel management. The areas of health and a safety need considerable thought. The need for research into employment conditions abroad will also have to be taken into consideration.

Organisational strategy should therefore be based on the following considerations.

- A statement of organisational criteria on management's interpretation of its overall strategy requirements, its policy on central or decentralised control, the basis of the structure and the geography it should embrace.

- A statement of intention in terms of matching functional organisation to its marketing, R & D, production and logistics strategies and the central administrative requirements of the business.

- An outline of the general shape of the organisation showing the structure of management lines of communications and central staff functions and services.

- A breakdown of individual functions, product divisions, business units etc around which the organisational structure is to be planned, with head count targets ascertained from the operational needs of each part of the structure.

- Development objectives in terms of matching skills to managerial and operational requirements. This will involve recruitment, training and development.

- Rationalisation objectives in terms of decreasing and redeploying employees. Policies regarding natural wastage, redundancy and re-training will need to be addressed.

- Policies for dealing with trade unions will need to be stated. These may have to be adapted on a country-by-country basis.

- Policies regarding internationalising management will include such aspects as expatriating national managers, training local managers, effecting exchanges between countries, recruiting management in different countries etc.

- Structuring remuneration and incentive schemes on either a local or international basis including such areas as extending share ownership and share-option scheme, pension plans, bonus schemes etc.

- Specific policies for central personnel control which might include: its organisation, health and safety, employee welfare, management recruitment, training services, legal issues, internal employee PR, international training awards, complaints and disciplinary procedures, head count monitoring, salary monitoring, relocation of personnel etc. These must be viewed from an international perspective.

- Financial implications of the organisational strategy should include forecasts of redundancy costs, recruitment, relocation, training, statutory and voluntary contributions to state institutions and company pension funds.

The strategic budget

The strategic budget is formed by translating the preceding strategies into a set of financial statements. By so doing it provides a vital tool for strategy planning.

- It provides a complete picture of projected revenue, expenses and capital-expenditure requirements against which the financial strategy can be formulated.

- It is a database against which future recommendations can be tested.

- It allows sensitivity analysis to be carried out to test and question individual elements of strategy.

- It provides a yardstick against which corporate performance can be monitored in terms of revenue achievements, expenses and capital expenditure over measured financial periods. This yardstick can also be used to test future annual budgets.

However, getting the strategic budget right presents its problems. It involves considerable input from a number of sources. The mere summing of constituent strategies may well present an unsatisfactory or unrealistic financial picture. It must therefore be used to:

- question back the validity of performance expectations, project costs, return on investment for marketing and capital expenditures etc; and

- force out longer-term performance objectives to improve investment outcomes, productivity, fill gaps in the business development programme and so on (conversely the strategic budget should not be used to compromise strategy to force out short-term performance at the cost of the longer-term development of the business).

The budget must be reviewed regularly by inputting forecast gains whilst ruthlessly pulling out those elements which are forecast to fall short of initial projections.

The value of the strategic budget should be to give management a reasonably reliable forecast of its future in terms of revenues and funding requirements.

Great emphasis has to be made in briefing managers that there needs to be a realistic approach to the numbers put into the plans because it will be used as the basis for the financial strategy. No doubt many companies new to this sort of discipline will need several tries before they get it to the level of reliability needed. The time invested initially in creating the database will pay future dividends. If the product of the exercise can be stored on computer it is there to be used for a whole range of projects, some of which have already been mentioned.

The financial strategy

No business strategy can be truly effected without a strategy to fund it and police its financial outcomes. A strategy for the Single Market will not only demand those investments and expenses sought in the individual marketing and resourcing plans but will bring with it the increased complexity and range of options the Single Market promises. These include: changes to the capital markets, new regulations involving mergers and takeovers and freedom in the movement of financial services. To these can be added all the risks and complexities involved with foreign exchange, differing rates of corporation tax, investment grants and so forth.

The financial strategy will therefore need to be formulated to find the best ways of funding the overall strategy of business development and at the same time seek to do so under complex and changing financial conditions.

- A statement of financial criteria against which the firm will define its financial performance objectives, policies relating to investments, financing risk, new share issues, retained earnings and earnings-per-share targets.

- A statement of intentions in terms of funding requirements, sources of funds, key financial ratios and dividend objectives.

- An organisation and structure to manage the financial affairs of the business throughout the organisation and the markets in which it operates.

- A capital expenditure plan:
  - cash and capital budgeting;
  - timing of investments; and
  - methods of financing investment (domestic currency, dollars or ECU instruments).

- Working capital plan to meet increases in expenditure:
  - financing increased working capital;
  - reviewing costing systems;
  - policies for current asset management: stocks, debtors, and cash management;
  - costing rationalisation; and
  - policies for foreign exchange management.

- Gearing policies to determine critical levels of debt:
  - sources of borrowed funds, domestic or foreign;
  - gearing ratios; and
  - trade-offs between equity dilution and financing debt.

- New share issue considerations:
  - effect on earnings per share;
  - consideration for share-price management;
  - effects on control; and
  - impact on shareholder confidence in the company.

- Dividend policy:
  - trade-off of financing from retained earnings and meeting shareholder expectations; and
  - share–price considerations.

- Deployment of funds:
  - focus of investment and expenditure; and
  - trade-offs from earnings within the corporate business portfolio.

- Risk management:
  - assessing and balancing risks;
  - cut-off criteria for projects;
  - foreign exchange policies;
  - monitoring systems;
  - interest rates;
  - trends in corporate taxation in all operating territories; and
  - security.

- Organisational requirements:
  - financial control structure on an international scale;
  - skills, particularly those concerned with export and international finance, taxation and treasury management;
  - information technology requirements;
  - internal services to the company's business units; and
  - internal auditing requirements for an international business.

Internal organisation to manage the Single-Market strategy

The role of the chief executive will be paramount in pulling all the strands of the business together to provide a unified single-market strategy. All managers have long learned that the propensity for things to go wrong increases in times of change, where the level of complexity rises and when the activities become riskier. The Single Market brings all these together at one go.

Chief executives will therefore be torn between keeping a 'hands-on control' of strategy formulation and implementation and exploiting the collective skills and wisdom of the management team. Without firm leadership managers may well pursue different courses of action in which each has implicit belief that what they are doing is right for the business.

A number of companies have therefore seen the value of putting a senior executive in charge of Single-Market strategy and implementation. Many consultants are recommending this strategy to their clients for three reasons.

Firstly, it allows the company to benefit from a senior executive who is freed from his day-to-day responsibilities and can therefore devote his full attention to the ramifications of the Single Market. Secondly, it permits the chief executive to oversee strategy through a single executive rather than through a group of individual senior managers and thirdly, it enables options and alternative strategies to be sounded before commitments are made to the chief executive.

The immediate dangers are obvious. Unless the executive responsible for championing the Single-Market strategy can win over his peers they are likely to feel both threatened and usurped. The experience, seniority and interpersonal skills of the executive will be important. The chief executive will need to be very careful in the selection of the candidate (whether it be an internal or external appointment) and in the level of support given.

Developing the strategy and effecting its implementation cannot be the work of a single individual. It will involve inputs from across all functions and from all levels of management. The method of strategic development will therefore stem from both upward and downward directions within functions and have to be co-ordinated across those functions. It is important however to ensure that the development of the Single-Market strategy is not seen to be a backroom staff function.

To get full co-operation and involvement from the management team will involve the formation of a strategic planning group within the company. The group should comprise senior functional managers and staff specialists – either under the chairmanship of the chief executive or the senior manager appointed to co-ordinate strategy.

The co-ordinating group is then charged with preparing strategy proposals (based on marketing, R & D, production, logistics, physical distribution and organisational strategies); creating the strategic budget; setting action plans and forming project groups; and diffusing internal communications about the Single-Market strategy throughout the organisation.

Many aspects of the process should not be confined to a few closeted senior managers. It should allow for inputs from the entire management chain in the same way as annual budgets are prepared. To do this, however, management has to be thoroughly briefed.

Cascade of management briefings

The purpose of management briefing is to trigger an action programme which will be carried through enthusiastically. Whether the chief executive decides to brief all levels of management at one time or whether a cascade of briefings down through the echelons of the business is favoured will depend greatly on practicality and management style. In all but the smallest of companies the cascade approach is recommended in order to tailor briefings to the interests of each function, business unit, department or team, ensuring that each group feels that it is making a contribution. In outline a model briefing might cover:

- a general scenario of the Single Market (see Chapter 1);

- management perception of opportunities and threats for their particular industry sector (see Chapter 2);

- the corporate mission (see Chapter 3);

- the focus of the company's competitive advantages;

- company strategic intentions based on business development criteria, new products, new markets etc;

- outline of the planning system to be used; and

- parts to be played by individual groups within the business structure.

A timetable for action

The opportunity to use the Single Market as a trigger for corporate activity is an absolute gift. It provides excitement and opportunities for people to contribute. It presents a new challenge that people can relate to. It lights a beacon for corporate direction. It can be turned into a powerful theme for internal communication.

Yet managements which seem to be doing nothing or attempt to tackle the Single Market without a co-ordinated, internally visible programme of activity will fail to capture the enthusiasm of their employees. People will become tetchy if they feel their company is missing opportunities. They will become anxious if they are kept in the dark.

By making 1992 a crusade it will add a fillip to morale and productivity.

The Single Market provides a unique theme around which corporate strategy, internal communications, training and development can occur.

So, for both the development of the business and internal motivational reasons the Single Market has to be a major corporate project – *a project which has to be strategic, co-ordinated and visible.*

Appendix: 1992 programme checklist

This checklist highlights some of the key proposals and directives which are likely to influence companies as a result of the Single Internal Market. Not all are included in the Single European Act but are nevertheless important. The way to use this checklist is to use the document references or text to call up data on either Spearhead or an EC on-line database.

Proposals by the Commission	References	Forecast date of adoption
Single European Act		1987
Company Law Proposals		
Fifth Company Directive	COM(72)887	(later than)
(Structure of Public Limited		1990
Companies)	COM(83)185	1988
Proposed Statute for a	COM(70)600	1990
European Company	COM(75)150	1990
Regulation – European	COM(73)2046	1985
Economic Interest Grouping	COM(78)139	
Cross Border Mergers	COM(84)727	1987
Amendments to the Scope of		
Present Directives on		
Company Accounts	COM(86)397	1989
Eleventh Company Law Directive		
(Taxation of Branch Offices)	COM(86)238	1988
Draft Merger Control Regulation		1989
Directives Concerning Takeovers	COM(69)5	1989
Approval of Persons Carrying		
Out Company Audits	84/253/EEC	1984
Arbitration Procedures		
Double Taxation	COM(76)611	1985
Drawing up and Distribution of		
Particulars for Companies		
Seeking Stock Exchange Listings	87/345/EEC	1987
Commonality of Taxation		
Companies and Subsidiaries		1985
Twelfth Directive for Single		
Member Private Limited Companies		1990
Harmonisation of Tax		
Liabilities – Transactions		
in Securities	COM(76)124	1986

Directive – Relationship of Undertakings in a Group		1990

Deregulation of Capital Movements

Implementation of Article 67 of Treaty of Rome (liberalisation of Capital Movements	Directive 88/361/EEC	
Proposal to Amend Directive 77/388/EEC to Provide for the Removal of Fiscal Frontiers	COM(87)322	1989
Liberalisation – Collective		
Investment Undertakings	88/220/EEC	1988
Transferable Securities	85/611/EEC	1988
Liberalisation Mortgage Transactions	COM(84)730	1987
Liberalisation of Issues, Placings		
Acquisitions of Securities – Risk Capital	Directive	
Long Term Credit	87/102/EEC	1987

Opening Up Financial Services

Second Directive Co-ordination of Credit Institutions		1989
Solvency Rate for Credit Institutions	COM(88)194	1989
Permitting Insurance Companies to Offer Services other than Life Assurance	COM(78)516 COM(78)68 Directive 87/343/EEC	1986
Co-ordination of Legal Issues Regarding Legal Expenses Insurance	COM(79)516 COM(82)43 Directive 87/344/EEC	
Credit Insurance Directive	COM(79)355 COM(80)854	1988
Winding Up of – Insurance Companies – Accounts of Insurance Companies – Third Directive Motor Liability Insurance		1989
Freedom to Offer Motor Liability Insurance		1989
Freedom to Offer Life Assurance Services		1991
Co-ordination of Regulatory and Administrative Provisions Collective Investment, Undertakings for Transferable Securities	COM(76)152 COM(77)227	1985

Information Requirements, Acquisition and Disposal of Major Capital Holdings	COM(85)791 COM(87)422	1988
Prospectuses for Securities Offered for Public Sales	COM(80)893 COM(82)441	1988
Directive Concerning Investment Advisors		1989
Banking Second Directive		

VAT and Excise Duties

Freeze on VAT Proliferation and Range Widening of VAT Rates		1986
Fourteenth Directive Deferred VAT on Imports	COM(82)402	1985
Flat Rates of VAT Farmers		1986
VAT on Passenger Transport		1986
Nineteenth Directive on Harmonising Laws on VAT	COM(84)648 COM(87)317	1989
VAT Schemes for Small Businesses	COM(86)444 COM(87)524	1986 1987
Seventh VAT Directive Dealings in Antiques, Works of Art, Second Hand Goods and Collectors Items	COM(77)735 COM(84)84	1986
Approximation of Taxes on Tobacco/Cigarettes	COM(87)326 COM(87)325	1989
Harmonisation of Duty on Oils and Alcoholic Drinks	COM(87)327 COM(72)225 COM(85)151 COM(82)153 COM(85)150	
Common Community Statistical Nomenclature and System for Relief from Customs Duty	Regulation 1315/88	1988
Harmonisation of Duty Free in International Travel	85/348/EEC	1985
Harmonisation of VAT Abolition of Certain Derogations (Article 28(3) Directive 77/388/EEC)	COM(84)649 COM(87)272	1990

Movement of People

Freedom of Movement of Workers in the Community	COM(79)737	
Derestriction of Residence Permits		1988

Pan European Vocational Training Card		1990
Functioning of General System of Mutual Recognition of Qualifications for Higher Education	COM(85)355 COM(86)257	1991
Mutual Recognition of Qualifications in Pharmacy	85/433/EEC	1985
Sixth Directive Exemptions in International Travel – Increase to 400 ECU	COM(83)117	1985
Mutual Recognition of Qualifications for Architects	85/384/EEC	1985
Seventh Directive Tax Free Sales	COM(83)166	1986
Personal Importation of Small Amounts of Taxable Goods	COM(83)730	1985
Directive to Reduce Border Controls of Member States	COM(85)224 COM(85)749	1985
Gun Control Approximation of Legislation	COM(87)383	1988
Abolition of Police Controls on Individuals Exiting and Entering Member States	COM(84)749 COM(85)224	1988
Directives on External Country Immigrants		1990
Directives on Refugees		1990
Directives on National Visa Policy		
Directives on Extradition		1991

European Broadcasting/Telecommunications

Co-ordination of National Laws	COM(86)768	1987
Regulation of Copyrights		1987
Transmission of Data		
Pan European Land Based Cellular Digital Mobile Communications	87/372/EEC	1987
Programme to Establish an Information Service Market	COM(87)360 COM(88)3	1989

Movement of Goods

Measures Leading to the Full Abolition of Import Formalities and Control on Goods Between Member States		1992
Harmonisation of Statistics		1990
Elimination of National and		

Regional Quotas and Protective Measures		1989
Single Administrative Document	COM(82)401	1985
Harmonisation of VAT and Excise Duty		1988/90
Abolition of Customs Presentation Charges	Regulation 1797/86	1986
Discontinuation of Transfer Advice Note and Guarantee to Simplify Transit Procedures	COM(79)456	1986
Regulations of Free Zones and Customs Warehouses	COM(85)468	
Duty Free Admission of Fuel Held in Commercial Motor Vehicle Fuel Tanks	COM(84)171	1985
Abolition of Quotas on Road Transport	Regulation 1841/88	1988
Freedom to Provide Services by Non-Resident Carriers	COM(85)611	1991

Public Procurement

Improvements to Directive Covering Public Procurement	Directive 88/295/EEC	1988
Widening of Categories Covered by Existing Directives – Energy and Telecommunications		1988
Electricity and Water		1990
Opening up of Public Procurement for Services for Priority Sectors		1989
Further Harmonisation Procedures for Procurement of Public Works		1990

Movement of Animals, Plants and Foodstuffs   1985/91

COM(71)64	COM(81)500	COM(84)288
COM(71)1012	COM(84)439	COM(80)14
COM(72)884	COM(83)655	COM(77)377
COM(81)795	COM(84)337	COM(82)883
COM(84)295	COM(81)504	COM(76)427
COM(84)530	COM(85)192	
COM(84)900	COM(79)649	
COM(83)584	COM(83)512	
COM(82)529	COM(84)500	
Directives	77/461/EEC	72/461/EEC
	72/462/EEC	80/215/EEC

77/99/EEC	71/118/EEC (Amended)
77/83/EEC	77/93/EEC
77/93/EEC	77/93/EEC
66/401/EEC	70/437/EEC
70/458/EEC	

(Regulation 1468/81 covers the mutual assistance between Member States to correctly apply the law on customs and agricultural matters.)

Product Standards and Liabilities

Approximation of Laws Relating to the Ranges of Nominal Quantities and Capacities for Prescribed Goods	Directive 87/356/EEC	1987
Approximation of Laws Relating to Machines	COM(87)56	1989
Toy Safety	No ref assigned	1988
Liabilities for Defect Products	Directive 85/374/EEC	1986
Harmonisation of Laws on Simple Pressure Vessels	87/404/EEC	1987
Products Endangering Health and Safety of Consumers	87/357/EEC	1987
Amendments to Directive 76/769/EEC Relating to Marketing Dangerous Substances	COM(88)7	1989
Directives Relating to Food Additives	87/55/EEC 86/354/EEC	1986
Directive on Consumer Protection in Respect of Prices on Non-Food Items	88/314/EEC	
Technical Standards Directive	88/182/EEC	1988
Technical Standards Road Vehicles Directive	86/360/EEC 85/3/EEC 88/218/EEC	1986 1984
Community Patent Convention		
Rules for Implementation of European Trade Marks	COM(80)635 COM(84)470 COM(85)793 COM(86)742	1990
Environmental Protection – Dangerous Substances Vehicle Exhausts Directive	67/548/EEC 88/76/EEC	1985 1987

Asbestos Directive	87/217/EEC	1987
Pollutants Directives	87/219/EEC	1988
	87/216/EEC	
Polychlorinated Biphenyls (PCBs)	COM(84)513	
Airborne Noise Omitted by	Directive	
Household Appliances	86/594	1986

Food Regulations

General Directive on Materials Commonly in Contact with Food		1986
General Directive on Nutritional Applications		1986
Food Labelling		1986
Pre-Packaging of Drinks	88/316/EEC	1988
Directives on Food Inspection, Analysis and Sampling	COM(84)39 COM(84)489	1985/87
Good Laboratory Practice Directive	88/320/EEC	1988
Inventory of the Source of Materials used in Food	88/320/EEC	1988
Flavouring	82/711/EEC	1982
Food Additives, Flavourings, Preservatives, Emulsifiers and Solvents	COM(80)286 COM(82)166 COM(83)626 COM(85)79 COM(81)712 COM(84)4 Directives 87/55/EEC 86/354/EEC 88/344/EEC 86/102/EEC	1986 1986
Chocolate Consolidation	COM(83)87	
Infant Foods	COM(84)703	1986
Labelling of Ingredients	COM(82)626	1990
Labelling Presentation and Advertising of Foods Stuffs for Sales to Ultimate Consumer	86/197/EEC	1986
Use of Plastic Packaging	COM(81)159 Directives 83/572/EEC 82/711/EEC	1985 1982
Consumer Protection Display of Pricing on Food Stuffs	COM(84)23 Directive 79/581/EEC	1985

General Directive Covering	
Irradiation of Food Products	1988
Use of Biotechnological Processes	1988

Data Sources Used in Compiling this Checklist were:

- DTI The Single Market
- Spearhead
- Management Accounting
- Guide to 1992
- Northgate Associates.

Useful Addresses

Commission of the European Communities
8 Storey's Gate
London SW1P 3AT
Tel: 01–222 8122

Commission of the European Communities
(Information Unit)
Millbank Tower
London SW1P 4QU
Tel: 01–211 7060

Commission of the European Communities
Windsor House
20th Floor
9–15 Bedford Street
Belfast BT2 7EG
Tel: 0232 240708

Centres for European Business Information

Birmingham Chamber of Industry and Commerce
75 Harborne Road
Birmingham B15 3DH
Tel: 021–454 6171

Centre for European Business Information
Small Firms Service
Ebury Bridge House
2–18 Ebury Bridge Road
London SW1W 8QD
Tel: 01–730 8115

Newcastle Polytechnic Library
Ellison Building
Ellison Place
Newcastle-Upon-Tyne NE1 8ST
Tel: 091–232 6002

Strathclyde Euro Infocentre
Scottish Development Agency
25 Bothwell Street
Glasgow G2 6NR
Tel: 041–248 7806

European Business Information Centre
Irish Export Board
Merrion Hall
P O Box 203
Strand Road
Sandymant
IRL Dublin 4
Eire
Tel: (353) 169 5011

European Business Information Centre
Shannon Free Airport Development Co
The Granary
Michael Street
IRL Limerick
Eire
Tel: (353) 614 0777

European Community
SME Task Force
Rue d'Arlon 80
1040 Brussels
Belgium
Tel: (322) 236 1676

Business Corporation Centre
BC Net
SME Task Force
Same as SME Task Force
above
Tel: (322) 230 3948

CEN
Rue Brederode 2
BTE 5–1000
Brussels
Belgium
Tel: (322) 519 6811

CENELEC
Same as CEN above

Chambers of Commerce with connections throughout Europe

American Chamber of Commerce
75 Brook Street
London W1Y 2EB
Tel: 01–493 0381

Association of British Chambers of Commerce
Sovereign House
212a Shaftesbury Avenue
London WC2H 8EW
Tel: 01–240 5831

Austrian Commercial Delegate
1 Hyde Park Gate
London SW7 5ER
Tel: 01–584 4411

Belgo–Luxembourg Chamber of Commerce
6 John Street
London WC1
Tel: 01–831 3508

Canada–United Kingdom Chamber of Commerce
3 Regent Street
London SW1Y 4NZ
Tel: 01–930 7711

French Chamber of Commerce
Knightsbridge House
197 Knightsbridge
London SW7 1RB
Tel: 01–225 5250

German Chamber of Industry & Commerce
12–13 Suffolk Street
London SW1Y 4HG
Tel: 01–930 7251

*International Chamber of Commerce
(British National Committee)*
Centre Point
103 New Oxford Street
London WC1A 1QB
Tel: 01–240 5558

Italian Chamber of Commerce
Walmar House
296 Regent Street
London W1R 6AE
Tel: 01–637 3153

London Chamber of Commerce & Industry
69 Cannon Street
London EC4N 5AB
Tel: 01–248 4444

Netherlands British Chamber of Commerce
Dutch House
307–308 High Holborn
London WC1V 7LS
Tel: 01–242 1064

Norwegian Chamber of Commerce
Norway House
21–24 Cockspur Street
London SW1Y 5BN
Tel: 01–930 0181

Portuguese Chamber of Commerce & Industry
New Bond Street House
1–5 New Bond Street
London W1Y 9PE
Tel: 01–493 9973

Spanish Chamber of Commerce
5 Cavendish Square
London W1M 0DP
Tel: 01–637 9061

Swedish Trade Council
73 Welbeck Street
London W1M 8AN
Tel: 01–935 9601

Department of Trade and Industry (DTI)

Department of Trade & Industry
1–19 Victoria Street
London SW1H 0ET
Tel: 01–215 7877

Department of Trade & Industry
(Export Licensing Branch)
Millbank Tower
London SW1P 4QU
Tel: 01–211 6611

DTI Regional Offices

Department of Trade & Industry
Industry Department
New Crown Building
Cathays Park
Cardiff CF1 3NQ
Tel: 0222 825396

East Midlands Regional Office
Severns House
20 Middle Pavement
Nottingham NG1 7DW
Tel: 0602 506181

Industrial Development Board for Northern Ireland
IDB House
64 Chichester Street
Belfast BT1 4JX
Tel: 0232 233233

Industry Department for Scotland
Alhambra House
45 Waterloo Street
Glasgow G2 6AT
Tel: 041–248 2855

North Eastern Regional Office
Stanegate House
2 Groat Market
Newcastle-Upon-Tyne NE1 1YN
Tel: 091–232 4722

North West Regional Office
Sunley Tower
Piccadilly Plaza
Manchester M1 4BA
Tel: 061–236 2171

South East Regional Office
Ebury Bridge House
Ebury Bridge Road
London SW1W 8QD
Tel: 01–730 9678

South West Regional Office
The Pithay
Bristol BS1 2PB
Tel: 0272 272666

West Midlands Regional Office
Ladywood House
Stephenson Street
Birmingham B2 4DT
Tel: 021–632 4111

Yorkshire & Humberside Regional Office
Priestley House
Park Row
Leeds LS1 5LF
Tel: 0532 443171

Central Office of Information
Hercules House
Westminster Bridge Road
London SE1 7DU
Tel: 01–928 2345

British Overseas Trade Board Regional Offices (BOTB)

British Overseas Trade Board
1 Victoria Street
London SW1H 0ET
Tel: 01–215 5320

For regional BOTB offices contact regional Department of Trade and Industry Offices.

Simplification of International Trade Procedures

Simplification of International Trade Procedures Board (SITPRO)
Almack House
26–28 King Street
London SW1Y 6QW
Tel: 01–930 0532

Export Credit Guarantee Department Regional Offices

Export Credits Guarantee Department
Aldermanbury House
Aldermanbury
London EC2P 2EL
Tel: 01–382 7000

River House
High Street
Belfast BT1 2BE
Tel: 0232 231743

Colmore Centre
115 Colmore Row
Birmingham B3 3SB
Tel: 021–233 1771

1 Redcliffe Street
Bristol BS1 6NP
Tel: 0272 299971

72–80 Hills Road
Cambridge CB2 1NJ
Tel: 0223 68801

Welsh Office
Crown Buildings
Cathays Park
Cardiff CF1 3NQ
Tel: 0222 824100

Sunley House
4 Bedford Park
Croydon
Surrey CR9 4HL
Tel: 01–680 5030

Fleming House
134 Renfrew Street
Glasgow G3 6TL
Tel: 041–332 8707

West Riding House
67 Albion Street
Leeds LS1 5AA
Tel: 0532 450631

Clement House
14–18 Gresham Street
London EC2V 7JE
Tel: 01–726 4050

Elisabeth House
St Peter's Square
Manchester M2 4AJ
Tel: 061–228 3621

VAT and Excise Duty

HM Customs and Excise
King's Beam House
Mark Lane
London EC3R 7HE
Tel: 01–626 1515

United Nations

United Nations
(London Information Centre)
14–15 Stratford Place
London W1N 9AF
Tel: 01–629 6411

Trade and Management Associations

Association of British Factors
Moor House
London Wall
London EC2Y 5HE
Tel: 01–638 4090

British Export Houses Association
69 Cannon Street
London EC4N 5AB
Tel: 01–248 4444

British Institute of Management
Management House
Cottingham Road
Corby
Northants NN17 1TT
Tel: 0536 204222

British Standards Institution
(Technical Help to Exporters)
Linford Wood
Milton Keynes MK14 6LE
Tel: 0908 320033

Confederation of British Industry
Centre Point
103 New Oxford Street
London WC1A 1DU
Tel: 01–379 7400

Institute of Directors
116 Pall Mall
London SW1Y 5ED
Tel: 01-839 1233

Institute of Export
World Trade Centre
St Katharine's Way
London E1 9AA
Tel: 01-488 4766

Institute of Freight Forwarders
Suffield House
9 Paradise Road
Richmond
Surrey TW9 1SA
Tel: 01-948 3141

Institute of Marketing
Moor Hall
Cookham
Maidenhead
Berkshire SL6 9QH
Tel: 06285 24922

Institute of Patent Agents
Staple Inn Building
London WC1V 7PZ
Tel: 01-405 9450

Institute of Practitioners in Advertising
44 Belgrave Square
London SW1X 8QS
Tel: 01-235 7020

Institute of Public Relations
1 Great James Street
London W1N 3DA
Tel: 01-405 5505

Institute of Trade Mark Agents
69 Cannon Street
London EC4N 5AB
Tel: 01-248 4444

Information Sources and Databases

Celex (EEC) Spearhead (DTI)
Accessible through:
Profile Information
Telecom Gold

Mercury Link Electronic Mail Service
One to One

British Library Business Information Service
25 Southampton Buildings
Chancery Lane
London WC2A 1AN
Tel: 01-323 7454

British Library Document Supply Centre
Boston Spa
Wetherby
West Yorkshire LS23 7BQ
Tel: 0937 546060

Market Research & Intelligence

CTA Economic & Export Analysis Ltd
96 London Road
Reading RG1 5AV
Tel: 0734 668381

Market Research Society
175 Oxford Street
London W1R 1TA
Tel: 01-439 2585

A C Nielsen Co Ltd
Nielsen House
Heddington
Oxford OX3 9RX
Tel: 0865 724724

Technical & Legal Advice

Technical Help to Exporters
British Standards Institution
Linford Wood
Milton Keynes MK14 6LE
Tel: 0908 220022

*British Institute of International and
Comparative Law*
17 Russell Square
London WC1B 5DR
Tel: 01-636 5802

Brebner & Co
107 Cheapside
London EC2V 6DT
Tel: 01-600 0885

Management Consultants

Ernst & Whinney
Becket House
1 Lambeth Palace Road
London SE1 7EU
Tel: 01–928 2000

Northgate Associates
Northgate House
40–42 Leys Avenue
Letchworth SG6 3EQ
Tel: 0462 677396

Sigma Management Consultants
Sigma House
51 Peach Street
Wokingham
Berkshire RG11 1XP
Tel: 0734 771855

Embassies

Belgium
103 Eaton Square
London SW1W 9AB

Denmark
55 Sloane Square
London SW1X 9SR

France
58 Knightsbridge
London SW1X 8PZ

Greece
1a Holland Park
London W11 3TP

Italy
14 Three Kings Drive
Davies Street
London W1Y 2EH

Luxembourg
27 Wilton Crescent
London SW1X 8SD

The Netherlands
38 Hyde Park Gate
London SW7 5DP

Portugal
11 Belgrave Square
London SW1X 8PP

Republic of Ireland
17 Grosvenor Place
London SW1X 7HR

Spain
24 Belgrave Square
London SW1X 8QA

West Germany
23 Belgrave Square
London SW1X 8PZ

Bibliography

Anzoff, I. (1975), *Corporate Planning*, Penguin Books.
Barronson, J. (May, 1970), Technology transfer through the international firm, *The American Economic Review*.
Beeth, G., Distributors finding and keeping the Good Ones, in H. P. Thorelli (ed.) *International Marketing Strategy*.
Bonoma, T. (1985), *The Marketing Edge*, The Free Press.
British Overseas Trade Board Annual Report (1986).
Brooke, M. Z. (1986), *International Management*, Hutchinson.
Business in Europe (Feb. 1988), Office for the Official Publications of the European Communities.
Cecchini, P. (1988), *The European Challenge 1992*, Wildwood House.
Christopher, W. F. (Nov./Dec. 1970), Marketing planning that gets things done, *Harvard Business Review*.
Conar, K. and Salaman W. J. (1987), Private labels back in fashion, *Harvard Business Review*.
Daniels, J. D. and Radebaugh, L. H. (1986), *International Business*, Addison–Wesley Publishing Company.
Davidson, W. H. and Haspeslagh P. (July/Aug. 1982), *Shaping Global Product Organisation*.
Department of Trade and Industry (1988), *An Introduction to the Single European Market*.
Directors Guide to Europe 1992 (June 1988), Institute of Directors.
Drucker, P. (1954), *Practices of Management*, Harper and Row.
Dudley, J. (1985), *Co-operation for International Marketing*, Director Publications.
Dudley, J. (1988), *How To Promote Your Own Business*, Kogan Page.
Dudley, J. (unpublished, private study), *Research into Small Businesses in the US*, James Dudley Management.
The Economist (July 1988), Survey of Europe's single market.
Elinder, E. (1961), International advertisers must devise international ads, *Advertising Age*.
Europe Without Frontiers (April 1987), Official Publications of the European Communities.
Evans, Dr. (1976), Trends in advertising client relationships, *Cranfield Research Papers in Marketing and Logistics*, Cranfield (UK) Institute Press.
Fannin, W. R. and Gilmore, C. B. (1986), Developing a strategy for international business, *Long Range Planning*, Vol. 19 No. 3.
Fitzpatrick, P. B. and Zimmerman A. S. (1985), Essentials for export marketing, *AMA Management Briefing*.
Glaxo Annual Report (1987).
Glaxo World (1986) No. 1.

Gray, R. (May 1988), *Management Accounting*.

Hardy, L. (1987), *Successful Business Strategy*, Kogan Page.

Harris, B. F. and Strong, R. A. (Nov. 1985), Marketing strategies in the age of generics, *Journal of Marketing*, Vol. 49.

Harris, G. (1984), The case against global advertising, *International Journal of Advertising*, Vol. 3 No. 3.

Heenan, D. and Perlmutter, H. V. (March/April 1988), Co-operate to compete globally, *Harvard Business Review*.

Johansson, J. K. and Nonaka, I. (May/June 1987), Market research the Japanese way, *Harvard Business Review*.

Johnson, G. and Scholes, K. (1984), *Exploring Corporate Strategy*, Prentice Hall International.

Kaynak, E. (1976), *Food Retailing Systems*, Cranfield Institute Press.

Keegan, W. J. (1974), *Multinational Marketing*, Prentice Hall International.

Killough, J. (July/August 1978), Improved pay-offs from transnational advertising, *Harvard Business Review*.

Kotler, P. (1984), *Marketing Management*, Prentice Hall International.

Kotler, P. (1985), Building a market driven company, *London Business School Journal*.

Kotler, P. (March/April 1986), Mega marketing, *Harvard Business Review*.

Kotler, P., Fahey, L. and Jatusripitak, S. (1986), *New Competition*, Prentice Hall International.

Lazzel, H. G. (Feb. 1976), *Management Today*.

Levitt, T. (Nov./Dec. 1962), Marketing myopia, *Harvard Business Review*.

Majaro, S. (1983), *International Marketing*, George Allen and Unwin.

Ohmae, K. (1985), *Triad Power*, The Free Press.

Peters, T. J. and Waterman, R. H. (1982), *In Search of Excellence*, Harper and Row, New York.

Porter, M. E. (1980), *Competitive Strategy*, The Free Press.

Porter, M. E. (1985), *Competitive Advantage*, The Free Press.

Ridgely, D. (1974/75), Managing new products, *Research Papers in Marketing and Logistics*.

Shapiro, B. P. (Sept./Oct. 1985), Rejuvenating the market mix, *The Harvard Business Review*.

Taylor, B. (June 1976), Managing the process of corporate development, *Long Range Planning*.

Turner, G. (1986), Inside Europe's giant companies – Nestlé finds a better formula, *Long Range Planning*, Vol. 19 No. 3.

Van Mesdag, M. (Jan./Feb. 1987), Winging it in foreign markets, *Harvard Business Review*.

Wiechman, U. (Winter 1974), *Columbia Journal of World Business*.

Index